THE BATTLE OF BRITAIN
ON THE
BIG SCREEN

THE BATTLE OF BRITAIN ON THE BIG SCREEN

'The Finest Hour' Through British Cinema

Dilip Sarkar MBE, FRHistS

AIR WORLD

THE BATTLE OF BRITAIN ON THE BIG SCREEN
'The Finest Hour' Through British Cinema

First published in Great Britain in 2022 by
Air World
An imprint of
Pen & Sword Books Ltd,
Yorkshire – Philadelphia

Copyright © Dilip Sarkar, 2022

ISBN 978 1 39908 823 7

The right of Dilip Sarkar to be identified as Author of this work has been asserted by him in accordance with the Copyright, Designs and Patents Act 1988.

A CIP catalogue record for this book is available from the British Library
All rights reserved.

No part of this book may be reproduced or transmitted in any form or by any means, electronic or mechanical including photocopying, recording or by any information storage and retrieval system, without permission from the Publisher in writing.

Typeset by SJmagic DESIGN SERVICES, India.

Printed and bound in the UK by CPI Group (UK) Ltd.

Pen & Sword Books Ltd incorporates the imprints of Pen & Sword Archaeology, Air World Books, Atlas, Aviation, Battleground, Discovery, Family History, History, Maritime, Military, Naval, Politics, Social History, Transport, True Crime, Claymore Press, Frontline Books, Praetorian Press, Seaforth Publishing and White Owl

For a complete list of Pen & Sword titles please contact:

PEN & SWORD BOOKS LTD
47 Church Street, Barnsley, South Yorkshire, S70 2AS, UK.
E-mail: enquiries@pen-and-sword.co.uk
Website: www.pen-and-sword.co.uk

Or

PEN AND SWORD BOOKS,
1950 Lawrence Roadd, Havertown, PA 19083, USA
E-mail: Uspen-and-sword@casematepublishers.com
Website: www.penandswordbooks.com

Contents

Introduction vi

Chapter 1 The Lion Has Wings 1

Chapter 2 The First of the Few 34

Chapter 3 Angels One Five 71

Chapter 4 Reach for the Sky 107

Chapter 5 Battle of Britain 142

Chapter 6 First Light 183

Chapter 7 'Last Light?' 213

Acknowledgements 215

Bibliography 216

Other Books by Dilip Sarkar 221

Index 223

Introduction

The Battle of Britain is an epic story. As a result, not least because of the need for expensive aeroplanes, it is a difficult one to translate to cinema. Writing this book and mapping the development of how the Battle of Britain has appeared in British cinema over the years, and considering the various influencing facts, has been an interesting, and I hope useful, exercise, especially the detailed 'reading' of certain key films.

It is perhaps surprising, though, that overall and with the exception of Guy Hamilton's 1969 *Battle of Britain* film, the summer of 1940, certainly in respect of the overall story, has been poorly served by cinema. Also, considering the importance of 'The Finest Hour' to the British national identity, it has been featured infrequently in television drama – Matthew Whiteman's excellent BBC2 docudrama *First Light* being the most recent, produced for the seventieth anniversary in 2010. It is doubtful whether this will change now, and so *Battle of Britain* and *First Light* may well represent the high points of the Battle of Britain on film.

While academic historians remain vexed and continue debating the merits or otherwise of history on film, there is an argument that unfaithful though some 'historical' films are to the actual facts, they can be of value through igniting interest in the viewer and inspiring a need to know more. All kinds of benefits for the historical record could arise from such a circumstance. Having first watched *Battle of Britain* as an 8-year-old schoolboy upon release in 1969, were that not the case, I would not be writing this …

Dilip Sarkar MBE, FRHistS, 2021

Chapter 1

The Lion Has Wings

To fully appreciate the backdrop against which *The Lion Has Wings* was made in 1939, we must travel back in time to Britain between the wars, a nation still shocked by the First World War's butcher's bill, and investigate the fear of bombing and state of Britain's aerial defences.

It was on Christmas Eve 1914, in fact, that the first German bomb was dropped on England – the small device exploding harmlessly in a Dover garden. From that point onwards, though, it was obvious that everything had changed: Britain could no longer rely upon the security provided by being an island nation and, of course, the Royal Navy alone. These primitive air attacks, however, soon intensified, culminating in the dropping of a one-ton bomb on London on 16 February 1918.

By the Armistice, German airmen had raided Britain over 100 times, killing 1,413 people. Indeed, because this deadly development in aerial warfare was both unprecedented and unanticipated, no shelters had been built to protect the public from German bombs. For the first, but not the last, time in history, London's deep underground network provided a safe haven for terrified Londoners; the bombing generating, according to Angus Calder, 'mass panics and near riots'. Although the total number of casualties involved would later equate to those suffered in just one night of the infamous *Blitz*, they were enough to generate an understandable fear of and respect for air power. Moreover, the air power doctrine that emerged between the wars confirmed the bomber as supreme. These two factors are vitally important to understanding events concerning attitudes to aerial warfare in Britain between the wars.

Britain was particularly vulnerable to air attack. Although surrounded by water, the British Isles are still close to the continent – from where any future threat was likely to be launched. Due to the relative smallness of the islands, no point within them was beyond a bomber's range – including not only crucial manufacturing centres and ports, but also the all-important capital. The successful attacks by German bombers in the Great War, however, had made clear that British aerial defences were inadequate. Consequently, the Prime Minister, Lloyd George, commissioned the South African General Jan Smuts to investigate the matter; his conclusion was that an Air Ministry should be formed immediately, responsible for all aspects of British air power, and that the existing air services should be amalgamated into an independent service. Hitherto British military aviation had been shared by the army-controlled Royal Flying Corps and the Royal Navy Air Service.

In spite of loud protests by both the Admiralty and War Office, the Royal Air Force was born on 1 April 1918. By the Armistice, the RAF was the largest air force in the world and enjoyed technical superiority. The new service boasted 22,000 aircraft and 188 operational squadrons. After the Paris Peace Conference in 1919, however, the world was eager to disarm. Britain lost no time in reducing the size of all three services. Consequently, by the end of 1919, the RAF had been stripped to just 371 aircraft of all types and a mere twelve squadrons – figures hardly justifying the RAF's status as an independent service. The RAF's first Chief of the Air Staff, however, Air Chief Marshal Sir Hugh Trenchard, believed strongly that a powerful air force could deter a potential aggressor. He therefore set about creating sound foundations upon which to build, and, if necessary, expand, the RAF.

Fortunate for the RAF though Trenchard's appointment was, it was bad news for Britain's fighter force: Trenchard was a 'Bomber Baron'. Many influential people in both the services and in civilian life now believed in the so-called 'knock-out blow' delivered by bombers. Indeed, such was the bomber's perceived power that Trenchard considered it unnecessary

> for an air force, in order to defeat the enemy nation, to defeat its armed forces first. Air power can dispense with that immediate step, can pass over the enemy navies and armies, and penetrate air defences and attack direct the centre of production, transportation and communication from which the enemy war effort is maintained. It is on the destruction of enemy industries and, above all, in the lowering of morale of enemy nationals caused by bombing that the ultimate victory lies.

Indeed, in 1932, Stanley Baldwin, then Prime Minister, emphasised the all-pervasive fear of bombing:

> I think it is as well for the man in the street to realise that there is no power on earth that can save him from being bombed. Whatever people may tell him, the bomber will always get through. The only defence is offence, which means that you have to kill more women and children more quickly than the enemy if you want to save yourselves.

What precious little spending there was on British air power between the wars, certainly until 1935, was overwhelmingly, therefore, focused on the bomber force. This is unsurprising, considering Trenchard's view in 1921 that the aeroplane was 'a shockingly bad weapon for defence', and that the use of fighters was 'only necessary to keep up the morale of your own people'. Trenchard's doctrine revolved almost entirely, in fact, around offensive operations: defence was side-lined with the absolute bare minimum of resources.

THE BATTLE OF BRITAIN ON THE BIG SCREEN

The first half of the 1930s saw Britain and other nations 'hell-bent', according to Sir Maurice Dean, 'for collective security and prepared to accept incalculable risks in that cause'. In 1932, Britain abandoned what was a miniscule rearmament programme. A year later though, Adolf Hitler and the Nazis came to power in Germany. Essentially, Hitler's main aims were to overthrow the hated 1919 Versailles *Diktat*, which severely restricted Germany's armed forces, and achieve 'living space' for the German people by aggressive territorial expansion. The Führer immediately set about contravening both Versailles' military restrictions and what were seen in Germany as territorial injustices, rebuilding the Wehrmacht in the process. Already, in fact, the Luftwaffe – prohibited by Versailles – was secretly rebuilding beyond the Russian Urals, far from prying Western eyes. In 1933, Nazi Germany withdrew from the League of Nations and the Disarmament Conference, and just two years later Hitler revealed his new air force to a disbelieving world.

In 1934, concerned by the potential threat posed by Hitler, Britain revisited rearmament, but the restricted spending involved suggests that rearmament was not a priority and nor, therefore, was the danger Hitler represented to world peace yet appreciated. It was not just a reluctance to rearm that had contributed to this sorry scenario, however. In 1929, the world had been plunged into an economic crisis when the Wall Street stock market infamously crashed, the resulting fiscal chaos directly affecting the next decade. In 1932, unemployment stood at 2.75 million, so clearly the British government between the wars had serious social issues at home to deal with. Against this calamitous backdrop Nazi Germany busied itself with rearmament, while Churchill later wrote that so far as British military spending was concerned, the years 1931–35 were those of 'the locust'.

Locusts or not, in November 1934, Baldwin told the House of Commons that Britain would 'in no conditions … accept any position of inferiority with regard to what Air Force may be raised in Germany in the future', and that Germany's progress in military aviation meant that the aerial defence of Britain no longer began at the White Cliffs of Dover but at the Rhine. In reality, though, the simple truth was that neither the British government nor people were ready to accept that another war was really coming, and pay the price required for aerial parity with Nazi Germany. Moreover, the price would also have to be paid for Trenchard's offensive doctrine. In the mid-1930s, the Air Staff still believed in a strict numerical ratio of fighters to bombers.

This was, however, meaningless, because, again as Dean wrote, 'the requirements of defence' should be 'determined by the area to be defended and the nature of the probable attack'. The size of the bomber force, of course, was dictated by quite different factors. In sum, the complete lack of substantial rearmament and deficiencies in doctrinal thinking were caused by three things: financial constraints; the indifference of, or opposition by, politicians; and bomber-centric air power doctrine. Information received in Britain during 1935, however, confirmed that although Germany was unlikely to be ready for war until 1939, Hitler's preparations towards that end were so substantial that the threat could no longer be ignored.

So it was that, albeit tentatively, Britain at last began to rearm. Germany, however, was already equipping with new, modern, monoplane bombers and fighters, whereas frontline RAF fighter squadrons still operated the now obsolete Gloster Gauntlet. Hitler was keen to test his new weapons and tactics, the opportunity for which arose in August 1936, when Hitler sent an expeditionary force, the Condor Legion, to support the fascist General Franco in the Spanish Civil War. Over Spain, the German fighters immediately established, and importantly maintained, aerial superiority, enabling ground forces to operate successfully. It was there, in what was undoubtedly the most significant event in military air power since the First World War, that Germany worked out the new tactical requirements of modern air fighting – Britain now seriously needed to catch up.

In July 1936, the defence of Britain was entrusted to a new formation: RAF Fighter Command, the first commander of which was

Air Chief Marshal Sir Hugh Dowding – whose previous appointment as Air Member for Research and Development perfectly positioned him to oversee the necessary major developments in aerial defence. Dowding had already been involved in both the commissioning and development of new monoplane fighters – which would become the Hawker Hurricane and Supermarine Spitfire – and Radio Direction Finding (better-known as radar), so appreciated, therefore, the strengths and limitations of these inventions, and how best to apply them. Fortunately, Dowding was opposed to Trenchard's obsession with the bomber, believing wholeheartedly that 'security of base must come first', arguing that unless the fighter force was strong enough to beat off an attempted 'knock-out blow', the battle would be lost before the bomber chief had an opportunity to strike.

In 1937, Dowding found a powerful political ally in Sir Thomas Inskip, the Minister for the Co-ordination of Defence, who asked him to state how many squadrons were required to defend Britain. A committee, chaired by Dowding, decided upon forty-five. It was not until a year later, though, that priority was at last given to the production of fighters. Like Dowding, Inskip believed that the RAF's priority was not the deliverance of a knock-out blow, but to defend Britain from such an attack, permitting the build-up of resources necessary to counter-attack. This made the RAF, in fact, the only air service to place such confidence in the fighter force. Exactly how the new fighters would be used once war broke out was still guesswork.

However, it was the bomber, not the fighter, that on 26 April 1937, was indisputably confirmed in the public's minds as the most feared weapon so far created by man. This was because of one word: Guernica.

Guernica was a Basque village with a population of around 5,000. Standing between Franco's forces and the capture of Bilbao, the location became crucial to the war in northern Spain. The town had no anti-aircraft guns, and defensive sorties by Republican aircraft were impossible due to recent heavy losses. The target on that fateful day was not the civilian population but one of military importance:

the road network and bridge in the suburb of Renteria. The aerial attack was a combined operation between the Germans and Italians, involving twenty-three aircraft carrying twenty-two tons of bombs.

After the bombing, German Me 109 and He 51 fighters strafed the roads around the target. Tragically, the raid failed to confine itself to the intended military target and also destroyed most of the village. At the time, civilian casualties were reported as 1,654, although more recent research indicates a death toll of up to 400. Nonetheless, the raid was perceived as a deliberate terror attack aimed entirely at a defenceless civilian population and confirmed the fear of air power prevalent throughout the remainder of the decade.

The world's media became virtually hysterical and Guernica's suffering was immortalised in Picasso's stark and emotive rendition of the tortured souls who suffered and died in this unprecedented air attack. In reality though, German air doctrine did not yet revolve around terror bombing. In fact, the indiscriminate bombing of cities was regarded as largely wasted effort and potentially counter-productive. In March 1938, however, the Italians unleashed heavy attacks on Barcelona which lasted several days. This time the civilian population was the specific target – 1,300 died.

Initially, the shocked survivors were demoralised, but once they recovered their main emotion was hatred of the enemy and defiance. This phenomenon made the Germans realise that such bombing could actually increase the enemy's will to resist. Consequently, *Luftwaffe* aerial doctrine concentrated on supporting land operations. Nonetheless, in Spain the bomber had always got through and the global fear of it appeared completely justified. So far as Dowding was concerned in England, events in Spain only served to convince him that a strong fighter force was an absolute priority.

Immediately he was appointed, Dowding set-to creating the System of Fighter Control, drawing together all components of his air defences. The System's key was the chain of radar stations around Britain's coastline, able to detect the approach of hostile aircraft and thereby provide early warning of an impending attack. At this time, however, radar was only outward-looking, so after enemy aircraft crossed the British coast it was no longer helpful. Inbound formations were visually tracked, cloud permitting, by the Observer Corps. Radar stations and Observer Corps posts communicated information to the Fighter Command Operations Room at Bentley Priory, which in turn passed filtered reports to the Group Operations Rooms. The Group Controller would then pass relevant information to the Sector Airfield Operations Rooms.

The British Isles was divided into group areas: 13 Group defending Northern Ireland and Scotland; 12 Group the industrial Midlands and northern England, while 11 Group was responsible for London and the south-east; in July 1940, 10 Group was added, defending the south-west. It was the Sector Controller's responsibility to order fighter squadrons into the air, and by radio telephony place them in the most favourable tactical position to intercept the enemy. Once enemy aircraft had been engaged, the aerial formation leader was then responsible for the actual combat. Anti-aircraft batteries, searchlights and the balloon barrage were also integrated in the defence, with representatives at Command, Group and Sector Operations Rooms. The System was as comprehensive and efficient as the technology of the day permitted – and the inclusion of radar would provide an immeasurable advantage.

Perhaps surprisingly, given fiscal and other constraints, the period between the wars was an exciting time for aviation, with various intrepid airmen making record-breaking flights of differing descriptions – exciting the public imagination. Most exciting of all was the Schneider Trophy. With seven-tenths of the world's surface covered by water, the Frenchman Jacques Schneider, son of an armament manufacturer, could not understand why marine-based aviation lagged so far behind land-based aviation. He saw the seaplane as being possessed of massive potential with water providing cheap airports.

As an incentive for aircraft designers to invest in seaplanes, Schneider presented his famous trophy for an international air race.

The winner would be the nation whose seaplane flew the fastest over a measured water course. Whichever country won the trophy three consecutive times would keep it. This was a time of emerging nationalism on a global basis, and so what undoubtedly remains the most emotive air race to date developed into a competition of immense national pride. More importantly, the races led directly to the Spitfire and Hurricane.

During the course of the Schneider Trophy competition, the Southampton-based Supermarine company's chief designer, Reginald Joseph Mitchell, produced sleek, bullet-like monoplane seaplanes, the all-metal construction of which was revolutionary. On 12 September 1931, Flight Lieutenant J.N. Boothman flashed over the cheering crowds at 340.08 mph – with the throttle not even fully open – winning the Schneider Trophy outright for Britain. That afternoon Flight Lieutenant G.H. Stainforth took up another S6B racer in which he set a new world record: 379.05 mph.

The depressed nation was delighted, British aviation reigned supreme. Dowding, then Air Member for Research and Development, recognising that these advances in design and performance could be applied to land monoplanes, invited tenders for two Air Ministry contracts. These were linked to Dowding's belief that the experience gained by designers during the Schneider Trophy races should be applied to military land-based aircraft led to the Air Ministry issuing Specification F.7/30 on 1 October 1931. The intention was for British aircraft designers to produce a new single-seat day and night-fighter to replace the Bristol Bulldog.

Cutting a long story short, two monoplane designs were eventually commissioned by the Air Ministry: Sydney Camm's Hawker Hurricane, and R.J. Mitchell's Supermarine Spitfire. The new fighters were very different to the biplanes previously flown by the RAF, being at least 100 mph faster, having enclosed cockpits, retractable undercarriage, and eight machine-guns. One common feature, however, was that the first Hurricanes and Spitfires had a wooden two-bladed fixed-pitch propeller – unlike the German Me 109 which by this time already enjoyed the benefits of the VDM Constant Speed airscrew, enabling the pilot to alter the airscrew's angle of 'bite' (pitch) in flight and thereby obtain the optimum setting for any situation. This disadvantage was later addressed by the fitting of first a two-pitch De Havilland propeller, then a Rotol Constant Speed propeller – just in time for the Battle of Britain.

The Hurricane entered service in November 1937, with a top speed of 316 mph and service ceiling of 33,200ft. Although the more advanced and superior Spitfire did not reach squadrons until August 1938, Mitchell's fighter could achieve speeds of up to 367 mph and an altitude of 34,400ft.

The German Me 109E, however, had a maximum speed of 350 mph and an impressive service ceiling of 36,000 feet – and in due course, in modern fighter combat, height and sun would prove to be everything. The 109 also enjoyed two other significant technical advantages over the new British fighters: fuel injection, meaning that its engine was unaffected in the dive, unlike the gravity-fed Rolls-Royce Merlin, plus the benefits of the combined armament of two 7.9mm machine guns and a pair of hard-hitting 20mm Oerlikon cannons. The Hurricane and Spitfire were faster, though, than the German monoplane bombers – which would be their primary target (Ju 87: 232 mph; He 111: 255 mph; Do 17: 265 mph; Ju 88: 286 mph).

By September 1939, Fighter Command was equipped with twelve squadrons of Hurricanes and eleven of Spitfires; the *Luftwaffe*'s total strength was 3,750 aircraft of all types, including 850 Me 109s. By the time the Battle of Britain began on 10 July 1940, Dowding had twenty-five Hurricane squadrons but only nineteen of Spitfires. This was because Supermarine was too small a facility to produce the quantity of fighters now required by the Air Ministry, and, it must be said, the more advanced Spitfire took more than twice the man hours to produce than the Hurricane. It was, however, the Spitfire that had immediately won the hearts and minds of the public.

Mitchell's fighter, being a direct descendant of his Schneider Trophy-winning seaplanes, was a world-beater the second his prototype was revealed to the public. Whereas the Hurricane was essentially a monoplane version of Hawker's Fury biplane fighter, relying on traditional construction methods of bracing wires and fabric, the Spitfire was of a monocoque construction covered in sheet aluminium. In the minds of many, it was, quite simply, the most beautiful aeroplane ever created and destined to become an enduring icon of British national pride. Naturally, any technical deficiencies or German advantages were concealed from the British public, for here, they must believe, was the shining sword to protect them from German bombers.

After years of uncertainty, the storm eventually broke on 1 September 1939, when Hitler invaded Poland. Two days later, with Hitler having ignored an ultimatum to withdrew his troops, Britain and France declared war on Nazi Germany. The years of waiting and preparation were over – for both sides. So afraid were people of air attack that between the end of June and the first week of September, some 3.75 million people were evacuated – these movements in September alone affecting up to a third of Britain's population. It was fully expected that Germany would immediately attempt to deliver the much talked about and dreaded knockout blow – and Londoners certainly believed that Armageddon had arrived when the sirens wailed at 11.27 hours the very day war broke out; fortunately, it was a false alarm, the first of many, caused by an unannounced French aircraft.

While, in anticipation of air attack, the British dug deep shelters, bagged up sand and taped windows as a precaution against glass splinters, Poland suffered. On the campaign's first day, the Luftwaffe destroyed much of the Polish Air Force on the ground in surprise attacks. By the second, the Germans achieved total air superiority. From then on, the Luftwaffe was able to concentrate on supporting the army and destroying Polish ground forces. On 25 September 1939, Warsaw became the latest Guernica.

For two days the Luftwaffe bombed the Polish capital – long after the military objectives of the mission were achieved. Casualties among Polish civilians were substantial. Whereas the destruction wrought beyond military targets in Guernica was arguably largely accidental, there was no question that Warsaw's agony was entirely *intentional*. The bombing of Poland's capital naturally further fuelled the fear of aerial bombardment in Britain. The effectiveness of air power, and the destructive power of the German bombers, was clear. On 28 September 1939 – after just four weeks of fighting – Poland surrendered.

Although the anticipated Luftwaffe attack on Britain failed to materialise in September 1939, Fighter Command nonetheless suffered its first casualties in a tragedy called the 'Battle of Barking Creek' – not to the enemy, but to so-called 'friendly fire' on 6 September 1939. The incident, in which two Hurricane pilots were shot down and killed by Spitfires, indicated how tense the overall situation was, and highlighted deficiencies in the System – which could be rectified in time for the battle ahead. What also clearly needed urgent attention was increasing public confidence that German bombers were not invincible, and that Fighter Command was suitably equipped and had the defensive system necessary to protect Britain against sustained German air attack. And that is where cinema, and in particular *The Lion Has Wings*, came in.

Cinematography, Propaganda and War

The art of cinematography was discovered in the nineteenth century as a by-product of scientific research, and is essentially the rapid projection of still photographs onto a screen, providing an illusion of reality and movement. Cinema soon became enormously popular as a means of mass entertainment, and by 1914, the film studios of Europe, Russia and Scandinavia led the way. This new means of story-telling was big business, given the vast audience, and those companies involved began investing greater sums in increasingly ambitious productions, which were initially silent, black and white, 'movies'.

The First World War, however, disrupted the European film industry, cinemas in Britain being closed for the duration – suggesting that the authorities back then had yet to appreciate cinema's virtually unlimited potential for communicating news, information and propaganda to the public. And in war, propaganda is crucial to all sides, to promote their cause and rally the people. In simple terms, propaganda could be defined as a process of managing, aligning and widely sharing information to promote a specific goal and positively influence public opinion and morale – and because film reached all strata of society, it became pivotal to that process.

This had, in fact, already been recognised in Germany, where cinema functioned throughout the First World War and was utilised for propaganda purposes; with the ban on importing and screening foreign-made films, the German film industry burgeoned. How highly this medium was rated by the government as a propaganda tool became evident in 1917, when the German film industry was partially nationalised by the creation of *Universum Film AG* (UFA) – in part a response to the success of American cinema in the propaganda war. By this time, it was clear that war inexorably linked film with propaganda as a potent means of influencing public opinion and morale – and demonising the enemy. Indeed, N.J. O'Shaughnessy, a leading historian of propaganda, considers that 'in history the function of propaganda has often ultimately been the creation of a mind-set that facilitates the act of killing' and that propaganda frequently reflects a 'voracious need ... to demonise'. So crucial, in fact, did A.J. MacKenzie consider propaganda to be by 1938, that he considered it the fourth 'defence service', after land, sea and air.

After the First World War, American studios forged ahead and were dominating the industry by the 1930s, which became the 'Golden

Age of Hollywood'. By now, films had synchronised sound and, by the mid-1930s, some were even in colour. Throughout that decade and the next, cinema would be the primary form of popular entertainment, with people often attending cinemas twice weekly. The extent of the cinema's popularity is evidenced by the fact that 'Picture Palaces', essentially super cinemas, could accommodate up to 3,000 people in a single sitting. This was, of course, the pre-home television age, radio and newspapers providing news and entertainment – and these mediums were no match or substitute for the escapism Hollywood delivered.

In Germany, Adolf Hitler was in no doubt as to the power of propaganda, and praised the British effort during the First World War in his autobiographical *Mein Kampf*, published in 1926 and which outlined his political manifesto and vision for Germany. Hitler became Chancellor of Germany in January 1933, two months later making Dr Josef Goebbels Reich Minister for Popular Enlightenment and Propaganda (Reichsministerium für Volksaufklärung und Propaganda – RMVP). Goebbels clearly understood the power of film, stating in 1934 that 'film is one of the most modern and far-reaching methods of influencing the masses. A regime must not allow film to go its own way.'

That year, Goebbels legitimised complete state control of the German film industry through the Reich Cinema Law (Reichlichtspielgesetz), which permitted 'positive' censorship by the state. With any kind of criticism of the state now impossible, the German film industry was now an arm of the totalitarian Nazi state – which Hitler fully intended to maximise. Shortly after coming to power, Hitler approached Leni Riefenstahl, a popular German actress who had directed her first film in 1932, with a view to producing a documentary featuring the 1934 Nazi Nuremburg Rally, which would 'appeal to, impress, an audience which was not necessarily interested in politics'.

The resulting film – *Triumph des Willens* ('Triumph of the Will') – was an orgy of Nazi pageantry – and an unprecedented success.

There was absolutely no question by now of the infinite potential of the propaganda-based film – or, given this early exploitation of the medium by the Nazis, what Britain was up against in the propaganda stakes.

The Lion Has Wings

As mentioned, when the Second World War broke out the British public's greatest fear was of bombing. Clearly, inspiring public confidence that Britain's aerial defences were sound would be a high priority for British propagandists. Due to certain doom-laden and influential films made during the 1930s, however, this was not necessarily straightforward.

Given the international fear of bombing between the wars, it was no surprise that this terrifying subject attracted the attention of popular literature and film. The novelist H.G. Wells, for example, wrote a script for London Films called *Things to Come*, which was brought to the cinema screen by Alexander Korda, a Jewish immigrant from Hungary, in 1936. This foreboding and sinister film provided a futuristic look at a war beginning in December 1940 – in which 'Everytown' is flattened by hordes of enemy bombers. Unnervingly, 'Everytown' was deliberately made to look very much like central London. The film, however, was considered too frightening, too realistic, to be popular, and public attendance was comparatively low.

The following year, the prophecy of *Things to Come* appeared fulfilled, in fact, when newsreels were broadcast showing the suffering of Guernica. Appearing that same year, 1937, *The Gap* (written by E.V.H. Emmett, more of whom shortly) was hardly optimistic. An Air Ministry-backed film aimed at encouraging volunteers for Territorial Army anti-aircraft units, the film showed an enemy raid succeeding because of a deficiency of manpower in those units. Again, like *Things to Come* and especially so soon after the real, dreadful, spectacle of

Guernica, the public's reaction was that the film only emphasised that the 'bomber would always get through'.

Similarly, on 6 June 1939, *The Warning* was released in the hope of recruiting volunteers to the Air Raid Precaution (ARP) network, showing the development of a raid and the defenders' response. The new Spitfires and Hurricanes were filmed scrambling and were described as 'incredibly fast', but again, the imagined enemy raid, this time on Nottingham, was successful. RAF pilots were seen being shot down in obsolete Gladiator biplane fighters – which hardly inspired confidence and only reinforced the bomber's perceived invincibility. What was required now was an antidote to this doom and gloom – which would ironically be provided by Korda.

After *Things to Come*, Korda had negotiated with the Air Ministry to make an officially sanctioned film emphasising that from 1936 onwards the RAF had expanded and had the weapons and defence system to deal with any aerial threat. Perhaps significantly, the deal was agreed on 1 September 1939 – the day Hitler invaded Poland. Two days later, Britain and France declared war on Nazi Germany – and the government ordered the closure of all places of entertainment, including cinemas, so as to avoid concentrations of people who would be vulnerable in the event of air attack.

This was not good news for Korda, who had decided that the best means of delivering the Air Ministry's message was via a feature film. Fortunately, following complaints to the press, two weeks later the ban was lifted. Given that 1940 would record over a billion cinema admissions in Britain, a figure which increased as the war progressed, it was a wise decision. Consequently, Korda, who enjoyed a personal friendship with and had the support of Winston Churchill (then the newly appointed First Sea Lord), successfully garnered support for the project from both the Air Ministry and Ministry of Information, the latter having been formed on 4 September 1939 and responsible for promoting the 'national case to the public at home and abroad in time of war' through producing 'national propaganda and controlling news and information'. The resulting film was *The Lion Has Wings* – the first British film of the Second World War.

Produced in haste during the autumn of 1939, owing to the urgent need to bolster public morale, Korda recruited three directors: Brian-Desmond Hurst (whose later work included the 1945 Battle of Arnhem classic *Theirs is the Glory*), Michael Powell and Adrian Brunel, and set-to making the film at Denham Studios. The actor Ralph Richardson – in the process of becoming a Fleet Air Arm pilot and who had appeared as Mussolini in Korda's *Things to Come* – was recruited to play 'Wing Commander Richardson', and Korda's own wife, the beautiful Merle Oberon, became Richardson's on-screen spouse.

Interestingly, Ronald Adam was chosen to play the German bomber chief, the actor himself having been a fighter pilot in the First World War, during which he was shot down and wounded, possibly by the Red Baron, Manfred *Freiherr* von Richthofen, who sent compliments to the vanquished Camel pilot in hospital. In 1939, Adam returned to active duty in the RAF as a wing commander, serving as a Sector Controller at Hornchurch during the forthcoming Battle of Britain.

Narration (for the British release) was provided by E.V.H. Emmett, a veteran newsreader whose voice was well-known and reassuringly familiar to the public. The film's musical score was composed by Richard Addinsell (who later found fame for his *Warsaw Concerto* in Hurst's 1941 film *Dangerous Moonlight*). Screenplay was written by Ian Dalrymple, previously an experienced editor-in-chief with Gainsborough Pictures and Gaumont-British, whose contribution to the writing of the 1938 film *Pygmalion* had earned him an Oscar nomination.

Dalrymple, who in 1940 would head-up the new Crown Film Unit and produce official propaganda films, was conscious that he had a delicate balancing act: on one hand, too much detail regarding Britain's air defences could not be revealed, but, on the other, he felt passionately, and arguably quite rightly, that the public deserved to know 'everything that does not (a) inform the enemy, or (b) provoke untimely debate'. Korda was given the use of Hatfield aerodrome, with Hurst directing both the aerial scenes and those involving Richardson and Oberon. According to another of the directors, Michael Powell, Korda had promised Churchill personally that he would make this important film – which would be ready in just one month.

On the afternoon of that fateful day 3 September 1939, off Inishtrahull, a German U-boat sank the SS *Athenia*, a passenger liner out of Glasgow bound for Montreal. Over 100 passengers and crew lost their lives, including twenty-eight citizens of neutral America. Condemned as a war crime, the RAF was ordered to retaliate.

The following day, Powell was tipped off by Squadron Leader H.M.S. Wright, the film's RAF liaison officer, that 149 Squadron's Mildenhall-based Wellingtons were poised to attack German shipping in the Kiel Canal, along with the Blenheims of 9, 107, 110 and 139 Squadrons. Powell dashed off to Mildenhall with camera crew and filmed 149 Squadron's take-off and triumphal return. This was important. In addition to show-casing Britain's aerial defences, it was equally necessary to reassure the public that the RAF also possessed sufficient offensive capacity to hit back at Germany.

While this made for impressive film footage, the actual truth of the matter was that 149 Squadron was poorly prepared for war. Astonishingly, Flying Officer Bill McRae only noticed at the last minute before take-off that his aircraft's bomb bay was empty, and when, en route to the target, Squadron Leader Paul Harris ordered his gunners to test their weapons, all failed to fire. Nonetheless, what was lacking in preparedness was compensated by the aircrew's spirit: although defenceless, Harris had pressed on.

Naturally, however, the Spitfire – which had already captivated imaginations and won hearts and minds – was destined to be the star of *The Lion Has Wings*. On the afternoon of 6 September 1939, and all the following day, Hurst's crew filmed Flight Lieutenant 'Treacle'

Tracey's 'B' Flight of 74 'Tiger' Squadron at RAF Hornchurch, an important sector station North of the Thames in Essex.

Given that on the morning of 6 September two pilots of 74 Squadron's 'A' Flight were responsible for destroying two 56 Squadron Hurricanes in the so-called 'Battle of Barking Creek' friendly fire tragedy, it was perhaps a quirk of fate that the 'Tigers' were chosen for this starring role. Nonetheless, it was a welcome distraction for 'B' Flight, the pilots of which entered into the spirit of the thing, socialising and happily cooperating with the 'luvvies'. Hurst was impressed, especially when the Spitfires mischievously beat up the film crew at low-level, and later cooperated at close-quarters, enabling air-to-air footage to be filmed from an Avro Anson piloted by a female ferry pilot. Once cut and edited, these scenes certainly helped promote the message that the RAF, according to Powell, was perfectly equipped, able and ready to 'blow the *Luftwaffe* out of the sky'.

The Lion Has Wings: A Reading

The film begins with two British icons: 'Big Ben', followed by a Spitfire on an airfield, silhouetted against the sky, to stirring music – which gives way to a soothing melody as the scene changes to the harbour, white cliffs and castle of Dover.

From this point (0.1.45 – that is one minute and forty-five seconds), Emmett narrates the film's first twenty minutes which imparts numerous significant messages. Britain, we can see through the camera's lens, is a peaceful and prosperous land, which, we are told, had resisted invasion for 800 years and opposed any dictator threatening peace in Europe: 'This is Britain, where we believe in freedom, and also believe in peace.' We are shown a hard-working and healthy, 'clean-living', nation developing the industrial revolution's legacy for the benefit of all, and improving social conditions, a prosperous nation whose people, including its children, lead an idyllic existence, with work, good housing and living conditions, schools, leisure time and sporting facilities, and annual seaside holidays. 'Is this to stop,' we the audience are asked, 'because one man seeks to destroy civilisation?' (0.5.23).

With the scene set of a tranquil and peaceful Britain, the young men of which concentrated not on war but upon sporting competitions, the mood dramatically changes: enter martial drumbeats and marching Nazis parading in front of Hitler – a sinister and foreboding contrast to Britain's 'good fellowship' (0.6.46).

In this change of tack, it is emphasised that while Britain pursued a peaceful path, Germany prepared for war, led by Hitler and the Nazi system, which 'crushed the individual' (0.7.56). Now we are shown footage from *Triumph of the Will*, indicating a nation blindly following and worshipping their *Führer*. Hitler's ranting contrasts sharply with sporting commentary in Britain. Hitler is shown having to be 'protected by armed guards', while the British Royal Family are shown 'walking freely' among their people.

Cleverly, the (real) Royals are shown as a happy family, from archival film, singing and miming to the children's nursery rhyme *Under the Spreading Chestnut Tree*. Again, this harmless activity is contrasted with an explanation of Hitler's record of breaking treaties and reneging on his assurances of peace, while deliberately moving towards war. Quotes are read from Hitler's political testament, *Mein Kampf*, leaving the viewer in no doubt whatsoever as to who was responsible for the war, and Britain's moral superiority.

At 0.15.10, the viewer is told that Britain has no choice but to defend its freedom – and the might of the Royal Navy – 'the greatest navy the world has ever known' – is shown with impressive footage of British warships and submarines. Then, (0.15.33), the Household Division is seen Trooping the Colour, with Emmett reassuringly explaining that the peacetime army has been substantially expanded and reinforced, and that the army was fully mechanised with modern equipment provided by British industry – including artillery and tanks.

A great show is made of a Light Tank Mk VI, essentially a reconnaissance tank used for policing the Empire and, with only a .50-inch Vickers machine-gun as its main armament, designed only for fighting other similar vehicles. In 1939, the British Army was largely equipped with this type of tank – which would soon prove no match, in reality, for the heavier and better-armed *panzers*.

We now come to the main event: the RAF (0.17.0). Emmett tells us that the junior service had grown from 'a small experimental force to become masters of the sky'. This is hard to assimilate, however, given footage from Hendon Air Pageants featuring biplane fighters and other obsolete types – although Emmett concedes (0.18.10) that the scenes 'are already out of date'. This is surprising. It seems only natural that the RAF's best and most modern fighter – the Spitfire – should have been showcased here; certainly newsreel footage of 19 Squadron, the RAF's first Spitfire squadron, with their Spitfires was plentiful from 1938 onwards.

Nonetheless, again to stirring, upbeat, music, phalanxes of RAF aircraft are shown in pristine formation, endlessly passing overhead, and the skill of RAF fighter pilots demonstrating formation aerobatics is shown to full effect. This section of Emmett's narration is clearly to emphasise that Britain's armed forces are well-armed and perfectly capable of meeting any threat from Germany. The reality, however, was rather different.

At 0.19.01, with Emmet's overtly propagandised introductory narration finally over, we arrive at a recreated Hendon Air Pageant and see in the crowd two German men in civilian dress watching the aerobatics. There is 'Holveg' (Herbert Lomas) commenting that, 'These people are becoming air-minded', his be-hatted companion knowingly responding, 'Yes, but not *war*-minded.' The latter is 'Schulemberg' (Trevor Austin), the 'German Chief of Air Staff'.

Before the outbreak of war, there were various visits of senior Luftwaffe officers to RAF bases in Britain, apparently diplomatic to all intents and purposes, the actual motivation only becoming clear as war with Germany loomed; this scene alludes to that dishonourable intent.

At 0.19.07 we are introduced to 'Wing Commander Richardson' (Ralph Richardson), an RAF pilot, inquiring of 'Schulemberg' what he thought of the show. 'Wunderbar' is the reply, with the two dastardly Germans exchanging knowing glances as Richardson leaves them watching a squadron of Hawker Fury biplane fighters in line abreast. At the same time, Emmett's narration returns to uphold the RAF as, after expansion, being 'second to none, ready for anything, no matter how difficult and dangerous'.

Emmett then invokes the great sailors who made Britain a global power, 'Nelson, Frobisher and Raleigh', drawing a direct parallel between those national heroes and the RAF's pilots, 'these captains of the clouds', now called upon to defend Britain in the air. By 0.19.57, the Fury's have given over to Bristol Bulldog biplane fighters … but two seconds later become Furies again. The daredevil aerobatics continue, concluding with a perfectly executed 'Prince of Wales Feathers'. There is no question: the RAF's pilots are skilled airmen indeed.

At 0.20.26, the camera focuses on 'Mrs Richardson' (Merle Oberon) seated in the crowd with a young man, watching the display, who declares the performance to be 'Swell', and that it was worth him travelling 'all the way from little old Montreal to join these boys' – giving a nod to the Short Service Commission side of the 1936 Expansion Plan, which provided an opportunity for young men from the Empire and Commonwealth to join the RAF and learn to fly.

While mass formations of RAF aircraft continue passing overhead, at 0.20.54, the narration acknowledges the skill and dedication of the RAF's groundcrews, and the factories producing war materials, in this case fighter aircraft – and again England's august past is invoked by drawing a parallel between the RAF's modern aircraft and the longbow which won the Battle of Agincourt for Henry V.

Some excellent footage follows of Hawker Hurricanes and Supermarine Spitfires being built, making the point that the RAF's aircrews are provided only the best machines 'the tax-payer can produce'. At 0.22.20, the scene switches to the production of the Vickers Wellington bomber – 'the type that went out on the Kiel raid' – the public being assured that this aircraft carried a devastating bomb load at high speed and could penetrate long distances. In truth, the Wellington was a medium bomber, unlike the later four-engine heavy bombers, most notable among them the Avro Lancaster, which were capable of doing exactly what this film claimed the Wellington could do. Then, the fact that Britain was well protected by anti-aircraft guns is illustrated through factory scenes showing production of these weapons.

Integrated with searchlight defences, Emmet tells us that their fire is 'truly formidable'. Due acknowledgement is also given to factory workers tirelessly producing war weapons, including ammunition. When bomb manufacture is mentioned (0.24.42), Emmett points out that these are for attacking legitimate military targets, and not to terrify' civilian populations. The narration continues to explain that although Germany has been producing war materials for some time, Britain's industry has caught up and has the resources to continue with this scale of production far beyond those available to Germany.

Again, the moral superiority of a Britain upon which war has been forced by a despotic dictator is emphasised. It is explained to the viewer that Britain did not want war and 'hoped reason would prevail' over the Munich Crisis and Danzig Corridor, but that Hitler's invasion of Poland and refusal to remove troops left no choice but to declare war on Germany.

At 0.27.04, the broadcast to the nation by the British Prime Minister, Neville Chamberlain, announcing the declaration of war, is played. Various civilians are filmed listening intently to this historic moment, the broadcast again stressing that Hitler had continually broken his promises, meaning that no one was safe, and that now there was no other option but to go to war in order to preserve freedom and democracy – with welcome support from the Empire. In what may be considered a mildly eccentric, perhaps even extraordinary scene (0.28.22) to us today, 'Mrs Richardson' and 'June' (June Duprez) stand to attention in their own home upon hearing the National Anthem – at which point enter 'Wing Commander Richardson' and 'Bobby' (Brian Worth) a Spitfire pilot and Flight Commander in 'Squadron 229'. 'What was that?' asks the Wing Commander, 'Are we at war?' A nod of the head from his wife confirms the worst, their conversation then paying tribute to Mr Chamberlain's untiring efforts to avoid a violent confrontation with Hitler via his diplomatic policy of Appeasement.

The two RAF pilots are visiting fleetingly while travelling to a new station, the Wing Commander reassuring his wife that 'We have never been better prepared'. 'Bobby', however, has more amorous thoughts, proposing marriage to 'June' for when he 'gets back', which is accepted, and after which our two heroes of the air depart for an uncertain future.

At 0.30.37, after the two ladies watch the pilots drive away, suddenly the air raid siren wails: 'Air raid!' says 'June'; 'Already?' responds 'Mrs Richardson' – giving the film's first indication of how terrified civilians were of bombing. Emmett then resumes narration, explaining how that first 'air raid' was a false alarm – which was actually the case. Dramatic music then accompanies scaremongering billboards indicating German 'inhumanity', including 'Frightfulness in Occupied Poland' and 'Red Cross Train Bombed'.

'Whether we liked it or not', Emmett tells us, 'this was war' (0.31.18) as the scene now changes to show the Wellington bombers of 149 Squadron at Mildenhall in Suffolk, aircrew relaxing while awaiting 'orders to avenge the *Athenia*' in their 'battleships of the skies'. We then see orders for a raid being given over the telephone by the 'Chief of the Air Staff' (Robert Rendel) to a staff officer, who communicates those instructions to groups and ultimately squadrons.

At 0.32.46 the 'sky battleships' are shown being towed out of their hangars and prepared for the raid, refuelled and armed, while Emmett again emphasises that the war had been forced upon Britain and was of Hitler's making. Aircrews are shown being briefed before take-off by an officer (Robert Douglas), for a raid on German pocket battleships making for the Kiel Canal's mouth. Interestingly, the briefing makes clear that ten miles from the target is a hospital, which must under no circumstances be hit – again indicating Britain's moral superiority and desire only to wage both a reluctant and honourable war.

The squadron leader (Anthony Bushell), resplendent in clean white flying overalls, then issues final orders to his men before engines are run up, the crews climb aboard and the Wellingtons take-off. Then, we see controllers monitoring the raid's progress, and at 0.37.34 that information being telephoned through to Fighter Command HQ. In the air, the crews are shown doing their respective jobs, as the bombers drone towards Germany, exchanging a 'Good luck' signal with a British destroyer over the North Sea.

As the bombers close on their target, the pilots reduce height, ultimately making a low-level attack and effecting a direct hit on the target ship – which conveniently does not appear to return fire! At 0.43.05 the Wellingtons are in trouble, however, when a flight of 'Messerschmitts' (which are variously Spitfires of 74 Squadron or Fairey Battle light-bombers!) intercepts the Wellingtons, but the enemy attack is swiftly beaten off by the Wellingtons' air gunners. Emmett then again hammers home that this raid was made against a legitimate military target and not civilians.

The Wellingtons are then shown landing back at Mildenhall, this actually being the returning aircraft from the real Kiel raid. Clearly, then, RAF Bomber Command was well-equipped and trained, and perfectly capable of mounting successful and telling raids on legitimate targets in Germany.

We now turn to RAF Fighter Command, as the cameras roll (0.44.55) at RAF Hornchurch, outside the dispersal area of 74 'Tiger'

Squadron's 'B' Flight. At 0.45.07 we see the dispersal bell tent, 'The Tigers Den', adorned with Hitler 'Wanted' posters, while Flight Lieutenant 'Treacle' Tracey and his pilots, also in pre-war white flying suits, await the order to scramble. Meanwhile, armourers maintain the nearby Spitfires' guns and replenish ammunition. While Emmett explains that the RAF also has 'interceptors and pursuit planes', the camera pans around across a squadron of ... Battle light-bombers.

We are told that there is no shortage of recruits, and that the serving fighter pilots are every bit as good as the First World War's aces. 0.45.37 shows the balloon barrage, a new idea 'never before tried in warfare ... death to the invader'. 0.46.11 sees anti-aircraft guns and crews, the details of which are an 'official secret, closely guarded' – but these guns 'throw up a hail of metal changing the sky into an inferno'. The role of searchlights is explained, along with the Observer Corps. Now, the scene is set for the film's finale: a German bombing raid on Britain.

At 0.46.38, we are transported to Berlin, to watch as the German raid unfolds. First, we see our old friend 'Schulemburg', the 'German Air Chief of Staff' issuing orders, again by telephone, to the German bomber chief – perhaps ironically played by former First World War British fighter pilot Ronald Adam, who would later serve throughout the Battle of Britain as a Fighter Controller. At 0.46.52, we find that 'Holveg' commands the German bomber squadron tasked with this attack. The German aircrews are clad in black flying kit and stand to attention as their commander paces up and down their ranks, barking out orders in a scene, Emmett says, which is 'a contrast to Britain's friendly way'. The briefing concludes with a rousing 'Heil Hitler'. The scene then cuts to a row of obsolete Heinkel He 51 fighters, a type which had fought in Spain but had been withdrawn from service in 1938.

The film then alludes to intelligence work, with British spies passing on details of activity at 'Airfield AZ2' (0.47.22). This information concerning preparations for an impending attack is relayed to the Air Ministry, and ultimately the Chief of the Air Staff, who immediately issues orders activating the aerial defences. First, the balloon barrage is raised, then the underground Operations Room at Fighter Command HQ is shown, with the Air Officer Commanding-in-Chief (John Longden) being introduced as 'the brain' – in reality, this was Air Chief Marshal Sir Hugh Dowding, who had done so much to create the System of Air Defence now being explained by Emmett.

Over the great Operations Room map table, the narrator describes how information from all sources is received, analysed and acted upon accordingly from this nerve centre. At 0.49.05, the Chief of Air Staff calls the Fighter Command chief, informing him that an enemy attack will take place that night. With all in place, that night we join the Observer Corps, awaiting developments in the open air, with their range-finders. The central figure in this scene is Bernard (later Baron) Miles, who would go on to to appear in many wartime films, including *One of Our Aircraft is Missing* and *The First of the Few*. By 0.49.45, all Observer Corps posts report to Fighter Command HQ that they are also ready, as are the 'ARP' (Air Raid Precautions) and anti-aircraft batteries, who are ready to 'welcome the nasties'.

At last, at 0.50.55, we see what doubtless the cinema-goers had been waiting for: a close-up of a Spitfire on an airfield, silhouetted against the night sky. Flight Lieutenant Tracey emerges from his 'B' Flight dispersal tent, awaiting with his pilots the telephone call sending them into action. Tension builds.

Sound detectors are shown while searchlights probe the darkness. Emmett again invokes the august past, remarking that on this night civilians and soldiers stand shoulder-to-shoulder, as they did 300 years before when the Spanish Amada was defeated. The film then cuts to scenes supposedly depicting flaming beacons being lit, providing early warning of the Spanish ships and galvanising Britain's coastal defences into action. 0.52.48 gives us a veritable Elizabethan pageant, as 'Queen Elizabeth I' (Flora Robson) delivers a rousing speech to her 'people' – all scenes lifted from the 1937 feature film *Fire Over England*.

Now, the action starts – at 0.53.39 – when a mass formation of German bombers is shown inbound. Although these are real aircraft, and not models, they are, in fact, Junkers Ju 52 transport machines. Nonetheless, the raid is on.

At Fighter Command HQ, the atmosphere is tense as information begins coming in as various sources report the enemy's progress. At 0.54.47, 'Braxstead Fighter Station' and 'Squadron 299' is notified, the order 'Take-off' (0.55.11) sending the white-suited 'Tigers' running for their Spitfire Mk Is. Merlin engines roar into life and pilots clamber into their cockpits before racing across the airfield and becoming airborne. In reality, the Spitfire was designed as a daylight interceptor and was not a good aircraft for night-flying, on account of the glowing banks of exhausts either side and forward of the pilot, ruining night vision, and narrow-track undercarriage, which made night landings tricky. The truth was, however, that dedicated night-fighting aircraft simply did not exist at this stage of the war, and indeed nor would they for some time, and so the all-conquering Spitfire, so far as the public need to be concerned, will protect them by night and day – which, in fact, it did, along with Hurricanes, Blenheims and Defiants, until radar-equipped night-fighters arrived in the autumn of 1940. The Spitfires are also shown flying-by in the textbook 'vic' of three formation – which proved totally unsuitable, in the event, for modern air-fighting.

At 0.56.36 we see our Spitfire pilots airborne, communicating with each other over the radio-telephone, and receiving instructions from the Controller. For Spitfire enthusiasts, this is great footage, showing the original windscreen of the Mk I, which lacked the later armoured glass, and the ring and bead, as opposed to the later reflector sight.

The incoming raid is shown again at 0.57.28, the 'raiders' now being a squadron of RAF Battles. The Controller, being in receipt of up-to-date information regarding the enemy formation's progress, is able to successfully guide the Spitfires to intercept. At 0.57.57, all six Spitfires of Treacy's Flight, in two rows of three, line abreast, are shown bearing down upon the enemy.

The Spitfire leader sights the intruders, excitedly shouting into his microphone – the enemy aircraft now being a Focke-Wulf Condor passenger aircraft, flown by a grim-faced Nazi pilot, who is given bad news by a crew-member: 'Spitfires!'

With cries of 'Alright you lousy so-and-sos!' the gum-chewing Spitfire pilots engage the enemy bombers, which are now, in fact, RAF Blenheims. The Spitfires open up, their Browning machine-guns chattering away, killing the black-clad Nazi leader who slumps over his controls, his bomber crashing in flames.

At 0.59.10, three Spitfires pursue another German, this time a Ju 52. The rear-gunner opens up on his assailants but is no match for eight Brownings, and is immediately killed. And so it goes on … at 0.59.33 a Spitfire's bullets ripping through the swastika flash of an enemy aircraft – which also crashes. The Spitfire leader, 'Cornflower Red', then informs the Controller that two 'bandits' have been destroyed. Emmet then announces that the first raid have been driven back – but a second is on the way, the camera showing a formation of Hawker Fury biplanes.

The process of showing information incoming from the Observer Corps and plotted in the Operations Room is repeated, more Spitfires subsequently being scrambled, as searchlights and anti-aircraft guns also go into action, the heavy ack-ack guns banging away – soon shooting down more raiders. Then, the guns are ordered to cease fire as the Spitfires arrive on the scene, rapidly despatching another bomber.

Spitfires are shown landing (1.02.36) while Emmett makes the point that 'B' Flight has taken over in the air while 'A' Flight returns to refuel and rearm. 'Cornflower Blue', the leader of 'B' Flight, then reports to the Controller (now Wing Commander Richardson) that two more enemy aircraft have been destroyed. The Spitfires are then shown being replenished. Although the Flight Commander's aircraft has been hit in the fuselage by a single German bullet, there are no other RAF casualties. Next, we have 'German Raid Number 3', another formation of Ju 52s passing overhead (1.03.47). Again, the sequence of defence is repeated, He 51 fighters and the lone Condor being shown, the bomber being forced up higher by the balloon barrage, from which altitude, Emmett assures viewers, bombing would be less accurate.

Thwarted, the enemy withdraws – but the Spitfires of 'Squadron 301', also based at 'Braxstead', are scrambled to intercept the retreating Germans (1.05.10). The Spitfires chase after the bombers – now three Heinkel He 111s – sighting and attacking the Germans, leading to an aside from 'Wing Commander Richardson' that he has 'Some damn good chaps on this Station.' The 'bombers' – now Vickers Wellesleys – are engaged: 'Number 3 Attack. Go!' – resulting in four destroyed for no loss. A delighted 'Wing Commander Richardson' then orders the Spitfires home. 'Bobby' puts in a brief appearance in 'Wing Commander Richardson's' Operations Room during the action, but is told to go home and rest. The 'All Clear' is announced along with a signal from the Air Officer Commanding-in-Chief, congratulating everyone involved.

At 1.08.47, 'Wing Commander Richardson' is shown coming home, falling asleep reading the newspaper, as his wife returns from night-duty as a nurse, who wakes him and is naturally delighted to hear that 'everything had gone very much to schedule'. Instead of going to sleep, the 'Richardsons' decide to take their car down to the river, where they sit in the shade of a leafy tree near the Thames. At 1.10.28 'Mrs Richardson' explains how, together with her fellow nurses, she was getting fed up with nothing to do, because of all the false alarms. Merle Oberon then launches into a wistful consideration of how in years past women have had to give their menfolk to the land and sea, and now to the air – but without complaint, regardless of the cost: 'We must keep our land, darling, we must keep our freedom, we must fight for what we believe in: truth, and beauty, and fair play, and kindness' – profound words unfortunately lost on the 'Wing Commander', who after a hectic night's work has now fallen to sleep.

So concludes *The Lion Has Wings*, with Emmett again underlining why Britain is having to fight a war forced upon her by Hitler's Germany, as formations of RAF aircraft fly overhead. The last word: 'We can learn from the motto of the Royal Air Force, *Per Ardua ad Astra*: through ordeal to the stars, through endeavour triumph, through trial, to victory!'

Conclusion

The Lion Has Wings was made with a budget of £30,000 – equivalent today, given inflation, to a still comparatively modest £181,737. The three directors successfully interwove actors with real newsreel footage and Emmett's commentary to produce a documentary-style propaganda and morale-boosting film – the first of its kind made during the Second World War. What audiences wanted from cinema was entertainment – and Korda's film demonstrated to the government how the extraordinary reach and popularity of the cinema could be harnessed and manipulated to communicate messages and themes via an engaging storyline. It was, however, as Michael Powell later admitted, 'an outrageous piece of propaganda'. Indeed, at least one audience treated with contempt the claim by 'Wing Commander Richardson' that 'We have never been so prepared.' Nonetheless, overall the film was well-received by critics and the public, being shown at over 200 cinemas in November 1939, finding favour with 73 per cent of viewers – and became that month's top cinema attraction, the second most profitable film of 1939.

Clearly the film was a blatant and overt attempt to reassure the public that Britain's aerial defences were cutting-edge and perfectly capable of seeing off any aerial threat, in addition to striking back at Germany. If the intention was to reduce the public's fear and anxiety of bombing, it certainly helped – one young lady commenting to Mass Observation that having seen the film, she felt 'much safer'. The other thing, much more significantly, that had increased public confidence, however, was that by the time *The Lion Has Wings* was released, over two months after war broke out, the imminently expected and dreaded 'knockout blow' had failed to materialise.

Indeed, there had been an urgent flurry of activity when general mobilisation was ordered, the size and composition of the RAF, for example, literally changing overnight as ranks were swelled by countless auxiliaries and reservists, and the BEF and Advanced Air Striking Force had dashed over to France – but nothing had yet happened. On the Continent, British troops had dug in for the winter on the Franco-Belgian border, awaiting events. The initial surge of activity and anxiety had subsided, the so-called 'Phoney War' now in full-swing, and many evacuees had returned home; Cambridge, for example, accommodated 6,700 children in September 1939, but by November only half remained. Indeed, as Flight Lieutenant Brian Lane, a Spitfire pilot in Duxford's 19 Squadron, wrote, it was 'a queer war'.

The Lion Has Wings was authorised to be surprisingly open regarding the System of Air Defence – except in two crucial respects. Firstly, understandably, no mention is made of radar, the true significance of which the Germans had failed to appreciate even by the Battle of Britain, the film implying that the tracking of enemy aircraft was entirely reliant upon the eyes and ears of the Observer Corps and sound locating devices. Perhaps even more secret was the fact that in 1932, the Polish Cipher Bureau had cracked the German Enigma code, a machine used to send encrypted messages, although by 1939 the German system's complexity outstripped the Poles' capacity to keep up with it.

Before war broke out, Poland provided Britain and France with reconstructed Enigma machines and their knowledge of decryption, enabling British mathematicians and code-breakers to advance this work from the now famous Bletchley Park. At the time Korda's film was made, the Germans were still able to make much use of landline communications, but by the Battle of Britain signals traffic was constant. The Poles' pioneering work accelerated the Allies ability to eavesdrop on German messages, informing strategy and tactics. Exactly to what extent, owing to documents still being secret, we may never know, but nonetheless this, and radar, was something that the public could not be made aware of in 1939, for obvious reasons.

While, unlike the other films in this book, *The Lion Has Wings* does not show an interpretation of the actual Battle of Britain, which had yet to occur, it certainly predicted such an aerial assault – and was the first Second World War film to heroise the fighter pilot. For those reasons, and because investigating this film requires an examination of the broader context of air power and propaganda, it remains an important work – and hence inclusion in this book.

Chapter 2

The First of the Few

'We few, we happy few, we band of brothers.'
Henry V, *Act IV, Scene III*

'Never in the Field of Conflict Has So Much Been Owed to So Many by So Few.'
*Winston Spencer Churchill,
20 August 1940*

As *The Lion Has Wings* predicted, Britain was in due course subjected to a sustained aerial offensive, albeit not the dreaded 'knock-out blow'. The so-called 'Phoney War' persisted until April 1940, when Germany successfully invaded Norway, then 10 May 1940 saw Hitler's long-awaited and shocking attack on the West. This time, Rotterdam suffered Guernica and Warsaw's fate.

Owing to total aerial superiority, German forces swept through the Netherlands, Belgium, Luxembourg and France, by-passing the much-vaunted Maginot Line in a masterstroke of military strategy. By 26 May 1940, Lord Gort's BEF was in danger of envelopment and so the unthinkable decision was made to retire on and evacuate from Dunkirk – an operation which saw over 300,000 British and Allied servicemen rescued from the jaws of defeat. And, in spite of clever propaganda creating a victory out of this appalling shambles, what a defeat it was.

After six weeks of fighting, France, that great and historic military power, surrendered. The unthinkable had happened. As Winston

THE FIRST OF THE FEW

Churchill – who had dramatically succeeded Neville Chamberlain as British Prime Minister on the very day Germany surprised the West – rightly predicted: 'What General Weygand called the 'Battle of France' is over. The Battle of Britain is about to begin.'

Before Germany could mount a seaborne invasion of southern England however, aerial supremacy had to be achieved – which was the enemy's objective in the Battle of Britain. Later, according to the British Air Ministry, the sixteen-week aerial campaign began on 10 July 1940. The first phase saw attacks on convoys before the enemy's focus moved to the ports and radar installations, Fighter Command's airfields, and London. From 7 September 1940, Londoners were bombed around the clock, the pre-war assurance that the 'bomber would always get through' becoming an apparent reality. What did not become a reality, however, was the presumption that civilians under bombardment would lose the will to resist, and instead rise up against their own government. Quite the reverse occurred: the bombing only served to generate hatred of the enemy and bolster the nation's resolve behind Churchill's coalition War Cabinet to continue the fight. 'Britain Can Take It' became a new watch-word for courage – bombed out shopkeepers' signs indicating 'Business As Usual' emphasising the civilian population's resolve helped win the respect and admiration of the free world.

During the summer and autumn of 1940, some 2,000 aircrew of Fighter Command took on the so far undefeated Luftwaffe – these young men from Britain, the Commonwealth, and free men from the occupied lands being immortalised by Churchill in his speech of 20 August 1940: 'Never in the field of human conflict has so much been owed by so many to so few.' And so, the aircrew of Fighter Command who fought the Battle of Britain, which ended, according to the Air Ministry, on 31 October 1940, became forevermore known as the 'Few' – a clever allusion by Churchill, a master of the English language, to the victory of Henry V's outnumbered and disease-ridden army over the might of French nobility at Agincourt in 1415, and Shakespeare's words: 'We few, we happy few, we band of brothers'.

The climax of the Battle of Britain came on 15 September 1940, when mass raids were made around the clock, again on London. Although the number of German aircraft destroyed was inflated, everyone sensed a turning point.

Two days later, Hitler postponed the proposed invasion indefinitely. By the end of that month, the Luftwaffe was unable to continue sustaining such heavy losses to its bomber force, and switched the main assault to night attacks – the infamous Blitz on British cities, which reached its dreadful zenith on the night of 10/11 May 1941. The daylight battle was not over, however, as the fighters of both sides clashed until well beyond the Air Ministry's preferred end-date, until bad winter weather in early 1941 put a natural stop to things. Between the Battle of Britain's official dates, 544 of the Few were either killed in action or reported missing.

By beating off the enemy attack, however, Fighter Command had proved that the Luftwaffe could be beaten, and that the bomber was not invincible. Crucially, the Few had proved to the still neutral Americans that Britain, although alone under the German bombs, was far from beaten. The importance of the Few's achievement, therefore, cannot be underestimated, and indeed, as the war progressed and was ultimately won, the enormity of this deliverance would be increasingly understood and celebrated.

In 1939, *The Lion Had Wings* had conveyed its message through a 'docudrama' style, which had proved immensely popular, featuring determined and daring Spitfire pilots beating back an enemy raid; during the summer of 1940 there was no need for fictional interpretations – the battle in the air was happening for real, and with it came an insatiable thirst for news. Naturally, at the time, the 'fighter boys' were looked up to as the modern equivalent of heroic, chivalrous, knights, the glamorous duellists of the skies – and cinema was now well accepted as a powerful means of communicating news and propaganda.

THE FIRST OF THE FEW

The Ministry of Information capitalised on this through the production not of feature films but of 'shorts', providing the public with information, some featuring fighter pilots. More popular were newsreels, made by such companies as Pathé Gazette and British Movietone News. One newsreel made by the latter, appearing in 1940, was entitled *Well done! The Fighter Command.* Today, this, and other newsreels like it, provide us unique glimpses of the past. This particular newsreel (available on YouTube) comprises a number of separately entitled sequences, one, for example, being *RAF Fighters Ever on the Alert*, featuring Hurricanes landing and the pilots of 56 Squadron awaiting the call to scramble at North Weald.

Among the pilots featured lounging around at dispersal, awaiting the call to scramble, are Squadron Leader G.A.L. 'Minnie' Manton, Flight Lieutenant 'Jumbo' Gracie, and Flight Lieutenant Percy 'Squeak' Weaver, dating this footage as before 31 August 1940 – the date Weaver was reported missing over the Essex coast. Later, another sequence, using graphics, showed tactics used when a Spitfire intercepts a He 111 bomber, and real camera-gun footage of a Stuka under attack. Newsreels such as this were well-received and highly popular with the public, showing as they did, albeit censored, authentic images of the war in progress. During the Battle of Britain, of 250 newsreels, eighty-three featured the RAF. Although there was no shortage of cinematic exposure for Fighter Command, the Battle of Britain would have to wait until 1942 for its first British feature film proper.

Nonetheless, the Director, Brian Desmond Hurst, whose previous works included *The Lion Has Wings*, worked the Battle of Britain into his film *Dangerous Moonlight*, released on 26 June 1941. During 1940, the RAF's ranks had fortunately been increased by volunteers, many being trained pilots and airmen, from the occupied lands – men who had been evacuated or escaped, via various routes and means, to continue the fight. The largest national group among these freedom fighters desperate to liberate their oppressed homelands was the Poles, who fought with distinction during the Battle of Britain and beyond. In this love story, Hurst focuses on the fictional tale of 'Stefan 'Steve' Radecki' (Anton Walbrook), a Polish fighter pilot and gifted concert pianist who meets an American reporter, 'Carole Peters' (Sally Gray) in Warsaw. After the German invasion, 'Radecki' volunteers, but is not chosen, to fly a 'suicide mission' (hence the film's American release became *Suicide Squadron*). Nonetheless, he is among the last to leave Warsaw, ending up in New York, where he meets up with and marries 'Carole'.

The couple travelled to the UK for 'Radecki' to continue the fight to free his homeland, where he gives a concert – the scene famous for the *Warsaw Concerto*, written by Richard Addinsell. Later, 'Radecki' is shown as a pilot in a British Spitfire squadron, newsreel footage of 222 Squadron being among those clips used, and in action, for a full-on fourteen minutes, when he ultimately only narrowly survives ramming a He 111. Baling out, wounded and 'shell-shocked', 'Radecki' suffers memory loss. Recovering in hospital, our hero recalls the *Warsaw Concerto* and meeting his wife, whom he recognises and repeats the words spoken when they first met: 'Carole, it's not safe to go out with you when the moon is so bright' – and lived happily ever after. While *Dangerous Moonlight* became a box office hit in Britain, it was less well-received in America, and Walbrook was unhappy with his own performance. Again, this film was, though, important propaganda.

Released a few days after Hitler's invasion of Russia, *Dangerous Moonlight* was a timely reminder of Britain's achievement less than a year previously, when Fighter Command successfully defied the mighty Luftwaffe. The film was also an acknowledgement of the contribution made by foreign nationals, in this case the more numerous Poles. It is no surprise, however, that the Spitfire, yet again, was the featured fighter – the iconic aircraft's technical superiority, in addition to its charismatic good-looks, was well acknowledged by this time, and in 1941 the Spitfire had replaced the Hurricane as the RAF's front-line fighter. The type was also the focus of the immensely popular 'Spitfire Fund', in which citizens, corporations, businesses and other organisations at home and overseas were encouraged to raise money for the Air Ministry for the purchase of Spitfires. £5,000 was the figure set to donate an aircraft. Hundreds of such 'presentation aircraft' would ultimately arise from this propaganda masterstroke by Lord Beaverbrook, the press magnate and Minister of Aircraft Production – who provided the Home Front a means of hitting back at Hitler's bombers. The fact was, given all of this exposure in films, newsreels, shorts and the 'Spitfire Fund', the Spitfire had received unprecedented promotion, which had inspired the free world – and everybody wanted to see it.

On 26 September 1941, an American-made film, *A Yank in the RAF*, was released by 20th Century-Fox. Although not a British film, like certain other productions mentioned in this text, this cinematic story, based upon a story by Darryl F. Zanuck (under the pseudonym 'Melville Crossman'), is relevant to the development of cinema-goers' experience during wartime. When the film was made and released, America remained neutral, the Neutrality Acts preventing American citizens joining the armed forces of belligerent powers. Consequently those so-called 'Gun Jumpers', who were unable to wait for America to enter the war before playing their part, first had to travel to Canada and enlist in the RCAF.

In the film, 'Tim Baker' (Tyrone Power) is a self-focused but intrepid adventurer clandestinely ferrying American-built aircraft across the border to Canada, before similarly flying a Hudson to England, and rekindling acquaintance with his periodic girlfriend 'Carol Brown' (Betty Grable) who has joined the WAAF. Not to be outdone, 'Baker' joins the RAF but is disappointed at his posting to a bomber unit, and less impressed further still when his first operation involves not dropping bombs but leaflets. Cutting a long story short, 'Baker' answers Fighter Command's call for volunteers and finds himself operational on a Spitfire squadron in time for Dunkirk. After shooting down two enemy fighters, 'Baker' is himself shot down but manages to return to England – and, as inevitably as he ends up flying a Spitfire, gets the girl.

Although ostensibly not an overt propaganda film, *A Yank in the RAF* nonetheless drew attention to those American volunteers already fighting the Axis, and through a comparatively light-hearted look at the war and clever pairing of two of Hollywood's most popular stars, the film became the studio's second most successful film of the war (after *How Green Was My Valley*, about a Welsh mining community). Again, the storyline of the central character's desire to become a fighter pilot, and evocation of the dark days of Dunkirk, all helped to romanticise the Spitfire.

The wider RAF, however, was not being ignored by either newsreels, shorts, or film. Bomber Command had come into sharp focus when *Target for Tonight* was released on 18 August 1941. Produced by the Crown Film Unit, the popular film featured the story of a raid on Germany, from start to finish, showing the RAF at work. Interestingly, one of the Wellington pilots appearing in the film was Percy Charles 'Pick' Pickard, at the time a squadron leader serving with 311 (Czech) Squadron, but later killed flying Mosquitoes during the audacious raid on Amiens prison, Operation *Jericho*, mounted to release French Resistance prisoners.

One of Our Aircraft is Missing, released on 27 June 1942, told the story of a Wellington crew forced to bale out over the Netherlands and whose successful evasion was greatly assisted by brave Dutch civilians. Directed by Michael Powell (previously one of *The Lion Has Wings* three directors) and Emerich Pressburger, the film received two Oscar nominations and remains one of Britain's best-loved films of the Second World War. Nonetheless, it was behind two films in the box office ratings, namely *Mrs Miniver* and *The First of the Few* – both of which returned to Fighter Command and, of course, the Spitfire.

Mrs Miniver was not a British-made film but a Hollywood production, providing Americans a utopian view of an upper-class

THE FIRST OF THE FEW

British family's part in the 'People's War'. By the time Metro-Goldwyn-Mayer released the film on 4 June 1942, the United States had been in the war for over six months, following the surprise Japanese attack on Pearl Harbor on 7 December 1941 – and it was now equally crucial to maintain morale and public confidence in America. To that end, the US Department of War had already commissioned Frank Capra to direct a series of seven factual documentaries explaining why America was in the war, and why it had to be fought and won. The first of these, *Prelude to War*, was released on 27 May 1942; it explained the causes of the Second World War and placed the blame firmly at the Axis Powers' door. *Mrs Miniver* took this theme further through a storyline revolving around a peace-loving, functional and thoroughly decent British family.

'Kay Miniver' (Greer Garson) is the family's unassuming but wise and stoic matriarch, whose son, 'Vin' (Richard Ney, who in real life was to marry Garson) returns from university, meets, falls in love with and marries 'Carol' (Teresa Wright), the daughter of 'Lady Beldon' (Dame May Whitty). Determined to do his 'bit', 'Vin' joins the RAF, becoming, inevitably, a Spitfire pilot. 'Mr Clem Miniver' (Walter Pidgeon) takes his boat off to join the heroic 'Little Ships' assisting the Dunkirk evacuation, and upon return the 'Minivers' take in their stride being nearly killed when a bomb hits their home, and 'Mrs Miniver' capturing a fugitive Nazi airman (Helmut Dantine). After 'Vin' and 'Carole' are married and return from their Scottish honeymoon, the now two 'Mrs Minivers' accompany 'Vin' in his sports car to his nearby aerodrome, watching with concern his Spitfire squadron scramble.

Eventually, the ladies, with 'Mrs Miniver' senior driving, leave the airfield – comprising most unlikely timber-built buildings – and head home, through the blackout. On the way, they are forced to stop when the village is heavily bombed (clear message there: not a legitimate military target, and throughout the film the viewer has come to know some of the villagers and their peaceful, simple way of life). A German Stuka machine-guns the car – killing 'Carole'. 'Vin' returns from duty and surviving aerial combat to the devastating news that his wife of only a few days has been tragically killed by enemy action. The film's subsequent finale is sheer genius. The 'Minivers' and villagers are seen attending a service in the bombed-out local church, complete with Medieval knight's effigy, where the 'Vicar' (Henry Wilcoxon) takes his central theme from Psalm 91:5: 'You will not fear the terror of the night, nor the arrow that flies by day, nor the pestilence that stalks in the darkness, nor the destruction that wastes noonday.' The 'Vicar' then delivers a powerful and deeply moving sermon affirming their cause's moral right and emphasising that this, above all others, was the 'People's War'.

The roar (actually more of a whine, definitely not the Merlins supposed) of aero-engines then interrupts proceedings as through a gaping hole in the church roof we see an endless stream, or so it seems, of Spitfires heading out, presumably, to once more engage the Luftwaffe – to the rousing hymn *Onward Christian Soldiers*, and finally *Land of Hope and Glory*. The Battle of Britain is not specifically mentioned, but clearly this is an allusion to it, and so influential did America's President Roosevelt consider the final sermon that he ordered it produced as leaflets in various languages for dropping over enemy occupied territory, and had it published in the magazines *Time* and *Look*.

Mrs Miniver became the top box office attraction of 1942, making an initial profit of $4,831 and becoming the studio's most profitable film of the year. It was particularly well-received in America, which Churchill considered vitally important, and was named by 555 of 592 American film critics as the year's best film – doing great service in rallying support in America for Britain and the war.

In Germany, the film even won the admiration of Goebbels, who acknowledged that the propaganda power of *Mrs Miniver* was of a level only previously 'dreamed of', and that the anti-German sentiment was subtly achieved without one hostile word spoken against Germany. Although popular in Britain, the cinema-going public's reaction was mixed – but the film remains the benchmark for the nation's perceived popular memory of and identity during the Second World War.

More important than *Mrs Miniver* to British audiences in 1942, however, was *The First of the Few*.

The First of the Few

Given the enormity of the Few's achievement and the unprecedented place this unique victory had in the contemporary national consciousness, it is perhaps surprising that it would be two years before the event was celebrated and featured in a British feature film. Several ideas were considered but rejected until the Australian writer Henry C. James hit the right note with a story that had everything: the life, premature death and inspirational achievement of the genius Reginald Joseph Mitchell, tragic designer of the iconic Spitfire, who had died of cancer on 11 June 1937 – without ever knowing the immense contribution his Spitfire made during the Second World War.

Film-producer George King and his partner John Stafford bought the option to James's idea, and set up a company, 'British Aviation Pictures', covering the rights. Metro-Goldwyn-Mayer expressed interest but only if they controlled all rights, which was unacceptable to King. The British actor Leslie Howard was approached with a view to him playing the lead role of R.J. Mitchell, but Howard had no interest in working on another Hollywood-backed project.

After MGM left the arena, however, Howard agreed to the starring role – and also became both director and producer, buying the film's rights – which was then financed by Rank. Coincidentally, Howard, like Alexander Korda, although born in London was of Hungarian-Jewish heritage. When war broke out, Howard had returned to Britain from America, to assist the war effort by making morale-boosting films – and was now embarking upon what would prove to be his greatest contribution in that endeavour.

King and Stafford had already identified the genius of Churchill's use of language by eulogising Fighter Command's aircrew as the 'Few', and received the Prime Minister's consent to use his words on-screen. Knowing that this stirring film about the Spitfire needed Air Ministry and other official support to ensure the best possible result, Howard also enlisted Churchill's help, who endorsed the project in writing and even personally called Air Chief Marshal Sholto Douglas, Air Officer Commanding RAF Fighter Command, to impress upon him that all necessary cooperation must be provided to British Aviation Pictures.

With Churchill aboard, anything was possible: a Supermarine S6 Schneider Trophy seaplane was produced for studio scenes, along with a Spitfire fuselage, and access for Howard to experience the atmosphere and rituals of the RAF fighter station at Biggin Hill. Best of all, the film-makers were given permission to film at the 10 Group Sector Station airfield of Ibsley, near Ringwood in Hampshire – home to Squadron Leader Christopher 'Bunny' Currant's Spitfire-equipped 501 Squadron, and Squadron Leader Frank Howell's 118; both pilots were decorated Battle of Britain aces, and their men included more of the actual Few.

Filming was also to go ahead at RAF Warmwell, on the coast near Weymouth in Dorset. Unlike Ibsley, Warmwell, the satellite and forward airfield of the Middle Wallop Sector Station, had played an active part in the Battle of Britain. Howard now had Spitfires, pilots, a Blenheim for use as a camera-ship – and even use of an airworthy He 111 bomber! This aircraft had been shot-up by Spitfires on 9 February 1940 and made a forced-landing at North Berwick Law, East Lothian. Having suffered only minor damage, the German bomber was repaired and subsequently operated by the Air Fighting Development Unit based at Duxford, and 1426 (Enemy Aircraft)

Flight. Howard could not have asked for more, and was positioned, therefore, to make a spectacular British aviation film.

Another advantage Churchill's involvement secured was the temporary release from war service of the British actor David Niven – chosen to play 'Geoffrey Crisp', a composite character based upon various test pilots, in what would be his first major British film. Rosamund John became 'Diana Mitchell', 'RJ's' wife (although in real-life Mrs Mitchell's name was actually Florence).

The Russian-born Anton de Grunwald, who had worked with Howard on *Pygmalion* in 1938 and wrote the screenplay for his *Pimpernel Smith* of 1941, collaborated with the prolific screenwriter Sir Miles Malleson, producing a workable film script from the original story written by King and Stafford. Many years later, Dr Gordon Mitchell, son of 'RJ' and Florence Mitchell, considered that the eventual script pursued two key themes: first, 'the widely-held public image of the high-powered, highly intelligent 'boffin' and second, 'the idea of someone literally killing himself by grossly overworking to produce something of vital importance, in this case, of course, the Spitfire'. How accurate these themes were in relation to Mitchell's story, however, was a quite different matter.

Nonetheless, Howard's stage was now set.

The First of the Few: A Reading.

The film begins with a narration, setting the scene, the opening line of which determines the direction of travel: 'It is the twentieth century, but the old Medieval tyranny has once more risen in Germany.' A map of Europe graphically illustrates how much of Europe has been 'absorbed', 'obliterated', 'overrun' or 'invaded' by Nazi Germany, newsreel footage providing further impact. An American reporter cuts in, stating that Britain is alone and many in the US doubt the country can withstand Germany's onslaught. At 0.2.56 we hear a

THE BATTLE OF BRITAIN ON THE BIG SCREEN

German propaganda broadcast by the British traitor William Joyce, better-known as 'Lord Haw-Haw', played over newsreel footage of Hitler, Goebbels and Göring, in which the Nazi leaders make clear their plans to invade Britain by August 1940 – and to devastate London by bombing.

According to Joyce, 'England will be erased from history, it will be over in a few weeks'. Churchill's steady and familiar tone then takes over from Joyce's shrill, almost hysterical shrieking, reassuring the people of Britain that the nation had 'become the sole champions now in arms to defend the world's cause'. Scenes of quintessential rural England, and London's air raid shelters accompany the Prime Minister's words, which make clear that Britain will fight on against Nazi tyranny – whatever the odds. Clearly, the hour is grim indeed.

At 0.5.00 we come to 'Zero Day: 15 September 1940', the height of and great turning point of the Battle of Britain, and see a reconstruction of the activity in a Fighter Command Operations Room, with raid after incoming raid being plotted on the great map table. Models, contrived graphics and newsreel footage of mass formations provide visual images, the 'Controller' (Cyril Raymond) having to be reminded by a steel-helmeted WAAF to put on his 'Battle Bowler' with German aircraft overhead.

At 0.6.20 we see our first Spitfires, a Mk IIA and a cannon-armed VB of 501 Squadron, flaps down, coming in to land at Ibsley, the Controller telling us that this is '227 Squadron' at 'Seafield', a frontline fighter station.

Groundcrews are seen hurrying out to replenish fuel and ammunition, and at 0.6.41 we see our first fighter pilot, walking in after landing, mug of tea in hand. This is Squadron Leader Christopher 'Bunny' Currant DFC, one of the Few and commander of 501 Squadron, who confirms to his Intelligence Officer that he 'got a Ju 88 and had a crack at a Dornier'. Other pilots talk excitedly of their recent combat, including at 0.6.49 the moustachioed Flight Lieutenant Gillen of 118 Squadron.

Enter another of the Few (right, 0.7.02), Flying Officer Peter Howard-Williams, and Pilot Officer John Robson, both also of 118; 0.7.19 includes another of the Few, Pilot Officer David Fulford (left), as 'Bunny' expresses concern over the 'CO', who has yet to return. Interestingly, the (unidentified) fair-haired pilot at right is a sergeant-pilot – of which there were many, although in this film those featured are otherwise exclusively officers.

At 0.7.31 the CO's Spitfire appears, causing consternation because the pilot is trying to land without flaps (essentially air brakes), suggesting that he has been shot-up, coming in too fast. At 0.7.46 we see our first glimpse of Niven – 'Wing Commander Geoffrey Crisp', in this scene the Station Commander of 'Seafield' – leading the charge of those rushing to assist the crash-landed pilot. The pilot is groggy but manages to exit the Spitfire with the help of 'Crisp'. This is Squadron Leader Frank Howell DFC, CO of 118 Squadron and another of the Few – who doesn't want an ambulance but another Spitfire, 'as there are hundreds of them up there and probably more coming'.

At 0.8.24 we return to the Operations Room, Seafield's '654 Squadron' being scrambled despite having only recently landed. The pilots run to their machines in a mixture of uniform and flying clothing, these being real Spitfire pilots and not actors. 0.8.38 sees Bunny outside dispersal with a pipe-smoking Flight Lieutenant Brian Kingcome DFC, yet another of the Few. The two pilots join others of '227 Squadron', lounging outside the pilots' hut – including Fulford, Howard-Williams, Gillen and Robson, whom we have met before – and one more of the Few, Flight Lieutenant Tony Bartley DFC, seen sitting on the building's steps, reading a paper as Spitfires roar into the sky.

At 0.9.00 'Crisp' joins the assembly, confirming that the CO was not badly hurt and congratulating the pilots on that afternoon's 'bag' of six enemy aircraft destroyed. The conversation then turns to the Spitfire, Bartley remarking (0.9.33) that 'You can't see a

Spit without getting a kick out of it!' Banter follows with Robson and Howard-Williams ribbing Bartley ('Rembrandt') about being an artist – until 'Crisp' confirms that the Spitfire was 'designed by an artist ... R.J. Mitchell', 'A wizard', according to 'Rembrandt', 'who ... lives in Inverness' Gillen adds, while Flight Lieutenant John Bisdee (0.9.59), also of the Few, suggests that 'He's in Canada, MI5.' An unseen voice adds that Mitchell 'Works at Vickers', while Bunny hits the spot: 'He's dead, isn't he?' before Robson assures the gathering that Mitchell designed the Spitfire in just 'two hours' at a 'golf club' – turning to 'Crisp' for confirmation. Niven rightly responds that 'It wasn't as easy as that', before being interrupted by a Spitfire overhead, flying aerobatics – this aircraft being flown by Supermarine Test Pilot Jeffrey Quill and filmed at RAF Northolt in November 1941. 'Crisp' then wistfully reflects on the past, and begins to tell the pilots how the Spitfire really was created – the drama now flashing back to 1922.

At 0.10.47, the camera is on a cliff-top, looking up vertically into the sky and filming seagulls in flight. A few seconds later we see 'R.J. Mitchell' (Leslie Howard) for the first time, lying on the cliffs dreamily watching the birds through binoculars, and we meet his wife, 'Diana Mitchell' (Rosamund John). The conversation concerns how man must learn the art and science of flight from birds, the implication being that the seagulls are Mitchell's inspiration. Gordon Mitchell, who was present while these scenes were filmed and acted as script-reader for the actors between filming, was adamant that Howard's portrayal of his father was the 'complete opposite' to the character he knew – who was actually 'forceful, strong, quick-tempered and very much awake all the time'.

Unhappy with the scene, Gordon later sought the view of Supermarine Test Pilot Jeffrey Quill, who knew 'RJ' well and described him as 'a hard-headed, highly practical man', who, when 'seeking inspiration' or trying to solve a problem, would not have been hanging around 'watching bloody seagulls!' Indeed, in Gordon's view, had his father ever watched the scene, his reaction would probably have been 'unprintable'. These scenes, however, rather underpin the film, 'Mitchell' announcing his intention to one day design and produce an aircraft 'just like a bird' (0.12.13), sketching a monoplane seaplane – on the reverse of an invitation from the Directors of the Supermarine Aviation Co Ltd, his employers, for Mr and Mrs Mitchell to attend a 'Luncheon in the Works Assembly Shop on the occasion of the Schneider Trophy Race, Naples, August 12, 1922.'

By 00.12.46 we are at said function, with 'Commander Bride' (Ronald Culver), a Director, extolling the virtues of the Supermarine Sea Lion, a hefty-looking biplane seaplane, the Company's entry in that year's Schneider Trophy race – which was, according to 'Bride', 'The greatest international sporting event in the world.' Supermarine, based on the banks of the Itchen estuary at Woolston, near Southampton, specialised in making flying boats, the Sea Lion being a modified First World War Supermarine Baby, for which Mitchell, the Company's Chief Designer, and owner, Hubert Scott-Paine, had been responsible. 'Bride' provides the race's background detail, explaining that in 1921 the race was 'won by our Italian friends', who, if they were to win in 1922, would be the third and final consecutive win enabling Italy to keep the coveted Trophy – which Supermarine was determined not to allow. This is not correct; up to this point, Italy had not yet won twice.

The Mitchells, however, are not at the lunch, 'RJ' having been reluctant to make a speech, arriving at the Supermarine works (0.14.10) to hear, amid enthusiastic cheers, that the Sea Lion had won the Naples race in record time. In reality, the Supermarine entrant had beaten the Italians into second place by just 2.5 mph, with a top speed of 145.7 mph. 'Mrs Mitchell' then persuades her husband, amid rapturous congratulations, to show the Directors his monoplane design – but they have other ideas: without giving the designer an opportunity to reveal his plans, 'Mr Higgins' (David Horne) declares that Mitchell 'lacks practical experience' and will therefore spend a couple of years in the 'Assembly Shop'. Crestfallen, Mitchell drops his revolutionary sketch and, according to Niven's narration, 'That was the end of Mitchell's strange ideas.'

The film then jumps ahead to the following year's race (0.16.03), which was held at Cowes. At 0.16.21 we see some incredibly rare actual footage of the Sea Lion taking off from the Itchen estuary, and in flight, these clips supposedly being the race and interwoven with cheering actors on the ground. Unfortunately, the American Curtiss CR-3, beat the Sealion by 20 mph. Niven's narrative then explains how Mitchell spent the next year designing the same old biplanes while 'dreaming' of his monoplane.

This is simply untrue. The CR-3 was an advanced design, boasting several forward-thinking features, including a liquid-cooled engine, wing surface radiators and a metal propeller. In reality, Mitchell spent his time not 'dreaming' but designing the revolutionary S.4 – a monoplane seaplane even more advanced than the American machine. Unlike the CR-3, Mitchell's new creation was not reliant upon crude-looking bracing struts and wires – his monoplane was cantilevered. The single wing was made in one piece, covered not in the traditional doped fabric but plywood, the fuselage, of monocoque construction, being similarly covered, included a fin and tailplane. The bullet-like nose was sheeted in aluminium and housed a Napier Lion engine; the propeller was also metal. Far from being influenced by seagulls, and abandoning his monoplane dream, Mitchell's S.4 was the result of technological progress.

At 0.17.04, we see 'Crisp' appear as a civilian and old school friend of Mitchell's. An out of work former First World War fighter pilot, and test pilot, 'Crisp' seeks an appointment with the designer. Clearly a charmer, cutting a long and largely irrelevant story short, 'Crisp' rekindles auld acquaintance with 'Mitch'. Over dinner that evening, the two men enthusiastically pour over the S.4 designs, which, it is agreed, 'Crisp' will test fly. Unfortunately the Supermarine Board fails to agree with 'Crisp' that the monoplane is 'the future', 'Higgins' insisting that another biplane is required. Faced with such backward-thinking, 'Mitchell' resigns. Again, this is patently untrue.

In reality, Supermarine produced the S.4, which, on 13 September 1925, set a new air speed record over Southampton Water at 226.75 mph. Nonetheless, no need for facts to obstruct a good story, and in the film 'Mitchell' and 'Crisp' leave dejected. While Mitchell's resignation is not accurate, this artistic licence does indicate the man's strong-headedness.

The scene then changes to high tea al fresco style at the Mitchells' picturesque cottage home, with 'Mitch', 'Diana' and 'Crisp' (the Mitchells actually lived in a detached house called 'Hazeldine', which Mitchell himself designed, at Russell Place, Portswood, on the western side of Southampton). Mitchell returns from London having been unable to find a job, and laments having not been able to get 'Crisp' a job, or, indeed, keep his own. 'Diana', however, is stoic, and 'Gordon' is shown (and named) as a baby in a pram ('Hello, old boy'). Then (0.33.06) Mitchell receives a welcome call from Supermarine, and is given the recall – and permission to build the S.4 – although the Board remains far from unanimous in support. Mitchell returns to Supermarine the following morning – and gets back to work. At 00.34.35, the S.4 is rolled out and successfully test-flown. The Supermarine team is soon on the way to the next Schneider Trophy race – held at Baltimore, USA, on 26 October 1925.

We now come to the 1925 race, amid great excitement (0.35.09). The American Jimmy Doolittle looks favourite to win in the Curtiss, when up goes 'Mr Geoffrey Crisp' in the S.4. In truth, there were many test pilots involved with both Supermarine's Schneider Trophy entries and, indeed, the subsequent Spitfire, not least among them Captain 'Mutt' Summers and Jeffrey Quill, so 'Crisp' is a composite character based a little, no doubt, on each of these men and their achievements.

At 0.36.09, we see some now otherwise unavailable and extraordinary original footage of the S.4, taxiing out, recorded at

Southampton during trials. 'Crisp', however, crashes the S.4 in an high-speed dive from which he is unable to recover – although badly injured, the debonair pilot survives. There is some truth in this: the S.4 did crash inexplicably during the race, although later it was suspected aileron flutter the most likely cause.

Niven's narration tells us that it appeared as though Mitchell's hopes had perished with his 'curious machine' (0.39.15) – but his 'weird ideas were beginning to catch on, and he was given one more chance'.

The scene them jumps to 1927 – Venice – and that year's Schneider Trophy competition. The previous year, being after the S.4 crash, Mitchell had not, in fact, had time to produce an entrant for the 1926 race, which the Italians won – so now both the Italians and Americans each needed just one more victory to retain the Trophy forever. Britain's 1927 entrant was Mitchell's new S.5, which had a metal-covered fuselage smaller in cross-section to the S.4. Everything about the S.5 was intended to reduce drag, including flush rivets and a highly polished surface.

This entry was actually Air Ministry funded and flown by RAF pilots of the High-Speed Flight, formed specifically for the race – which was, we discover from the narration, is how 'Crisp' 'got back into this racket'. At 0.39.33 we see the British delegation, including the 'Mitchells' and 'Crisp', now in RAF uniform and a flight lieutenant. The Brits are subjected to a 'welcome' speech by an Italian fascist officer who reads a message from the Duce, Italy's dictator Benito Mussolini, predicting an Italian win. The atmosphere remains convivial, however.

At 00.42.41 we see 'Mitchell' leaving his wife at midnight to go to work on the S.5, final teething troubles and preparations for the race – the first indication we have of how hard the designer is starting to push himself. A few seconds later we see the S.5 at the flight sheds – this being an accurate full-scale model. The technical issue is resolved by morning and 'Crisp' romps home to a resounding victory – thus ensuring that the competition continues.

At 0.47.15 we are again treated to some otherwise lost footage of what is actually Mitchell's subsequent design, the S.6, filmed taxiing across Southampton Water in 1929. Two S.5s actually competed, winning first and second place, setting another speed record of 281.66 mph. Mitchell's team returned home in triumph – but the narrative explains that Mitchell was still not satisfied and 'hotted up' the S.5. As the film explains through newspaper cuttings (00.52.18), Flight Lieutenant S.M. Kinkead of the High-Speed Flight was 'anxious' to attempt a new air speed record in the improved aircraft. Unfortunately, Kinkead was killed in that attempt, when he crashed into the Solent. Mitchell was devastated, which is well portrayed in the film (0.52.29). Fortunately, 'Mitchell' is persuaded by 'Crisp' to keep going.

By now, the race was being held biannually, giving Mitchell more time to design a new machine. Certainly, the competition was fierce: in March 1928, the same month Kinkead crashed, the Italians increased the record to 318.57 mph. At 0.53.14, however, 'Mitchell' expresses concern over funding for the project – which is hardly surprising seeing as 1929 also saw the Wall Street Crash. By 0.53.15, however, we are in the office of 'Sir Ian McLaren' (J.H. Roberts), a character based upon the Scottish engineer and industrialist Sir Robert McLean, who had become Chairman of Vickers Ltd in 1928 – which purchased Supermarine – a deal, according to 'Sir Ian' in the film, well-worth the half-a-million price-tag just for Mitchell. McLean was forward-thinking, encouraging Mitchell, and in the film 'McLaren' takes on this mantle, offering 'Mitchell' 'unlimited facilities'.

This development, Niven's narrative explains, gave Mitchell a 'new lease of life', enabling him to design and produce the S.6, which was 'so far ahead of its time', ready for the 1929 race (0.55.58). This time Mitchell had designed his seaplane around a potent new engine made by Rolls-Royce.

At 0.56.03 we again see otherwise unobtainable footage, this time of the S.6 being run-up on dry land and subsequently taxiing across

Southampton Water. That year's competition was held at Calshot on the Solent – and was won by Flight Lieutenant H.R.D. Waghorn flying an S.6 at an average speed of 328.63 mph – meaning that Britain had also now won the imposing Trophy twice – which is shown at 0.56.21. After Waghorn's record-breaking flight, Squadron Leader A.H. Orlebar achieved speeds of 336.3 and 357.7 mph, setting a new record – confirming the S.6 as both the fastest and most advanced aeroplane in existence.

At the film's victory party, however, a yacht is shown flying an illuminated message between masts: 'Down With The Government – Wake Up England' (0.56.33). This statement is by the eccentric British patriot, political activist, suffragette and nationalist, Dame Fanny Lucy Houston, widow of a wealthy shipping magnate. 'Lady Houston' (Toni Edgar-Bruce), who attends the party and congratulates 'Mitchell', assuring him that Britain must be 'strong on sea and land' – while the designer adds 'And in the air'. This later proves significant – although this meeting between Mitchell and Lady Houston never actually took place.

We now jump forward to 1931 (1.00.33) and the House of Commons in session while 'Sir Ian McLaren' and colleagues wait outside the chamber, the debate within concerning continued government sponsorship of Supermarine's Schneider Trophy entry that year – a vexing issue, because Britain, like Italy and America, required just one more win to keep the prize – which had become a matter of great national interest and pride.

At 01.01.25, an anonymous, unseen, MP is heard presenting a Parliamentary Question: 'Is the government aware of the very serious effect withdrawal will have on the RAF's position throughout the world, and also the repercussion for the aircraft industry in this country?' A counter argument is stated by another unseen MP: 'Is the Government aware that there are 3 million unemployed in this country?' – implying that the £100,000 of tax-payers' money required to fund Britain's 1931 entry could better be spent elsewhere. The scene then jumps to a forlorn 'Mitchell' and 'Crisp', relaxing at the Royal Aero Club while awaiting the debate's outcome, then hearing from 'Squadron Leader Jefferson' (Derrick De Marney), leader of the High-Speed Flight (actually led by Squadron Leader A.H. Orlebar), that no public funds are being made available. Deliverance, however, is at hand from an unexpected source: Lady Houston. All of this requires further explanation.

As a result of the 1929 general election, Ramsay MacDonald's socialist Labour Party controlled the majority of seats in the Commons, and, with a Liberal alliance, formed a minority government – the second Labour administration, the first, elected in 1924, having lasted just ten months. In 1929, however, MacDonald's new government was rapidly consumed by the effects of the Wall Street Crash – which inflation and unemployment escalate to unmanageable proportions for which there appeared no solutions.

For these reasons, therefore, in January 1931, MacDonald had no choice but to withdraw public funding for Britain's Schneider Trophy entry. The Labour government was immediately attacked in the press and accused of being unpatriotic – although it is impossible not to sympathise with MacDonald, given the very serious fiscal and social issues affecting Britain that year.

The film then switches (1.01.38) to the Royal Aero Club's reception and the arrival of a stranger (Bernard Miles), seeking 'Squadron Leader Jefferson' on 'private' business. The receptionist is far from helpful, but then 'Mitchell', 'Crisp' and 'Jefferson' appear and are approached by the man – who proves to be 'Lady Houston's' agent and hands over her ladyship's gift of the £100,000 necessary to fund Britain's 1931 Schneider Trophy entry. Astonished, and very grateful, a small celebration then takes place.

There is some truth in this, although the money was not presented in a cheque to 'Jefferson'. Fully intending to embarrass the Labour government, Lady Houston actually offered the donation to the Prime Minister, concluding that 'I know I can confidently rely on the kindly help and cooperation of all who will rejoice if England wins.' Although the donation was accepted with alacrity, her Ladyship continued attacking the socialist government, who, she charged, was reducing Britain to a third-rate country. Given the immense difficulties faced by the government at that time, this would seem a somewhat extreme right-wing nationalistic perspective. Nonetheless, with only seven months to go, Britain was now back in the race.

We are then transported (01.03.18) to the race, which occurred at Calshot, on the Solent. Mitchell had not time to produce his proposed S.7, so instead beefed up the existing S.6 to become the S.6B. The film, surprisingly, fails to actually make much of the race, with just a couple of passes overhead of a model S.6B. In reality, Flight Lieutenant J.N. Boothman flashed over the cheering crowds at 340.08 mph – with his throttle not even wide open – winning the Schneider Trophy for Britain – Mitchell's fifth overall and third consecutive victory. That afternoon, Flight Lieutenant G.H. Stainforth pushed the world record in another S6.B to 379.05 mph. The depressed nation was delighted, British aviation supreme, and Mitchell was deservedly made a Commander of the British Empire (CBE). It really was a vitally important victory for Britain, as Gordon Mitchell explained:

> People who were sick and tired of the hopeless struggle to find work and the humiliation of the dole queues longed for some excitement to relieve the monotony of everyday life. The sight of Mitchell's seaplanes thundering across the sky at breathtaking speeds raised a cheer from lips with had forgotten to smile. England might be in a depression, but in the world of aviation she still had something of which to be proud.

In the film, Mitchell's victory is announced to the viewer (1.03.27) by way of newspaper front pages: 'Britain Keeps Schneider Trophy ... Supreme in the World of Speed.' According to Niven's narration, it was a victory of 'a far-sighted individual over a near-sighted government', thus perpetuating the anti-socialist government feeling.

The film then jumps to 1933 (1.03.52), 'Crisp' reappearing in 'Mitchell's' life as a 'disturbing influence' once more, while the designer harmlessly works on his garden. 'Mitchell' surprises his friend by saying that for the first time, he is 'taking it easy' on account of ambitions being fulfilled. 'Crisp' persuades the 'Mitchells' to go on holiday – to, of all places, Germany; 1933 was, of course, the year in which Hitler and the Nazis came to power. Among other things, the nation's youth was encouraged to be patriotic and nationalistic, and organised into Nazi movements, including the Hitler Youth. As previously outlined, although Germany was banned from having an air force by Versailles, the Luftwaffe had been secretly rebuilding for some years in Russia, and German youth was encouraged to be air-minded and introduced to gliding – as future recruits for Hitler's new air force.

At 1.05.15 we see a Göppingen Gö-1 glider passing overhead – a type commonly used in Germany for the introductory flying experience. A Bavarian brass band plays Wagner's *The Ring of the Nibelung* – enthusiastically for the British visitors' benefit – which is no coincidence: Wagner was Hitler's favourite composer and a confirmed anti-Semite. The local Sturmabteilung (SA) leader extols to the Mitchell party the benefits of 'strength through joy', revelling in show-casing the excellence of Nazi organisation and the Führer's will, subtly putting down the British until 'Crisp' points out, politely and equally subtly, that Britain did not need gliders as it had powered aeroplanes capable of achieving 400 mph – much to the Nazis' chagrin. Everybody is happily drinking good Bavarian beer when the band and Hitler Youth march off.

We join the British party at 1.07.25, at a dinner hosted by German general 'Von Straben' (Fritz Wendhausen, whose tunic is complete with an absurdly outsize national breast eagle) at the 'Richthofen Club'. Again, the atmosphere is convivial, and 'Mitchell' thanks his hosts, expressing appreciation of what he has seen in Germany: 'well organised youth, and a peace-loving people'.

Enter, at 1.09.33 the German designer 'Dr Willy Messerschmitt' (Erik Freund), in due course designer, among other things, of the German Me 109 fighter, who is introduced to 'Mitchell'. In conversation, 'Messerschmitt' gives a wry look when 'Mitchell' mentions having seen gliding clubs, which the German says 'have their uses' – implying that something more sinister was actually afoot with secret powered flight. Over after-dinner Cognac and cigars, 'Mitchell' again refers to his admiration for birds in flight (1.11.16), and a German officer present (Gerard Heinz) openly admits that Germany is not just making gliders – or only commercial aircraft – and that Germany has forgotten the Versailles Treaty. 'Messerschmitt' adds that important to aviation though Mitchell's achievements have been, nothing compares to the significance of Hitler coming to power in Germany. The Germans maintain they have 'had enough of being under-dogs' and state that Versailles is 'history', 'dead', and that now they intended to be 'overlords' with aggressive intentions, with more guns, tanks and powered aircraft than their enemies. 'Von Straben' realises that the conversation has gone too far, and puts a stop to it – but the damage is done; while the host reassures the British guests that 'England is our friend', a young, drunk, German, 'Von Crantz' (Victor Beaumont), laughs hysterically. Fortunately 'Diana Mitchell's' reappearance puts a stop to what has become both an awkward and disturbing conversation. As the three British guests make their way back to their hotel, 'Mitchell' and 'Crisp' are morose, realising the implications for Britain and peace involved – 'Mitchell' announcing that the holiday is over and that they must return home – 'Tomorrow'.

While gliding was used in Germany to encourage air-mindedness, and Versailles was being contravened in secret, the fact is that R.J. Mitchell never visited Germany – or met Willy Messerschmitt. Gordon Mitchell remembered that once the family enjoyed a holiday 'for pleasure only' in Austria. The Vickers Chief Test Pilot, Captain 'Mutt' Summers, however, did cultivate contacts in the German aviation industry and in the course of visits to Nazi Germany, Gordon affirms, 'managed to see aircraft not intended to be seen by British visitors'. Nonetheless, the film version has more impact than a picture of German intentions being assembled in Britain via diverse intelligence sources. If, however, 'Mitchell' lacked purpose when 'Crisp' reappeared in his life, his experience in Germany had convinced him, we are told at 1.15.37, that he now had 'more urgent' work to do than ever ...

Back home, 'Mitchell' recounts his experiences in Germany to 'Sir Ian MacLaren', at 1.16.30 making clear his intention: 'I want to build a fighter. The fastest, deadliest fighter in the world'. These are, however, what Churchill described as the 'years of the locust', when defence spending was massively reduced and disarmament was the watchword – not building a strong and modern air force. 'Sir Ian' refers to the (MacDonald) government having no interest in rearmament, opining that the only option was to 'Hatch a conspiracy against the government ... to make it raise the money for defence of the country.' 'Mitchell' agrees to champion the cause and persuades the Air Ministry to contribute £7,500 to help him develop his ideas – which, 'Mitchell' retorts is 'No use at all'.

It was, however, all the Air Ministry's coffer could stretch to. 'Mitchell' then meets with 'Sir Henry Royce' (George Skillan), telling the engineer of his intention to build a land-based fighter along the lines of his Schneider Trophy-winning seaplanes – for which he needed a new engine. Royce agrees to fund the development of the required engine, and suggests his new powerplant, 'The Merlin', which, 'Sir Henry' tells 'Mitchell', is named after 'Merlin ... That fellow at the court of King Arthur who worked wonders. Now my engine and your plane are going to do just that.' It was certainly clever story-telling to connect the Rolls-Royce Merlin engine with the legendary King Arthur, but in truth the engine was named after a bird of prey, joining other Rolls-Royce aero-engines including the similarly named Kestrel and Goshawk. There is, however, much more to all of this.

The Air Member for Research and Development was Air Marshal Sir Hugh Dowding, in due course Fighter Command's chief and who shaped Britain's aerial defences. Dowding, who had flown fighters during the First World War, was a technocrat who had recognised the monoplane's superiority. He was averse, however, to the effort and funding invested in the Schneider Trophy contest, arguing that such float-planes were useless for military purposes. What Dowding wanted to do was 'invite private tenders from two firms to cash in on the experience that had been gained in aircraft construction and engine progress so that we could order two of the fastest machines which it was possible to build with no restrictions except landing speed, and that had to be on grass airfields.'

This far-sighted proposal was agreed by the Air Ministry, leading to Specification F.7/30 being issued on 1 October 1931. Various companies submitted tenders, but Mitchell's submission, the Type 224 monoplane, fell short. The competition was won by Gloster Aircraft with a radial-engine biplane, the SS37; this never actually entered production, however, because the Air Ministry appreciated that its top-speed of 238 mph was an insufficient margin over existing service types. Mitchell had actually found F.7/30 too restrictive. Instead, Supermarine and Rolls-Royce agreed to collaborate, as a private venture, on 'a real killer fighter' – without Air Ministry restrictions or interference.

In November 1934, Mitchell was authorised to start work on his next proposal, the 'Type 300 Fighter', while concurrently Rolls-Royce improved its new PV XII engine – later called 'Merlin'. So, Mitchell did not have to garner support or raise funds for his fighter. The initiative actually came from Dowding at the Air Ministry – Mitchell was knocking at an open door from the outset. What is true, however, is that work on the 'Type 300' – which would later be called 'Spitfire' – did begin as a private venture, for the reasons now explained.

At 1.19.45, the charming womaniser 'Crisp' is off-duty, discussing his love-life with a barmaid when interrupted by 'Miss Harper' (Anne Firth) – 'Mitchell's' secretary – who has arranged a fifteen-minute free window, between 22.00 hours and 22.15 hours before the test pilot's date arrives, assuring him that they must speak on a 'very important' matter. 'Crisp' is not keen until 'Miss Harper' blurts out: 'It's about Mr Mitchell!' The pair then sit down and 'Miss Harper' explains her concern that the designer is working far too hard, over-working dawn to dusk every day. Indeed, even at that late hour, 'Mitch' is in the drawing office. 'Miss Harper' explains that this has gone on for months. Galvanised into action, 'Crisp' sweeps up 'Miss Harper' for the pair to 'Go and get him'. 'Mitchell' is found poring over his designs in an otherwise deserted office, and, tired and rather listless, is taken home to 'Diana' – and falls asleep in an armchair.

Awoken by 'Diana' with soup and rolls, 'Crisp' implores his brilliant friend to 'ease up a bit', which 'Mitch' rejects as impossible. What he wants is 'just out of reach', and has to 'do 400 mph, turn on a sixpence, climb to 10,000ft in a few minutes, dive at 500 (mph) without the wings coming off, carry eight machine-guns' ... which, 'Diana' reminds him, has all arisen from 'watching those birds' on the clifftop. Not so.

The specification for the RAF's new modern fighters was produced by the Air Ministry, and Dowding in particular. Mitchell therefore designed his fighter around that requirement. 'Mitchell' is, he says, designing 'A bird which breaths out fire and death and destruction ... A "Spitfire" bird.' Again, this is artistic licence. Ultimately, Mitchell's fighter was named 'Spitfire' by Sir Robert MacLean, after his daughter, Anne. Mitchell preferred calling his 'Type 300' the 'Shrew', but Spitfire was chosen by the Air Ministry in 1936 – much to Mitchell's annoyance, who observed it was 'Just the bloody silly sort of name they would give it.'

In the next scene, 'Sir Ian' wants to see 'Mitchell' (1.25.50) but is surprised to learn that the designer is not at work, and nor was he the previous day. Nonetheless, 'Mitchell' is summoned for a meeting that afternoon with 'Air Commodore Button' – but no one at the works has seen 'Mitchell'. 'Diana' is contacted and confirms that her husband left for work that morning as usual. 'Mitchell' is actually at a meeting with his doctor (1.26.18), a specialist (Brefni O'Rorke), who confirms the worst: 'You're a rather sick man, Mr Mitchell' – who is told to stop 'overdoing it' and completely stop working.

Advised to 'take a year off', 'go on holiday', that may make it possible for the designer to 'carry on for years'. The alternative, 'Mitchell' is gravely told, is that he will only live another year, at worst 'six to eight months'. After the shattering news, 'Mitchell' attends the meeting with 'Sir Ian' and the 'Air Commodore' (actor uncredited), who explains to the ailing genius that he has 'stirred up a hornets' nest', so much so that the Air Ministry wants his new fighter – and wants it in 'twelve months'. 'Mitchell', however, replies that it will be delivered in 'eight months' – we, the viewers, being aware of the dire and tragic reason why. So, how much of this is true?

As we have seen, Mitchell did not 'stir up a hornets' nest' to pressurise the Air Ministry into commissioning a new fighter. That initiative had already come from Whitehall and involved various aircraft manufacturers. Mitchell, a heavy cigarette and pipe smoker, had, however, been diagnosed with rectal cancer and underwent a colostomy operation in August 1933. He was certainly working on the Type 300, but not as feverishly as imagined by the film, knowing that he was a dying man who had to provide Britain the shining scimitar to defeat German bombers with. As Gordon Mitchell remembered:

> there was never any suggestion that his life might be prolonged if he worked part-time in future, or even stopped

working altogether. In fact, I recall that Father could not wait to get back to the work he loved and enjoyed so much, and undoubtedly his medical advisors knew full-well that such work could only be beneficial, particularly in relation to his mental well-being ... He obtained his pilot's licence in 1934 and in fact led an extremely active life. He did indeed work hard but he also played hard and enjoyed his leisure and social activities to the full. Hardly, I submit, the life led by a man who was seriously overworking to the detriment of his health.

From 1.28.36 onwards, Mitchell and the Supermarine work-force work feverishly to produce the new 'killer fighter' – these actually being wonderful scenes of Spitfire production at Supermarine. An issue arises and an engineer, 'MacPherson' (Herbert Cameron), requires a solution in three to four days; 'Mitchell', however, will ensure that he can 'have them the following morning'. Back home, at daybreak, 'Mitchell' is clearly becoming exhausted but is quizzed by 'Diana' – who has guessed 'something is the matter, you are not well'. Now, 'Mitchell' breaks the news that he has secretly seen a doctor, 'some fellow in Harley Street' – but impresses upon her that the work he is doing is 'more important than us'. 'Diana' works it all out: 'If you don't stop working – you'll *die*!' 'Mitchell' makes it clear that his work has to continue, amid his wife's tears, because the work is 'important' and 'we don't know when we've got to pack up'.

As if appealing to her husband's paternal instincts, 'Diana' produces and reads a letter from their son, Gordon, who is away at boarding school and has made the 1st XI but needs a hand-out – before berating her husband for working himself to death for 'something that may never happen'. As a compromise, 'Mitchell' offers up a holiday in Cornwall, after which he can return and finish the job, before a long holiday, 'anywhere in the world until I'm fit again' – at which 'Diana' breaks down. The moment, however, is lost when 'Mitchell' sees the *Evening Standard*'s front page: 'German Bombers Wipe Out Spanish Town' (1.33.59) – this, of course, referring to Guernica, leaving 'Mitchell' in no doubt of the need for him to finish his work, and the urgency of it: no holiday, but 'Diana' understands.

Next, we have more terrific footage of building Spitfires, with 'Mitchell' looking on (1.34.44). This is, of course, only supposed to be the prototype, K5054, which was built by Supermarine in Woolston. At 1.35.04 is a great shot of a fixed-pitch propeller being assembled, as fitted to the first Spitfires. The mighty Merlin, installed in the airframe is run-up – and at 1.35.18 we see the Spitfire in the gun butts, having its eight machine-guns harmonised – indicating the destructive power involved. At 1.35.28, the end-result is rolled-out: the Spitfire! This is an interesting machine. It has been suggested elsewhere that this is a Mk IIA, fitted with the Watts fixed-pitch propeller; the aircraft has all the attributes of a later mark than K5054, obviously, including the later radio mast and armoured windscreen, but the 'fishtail' exhaust are inconsistent with the 'kidneys' of the Mk II and more applicable to a Mk VB, very likely a Mk I converted to Mk V specification. However, there are no wing blisters accommodating the ammunition drum for the 20mm Hispano cannon of the VB, so it could well be a later Merlin fitted to an earlier airframe.

At 1.35.45 we see a now wheelchair-bound Mitchell, exhausted and ill after his marathon effort designing and seeing the Spitfire produced, sitting in his garden, anxiously awaiting news of his creation's maiden flight – although, according to his nurse (Leslie Ruth Howard, Leslie Howard's daughter), 'Mrs Mitchell is there and can bring you back all the news.' At 1.36.19, outside the flight shed at Eastleigh, 'Crisp', who is preparing to test-fly the new Spitfire, assures 'Mrs Mitchell' and 'Miss Harper' that he'll 'show that old crate off'. As the Spitfire takes-off, the serial number 'K5054' can be seen, which is that of the prototype, although the real '54 was not camouflaged, she appeared in natural finish, and the aircraft shown airborne with 'Crisp' at the controls has no armoured windscreen and a curved canopy.

Meanwhile, 'Mitchell' is admonished by his nurse for not resting – and removes his burning cigarette from his hand. Inevitably, in this fanciful scene, we hear the Merlin's roar – and 'Crisp', having performed an astonishing aerobatic display for the dignitaries assembled at Eastleigh – exceeding 500 mph in the dive – 'without pulling the wings off' and leaving those on the ground ducking for cover. The senior RAF party assembled adjacent with 'Sir Ian' are naturally delighted. Poor old 'Mitch', looking glum in his wheelchair, suddenly has a great fillip when the Merlin's growl is heard in the distance, gathering to become a full-blooded lion's roar as 'Crisp' takes a detour and gives the fatally ill designer a flypast, giving 'Mitch' a thumbs up and a wave – indicating all is well – and the cancer-ridden designer knows his work is done.

'Crisp' lands – now in a completely different Spitfire and apparently a Photographic Reconnaissance Unit aircraft resplendent in pale blue finish – and is congratulated by the senior RAF officer, 'Air Marshal Bradford' (Robert Rendel, although unaccredited) for 'one of the best shows' he has ever seen – which is repeated to 'Diana', in her husband's absence: 'Will you thank your husband, and tell him that he has given England something that she badly needs.' Having seen his Spitfire fly, however, 'Mitchell' passes away, peacefully in his wheelchair, having literally worked himself to death in order to provide his country this potent fighter. How true, though, is all of this?

The prototype Spitfire, K5054, had begun taking shape throughout the summer of 1935, and Mitchell was on hand daily to oversee production. George Pickering, a test pilot at Supermarine, was a close friend of the designer's, and, concerned that Mitchell was overworking, would take him out for a beer. Here we see, again, then, how 'Crisp', who takes Mitchell for a stress-relieving drink, is an amalgam of various test pilots. K5054 was built at Woolston, then transported, in pieces, to nearby Eastleigh airfield where it was reassembled – and first flew on the afternoon of 5 March 1936, in the presence of, among others, R.J. Mitchell.

The historic maiden flight was made by Captain 'Mutt' Summers, who, fellow Supermarine test pilot Jeffrey Quill recalled, 'took the aeroplane up to about 3,000ft, checked the low speed handling, then came straight back to land'. So, no thrilling aerobatics, as in the film, and Mitchell was actually present – although his wife, secretary and bevy of Air Ministry 'brass hats' were not. Afterwards, K5054 went to the RAF Aeroplane and Armament Experimental Establishment at Martlesham Heath for evaluation; all went smoothly and Supermarine received its first order, for 310 Spitfires on 3 June 1936 – the first batch of 22,000 ultimately built throughout a range of twenty-four different variants.

Mitchell, however, did not expire, exhausted, once the Spitfire had first flown successfully, or after it had been ordered in numbers by the Air Ministry. In fact, he devoted his time to another Air Ministry specification, B.12/36, for a four-engine bomber. The resulting design was far in advance of the iconic Avro Lancaster, which entered service in 1942, and two prototypes were ordered by the Air Ministry – which were unfortunately destroyed when Supermarine was badly bombed on 26 September 1940. Mitchell, however, was aware that if he survived four years without his cancer returning, his longevity would be somewhat more assured.

Unfortunately, throughout the autumn of 1936, some months after the Spitfire's maiden flight, Mitchell suffered increasing bouts of severe pain, which took him away from working on the new bomber, and by February 1937 he was forced to accept that the end, tragically, was nigh. On 29 April 1937, in desperation, Mr and Mrs Mitchell flew to Vienna for a consultation with Professor Freund, a world-leading cancer specialist. Before leaving, Mitchell paid what he knew would be his last visit to Supermarine and bid individual farewells to his design team and secretary, Miss Cross. Last-minute treatment was received from Freund, all to no avail: Mitchell sat in his garden at 'Hazeldene' for the last time on 6 June 1937, became unconscious two days later, and died at midday on 11 June 1937; he was 42. If anything, therefore, the designer's end of life was actually more moving, in some ways, that the film's version of events.

We now return to 'RAF Seafield' (1.47.07) and a deeply moved 'Wing Commander Crisp', having now finished his flashback relation of the Spitfire story to his pilots. Suddenly, the Tannoy blasts into life, ordering 'Hunter Squadron scramble!' Chairs go flying in the pilots' haste to rush off to their nearby Spitfires. Groundcrews help the pilots into their aircraft, which take off in haste. The previously injured squadron commander, however, is unable to fly, and so 'Crisp' takes his place. We then see some great scenes of Pilot Officer Robson, Flying Officer Howard-Williams, and Squadron Leader 'Bunny' Currant chatting on their radios while climbing to meet the enemy. 'Crisp' is ordered by 'Bunny', the formation leader, to formate as his wingman, and calls 'Flapper Control' for information as to the enemy's position. The Controller (Cyril Redmond) vectors 'Hunter Squadron' to intercept a raid of '100 plus' incoming over Beachy Head at 'Angels-one-five', which is to say an altitude of 15,000ft.

More great images of pilots and Spitfires in flight follow, some of the latter filmed specifically for *First of the Few*, other clips being from newsreels. The raid's progress is shown on the plotting table, and at 1.49.50 'Bunny' sights the enemy, shouting 'Tally Ho! Tally Ho!' The Spitfires attack, more great aerial scenes, including a *Schwarm* of Me 109s and a close-up of a German fighter pilot sighting the threat and shouting '*Achtung! Schpitfeur*!' At 1.50.10 a clip showing a formation of real He 111 bombers in flight appears, which 'Hunter Squadron' engages, before a graphic, contrived, studio image of massed German bombers and fighters – indicating the overwhelming odds faced by the Spitfire pilots.

Superb Spitfire aerial shots follow, including a close-up of SD-N performing a 'Victory Roll' at 1.50.25. We then see a close-up of the captured He 111 made available for the film, which is attacked by 'Bunny'. Real cine-gun footage is shown of a He 111 being shot-up, this actually being footage from the gun-camera of the great South African ace 'Sailor' Malan. At 1.50.38. newsreel footage of a crashing Do 17 is cut in, and more excellent, albeit fleeting, images of Spitfires and the He 111 in flight, and the He 111 under attack, as viewed through the Spitfire pilot's reflector gunsight (1.50.53).

Excited radio transmissions from the Spitfire pilots indicate to 'Flapper Control' a successful combat, and the plotting table shows that the raid has been turned back (something which never or rarely occurred, in fact). More air-fighting scenes conclude in more successful attacks and victory rolls, until (1.52.06) 'Crisp' urgently warns 'Bunny' that he is about to be attacked from the rear by a '109'.

The warning is too late: 'Bunny' is shot down, but 'Crisp' resolves that he will 'Get that swine if it's the last thing I do!' and, grim-faced, does exactly that – with incredible close-up footage of Spitfire Mk IIA, SD-L, P8074, bearing a squadron leader's pennant, letting rip with all eight Brownings over the coastline. Naturally, 'Crisp' gets his German, and 'Hunter Squadron' is recalled by 'Flapper Control'. Cue 'Crisp', somewhat cringeworthily, gazing up into the clouds (1.52.42): 'Mitch! They can't take the Spitfires, Mitch! They can't take 'em!', and his lone Spitfire flying off into a symbolic sunset – followed a second later by the survivors of 'Hunter Squadron' – leaving us in no doubt whatsoever of Mitchell's apparent legacy.

Finally, at 1.53.25, Churchill's words appear across the screen 'Never in the Field of Human Conflict was so much owed by so many to so few', concluding the film.

Conclusion

As we have seen, *The First of the Few* substantially distorts the actual facts of the Spitfire story, but this was unknown at the time – reviewers and cinema-goers accepting the tale as a truth. The film was premiered at the Leicester Square Theatre via a charitable performance supporting the RAF Benevolent Fund on 14 September 1942 – eve of the second anniversary of 'Battle of Britain Day'. Reviews were overwhelmingly glowing. Indeed, together with Air Ministry publications and official newsreels, *The First of the Few* did so much to cement a particular perception of the Battle of Britain in the national consciousness – and in the process mythicised the Spitfire story to an almost unimaginable level.

What the film does not allude to, however, is that the Spitfire was not unique as a new eight-gun monoplane fighter for the RAF, and nor was it Britain's sole saviour in 1940. Sydney Camm of Hawker submitted a design for Specification F.36/34, which became the Hurricane – which flew before the Spitfire, on 6 November 1935 – and entered service in November 1937. So the Hurricane was in front of the Spitfire, although it was not so advanced a design, and its performance was inferior.

Nonetheless, during the forthcoming Battle of Britain of summer and autumn 1940, there would be thirty-two squadrons of Hurricanes but only nineteen of Spitfires, which entered service at Duxford on 4 August 1938. Unfortunately Supermarine was too small a concern to produce Spitfires in the numbers now required, and the more technically advanced Spitfire took longer to build than the Hurricane. That being said, the Spitfire's great advantage was that it could perform at high altitude – which the Hurricane could not. The enemy's Me 109 was also able to fly and fight very high up, and so without the Spitfire's protective high-altitude umbrella, enabling Hurricanes to operate lower down, the Battle's outcome could have been very different – height, of course, being crucially important in fighter combat.

The film also gives the impression that the Spitfire was an all-conquering and perfect machine. It was not. In fact, even by the Battle of Britain the Me 109E enjoyed certain significant technical advantages over both the Spitfire Mk I and II in service at that time. It is wrong, therefore, to think that the Spitfire was the RAF's only modern fighter of the day, or that it was technically superior to all other machines. In 1942, however, from a propaganda perspective the objective was to pay tribute to Fighter Command's victory during the Battle of Britain, and inspire the public through a morale-boosting and moving story. Consequently, the Spitfire, in a way no other aircraft was, also became a potent weapon in the propaganda war.

Sadly, on 1 June 1943, Leslie Howard was lost when the DC-3 passenger aircraft he was travelling on from Lisbon to Bristol was shot down by a German Ju 88C6 fighter flown by *Oberleutnant* Herbert Hintze over the Bay of Biscay; Howard was 50 years old and a great loss to British cinema. Just eleven days later, *The First of the Few* was released in America under the title *Spitfire*, where it was also well-received, being behind only *Mrs Miniver* in the box-office ratings. In Britain, Howard's film, according to *Kinematograph Weekly* was the most popular film of 1942, beating *Mrs Miniver* into second place. The reach achieved by *The First of the Few*, therefore, cannot be underestimated – or the positive contribution to Allied propaganda.

Returning to the Spitfire pilots appearing in the film, it is also sad to think that Flying Officer (as he became) David Fulford DFC was shot down over the French coast on 2 November 1942, and remains missing. In his foreword to my book *Spitfire! Courage and Sacrifice* (2006), Gordon Mitchell wrote that 'My father was heard to say on a number of occasions that "A Spitfire without a pilot is just a lump of metal", which showed the high regard and respect he had for the pilots whose job it was to fly his "lump of metal".' It is perhaps appropriate that 'RJ's' sentiment should be the last word here – and that the gifted but tragic designer be remembered as 'The First of the Few'.

Chapter 3

Angels One Five

Considering what a huge box-office success *The First of the Few* was in 1942, it is perhaps surprising that the British film industry did not rush to make more films featuring Fighter Command – although in terms of newsreels, shorts and general press coverage, the 'Fighter Boys' were hardly in danger of under-exposure. An interesting – and now virtually forgotten – film for our purposes, however, is *The Flemish Farm*, made in 1943.

Whereas *Dangerous Moonlight* had focused on the Poles, Jeffrey Dell's *The Flemish Farm* was a nod towards free Belgians. The story concerns a Belgian fighter squadron forced to flee their homeland, who first continue the fight in France before arriving in England and fighting in the Battle of Britain. Before escaping from the continent, however, the hero, 'Jean Duclos' (Clifford Evans) buries the squadron's colours on a Flemish farm – and resolves to return and retrieve the flag. Having parachuted into enemy occupied Belgium, 'Duclos' recovers the banner and returns to England, with help from the resistance. Upon return, the precious flag is formally presented to the Belgian Air Force in exile.

The interesting thing about *The Flemish Farm* is that although there is footage of a Spitfire landing, the film revolves around Hurricanes. While no aerial combat is recreated, there is some good footage of Hurricane Mk IIs – a departure from the 'Spit-centric' films to date.

The release of a particular American information film *The Battle of Britain*, the fourth in a series explaining to American servicemen and women, and the public, why their country was at war, also occurred in 1943. The Director was Frank Capra, an Italian-born American citizen, who, although established in Hollywood, volunteered to serve after the Japanese attack on Pearl Harbor. Capra was tasked with making the series of *Why We Fight* films by the Chief of Staff, George C. Marshall.

Capra had watched, and been intimidated by, *Triumph of the Will*, which, he considered, even 'Satan couldn't have devised a more blood-chilling super spectacle' upholding Germans as the invincible master race. Capra decided to counter-attack using a simple strategy: using original footage to let America's enemy demonise themselves through actual hostile events. *The Battle of Britain* used existing archival material, much of it German and very rare, cut together to tell the story together with a powerful voiceover by well-known Canadian actor and entertainer Walter Huston.

The film projected what is now the traditional narrative of the Battle of Britain: 'Showing the gallant and victorious defence of Britain by the Royal Air Force, at a time when shattered but unbeaten, the British were the only people fighting the Nazis.' Like *The Lion Has Wings*, Capra's film explains how Britain aerial defences worked, and predominantly, but not exclusively, featured many clips of Spitfires. These include a few seconds showing Johnnie Johnson, at the time of filming a flight lieutenant on 616 Squadron, exiting his Spitfire and telling the waiting intelligence officer that he got 'a 109 destroyed'.

Some superb footage shows German aircraft from the early war period in action – and somehow disturbing cine-gun camera film showing Spitfires under fire – and being fatally hit – by an Me 109. On 15 September 1940, the viewer is told that Fighter Command met the Luftwaffe's 'challenge by throwing in everything they had' – which, of course, is simply untrue. Certainly Air Vice-Marshal Park committed 11 Group to battle, with reinforcements from 10 and 12 Groups, but plenty of resources remained in the latter two and 13 groups. This is an underpinning pillar of the 'David and Goliath' popular narrative.

Capra's film, however, does not ignore Bomber Command's early efforts, or the stoic response of British civilians to the night Blitz. Cleverly, the final scene is borrowed from *Mrs Miniver*, showing the mass formation of Spitfires seen through the bombed church's holed roof. Finally, the Chief of Staff's words appear, leaving viewers in no doubt as to why the war was being fought, and to what end: 'victory of the democracies can only be complete with the utter defeat of the war machines of Germany and Japan'. It was powerful stuff – but this was a narrated documentary, not even a docudrama like *The Lion Has Wings* – and it was also another American production.

The following year, 1944, saw the British film *Tawny Pipit* released, which alluded to the Battle of Britain, and, albeit briefly, the Spitfire. The film concerned a recovering RAF fighter pilot, 'Jimmy Bancroft' (Niall MacGinnis) on a walking holiday with his girlfriend, formerly his nurse, 'Hazel Broome' (Rosamund John), who discovers a rare pair of nesting tawny pipits near the quintessential English village of 'Lipsbury Lea' (actually Gloucestershire's Lower Slaughter, in the Cotswolds). Military manoeuvres, however, threaten the birds, as do the uncaring ploughs of the War Agricultural Executive Committee. Bird lovers 'Jimmy' and 'Hazel' galvanise the villagers into action, protecting the tawny pipits and winning the day for conservation and wildlife.

The film's conclusion – another church service – shows 'Jimmy', now returned to his squadron, flying overhead in a Spitfire, dipping his wings and waving to the nesting rarities – his aircraft named *Anthus Campestris* – the bird's Latin name. Yet again, we see the fighter pilot as a gallant, heroic, figure, the Spitfire his knightly aerial steed – but embedded in a film of broader storyline and meaning, which certainly does not include any attempt to tell the Battle of Britain story. What it did, and which becomes relevant in due course, is present an image of all classes of society uniting against a common enemy – being a metaphor for how it was, and still is, popularly perceived Britain had responded to the threat of invasion in 1940 and, indeed, the Second World War generally.

THE BATTLE OF BRITAIN ON THE BIG SCREEN

The next British-made film featuring the RAF, *The Way to the Stars*, was released a month after the cessation of hostilities in Europe, in June 1945. This was the first retrospective film about the Second World War, in which we witness life and death on a Blenheim bomber squadron through the eyes of 'Flying Officer Penrose' (John Mills). Joining his unit during the Battle of Britain, fresh from training, shortly after 'Penrose' arrives the airfield is attacked – and Hurricane Mk IIs scramble to defend it.

After the raid, a Hurricane beats up the airfield at low-level before performing a victory roll – prompting an acerbic remark from 'Squadron Leader Carter' (Trevor Howard): 'Line shoot. These fighter types, you know, top button undone, victory rolls, bad show, I think.' Unlike that epic, however, not one Spitfire appears in *The Way to the Stars* – which remains in the opinion of many the best film about the wartime RAF. Be that as it may, this was still no attempt to tell the Battle of Britain story.

In America, the air war featured in cinema four years later, in 1949, when 20th Century-Fox released Henry King's *Twelve O'Clock High*. Starring Gregory Peck as 'Brigadier Frank Savage', the film revisited the United States Eighth Air Force's early missions, flying from bases in England. Owing to the lack of a long-range offensive escort fighter, losses among the American bomber crews were high, leading to division in public opinion at home regarding the wisdom of the daylight bomber offensive.

The Americans literally stuck to their guns, however, and this film paid tribute to the bravery and sacrifices of the aircrews involved. According to the *New York Times*, *Twelve O'Clock High*, which won two Academy Awards, was in the year's top ten films, and even in 2009 was considered among the best 1,000 films ever made. Clearly, air war films generated more than sufficient commercial interest in the new post-war world to attract investors, which Hollywood had certainly proved and cashed in on with *Twelve O'Clock High*, which firmly focused on America's pivotal contribution to the strategic bombing offensive.

Conversely, although Fighter Command's victory in the Battle of Britain was infinitely more significant strategically, and universally upheld as the nation's 'Finest Hour', it was not until 1952 that a film, British or otherwise, featured the epic aerial conflict as its central theme.

That film was *Angels One Five*.

Angels One Five

It was actually the English film producer and actors' talent agent Cecil Gordon Tenant who floated the idea of a Battle of Britain related film, with a view to finding a suitably commercial project for two of his clients, namely John Gossage and Derek Twist. Gossage's film credits, as producer, associate producer and production manager dated back to 1936, and included *Hamlet* (1948), in which Laurence Olivier's genius was demonstrated as both actor and director.

Twist was an even more experienced industry professional, whose work as an editor included *The 39 Steps* (1935) and *The Lion Has Wings* (1939), and as a writer eight previous films including the comedy *Green Grow the Rushes* (1951), on which he had worked with Gossage and also directed. Both Gossage and Twist had served in the wartime RAF – and Tenant's suggestion piqued their interest. The pair set up Templar Productions to front the project, receiving the backing of the Scottish film executive Robert Clark, head of production at the Elstree-based Associated British Picture Corporation, for a project entitled *Battle of Britain*.

With the summer of 1940 only eleven years distant at the time preparations for this film were being made, the often-traumatic events involved remained crystal clear in the memories of many, including both survivors and those who had lost loved ones. The 'Finest Hour' also enjoyed a unique status in the British popular memory of the Second World War and national identity, so the subject had to be treated both sensitively and, indeed, reverentially.

For this reason, Gossage and Twist resolved that the only way forward was to produce as authentic a film as possible – and to do that, they needed as many people who had actually served in the RAF both behind and in front of the cameras. The chosen director, for example, George More O'Ferrall, had been an army liaison officer at Fighter Command HQ. A former Shakespearean and West End theatre actor, O'Ferrall had also directed plays and in 1936 became the BBC's first drama producer, directing the 1948 television adaptation of *Wuthering Heights* and receiving a Royal Television Society award for his two-part *Hamlet* production. This new project, however, was his first film as director.

Battle of Britain also needed an informed screenplay, which would be written by Twist, who chose as the basis for this the book *What Are Your Angels Now?* by Wing Commander A.J.C. Pelham-Groom – a retired Fighter Command staff officer and Biggin Hill Sector Controller, since turned actor and writer. Typically, Pelham-Groom's novels, including *David Farlow Takes the Air*, *The Little Hanging Men* and *The 'Black Eagle'*, were tales of aerial high adventure and mystery, aimed at boys, so unsurprisingly Twist had to rework Pelham-Groom's Battle of Britain book to produce a more serious script suitable for an adult audience. Nonetheless, it was a break for Pelham-Groom, who also acted as the film's technical advisor and, by all accounts, was quite a character.

Other former RAF officers involved included Ronald Adam, who played the 'Group Controller'. Adam had served as Hornchurch Sector Controller during the Battle of Britain – as had Cyril Raymond, who would play 'Squadron Leader Barry Clinton', apparently had at Kenley. Humphrey Lestocq, who had become famous as a radio comedian for his 'Flying Officer Kite' character on the *Merry Go Round* series, was chosen as 'Flight Lieutenant "Batchy" Salter', a Hurricane pilot – the aircraft being a type flown by Lestocq during the war (he also flew Typhoons operationally with 609 Squadron). Indeed, so soon after the war, finding actors with service backgrounds was straightforward – but the producers would find sourcing aircraft somewhat more difficult.

The Air Ministry was supportive on the grounds that such a film could encourage recruitment during what was now the so-called 'Cold War', and provided the film-makers access to RAF Kenley, a crucial 11 Group Sector Station defending London in 1940, which remained operational, and Air Vice-Marshal Park's underground operations room at Uxbridge, in addition to seconding a number of personnel to the project. What the Air Ministry was unable to conjure, however, was numbers of period aircraft – a somewhat essential ingredient to a film telling the Battle of Britain story. Few Hurricanes were available: Mk Is L1591, used for in-studio cockpit shots and dressed in 56 Squadron codes as US-N – but criminally broken up after filming; L1592, dressed as US-D and used as a static aircraft, while P2617 taxied as US-B. Hawker Siddeley Aircraft Ltd provided the airworthy Mk IIC PZ865 (under civilian registration G-AMAU), masquerading as US-P, and apparently the RAF LF363, although no evidence of the latter has been identified on-screen. At the time, authentic Spitfires were similarly scarce, but salvation was at hand from an unanticipated source: the Portuguese Air Force still operated Hurricanes and provided five Mk IICs for the film. So it was that the Hurricane – not Spitfire – for once became star of the proposed film.

By now, Twist had substantially worked the screenplay, the film's title morphing from *Battle of Britain* to *Hawks in the Sun, Angels Fifteen,* and finally settling on *Angels One Five*, a derivative of Pelham-Groom's book title upon which the production was loosely based. The producers also emphasised that the film's focus was on people, not aeroplanes, and the title changes may have been because the lack of available aircraft prevented the making of an aviation-based extravaganza. The screenplay sought to tell the story of one fighter station's experience under attack during the summer of 1940, and that of a new pilot in particular, rather than a blow-by-blow account of the Battle of Britain as a whole. Although a lack of authentic aircraft may have influenced the change of tack, the film's budget was comparatively small anyway and incapable of funding extensive flying scenes. The final title was one heard many times in pilots' headphones as they scrambled and were directed by the controller towards the enemy – 'Angels', in the radio jargon of the day being height measured in thousands of feet.

With screenplay, actors, aircraft, and locations all good to go, *Angels One Five* was filmed in July 1951 – later than anticipated owing to a poor spring, postponing the anticipated release from 4 August 1951 to 19 March 1952.

Angels One Five: A Reading.

Starting as it means to go on, *Angels One Five* begins with a graphic of the RAF crest engraved into a hammered metal background, set to the rousing martial music of the *RAF March Past*. From the outset, therefore, the viewer can be clear that this film is about the RAF – and very much a tribute to the service. Due acknowledgement is given, in writing, by the producers' in respect of the cooperation provided by the RAF, Hawker Siddeley, and the Portuguese Air Force.

At 0.02.01, Churchill's oft-used and famous words once more appear, against a backdrop of cumulus clouds filmed from an aircraft in flight: 'Let us therefore brace ourselves to our duties, and so bear ourselves that, if the British Empire and its Commonwealth lasts for a thousand years, men will still say ... This Was Their Finest Hour'.

At 0.02.19 we see the Houses of Parliament and Big Ben through a roll of barbed wire: June 1940. A desperate time for Britain indeed, given that the BEF had ignominiously been forced to retire on and evacuate from the beaches around Dunkirk, France having fallen in a shocking blow to the Western democracies. Left behind in France are heavy weapons, artillery and tanks – and some 80,000 British and French soldiers have been captured by the victorious Germans. A disaster – but the British fight on.

There is a superb air-to-air shot of a pair of the Portuguese Hurricanes at 0.02.30, with the spurious serials and codes AV-X, K1694, and AV-P, N6542, 'on patrol' above the Sussex coast's iconic 'Seven Sisters' cliffs, keeping watch over an essential convoy. Then, at 0.2.40, we are shown radar masts for the first time in such a film, RDF having been top secret during wartime and therefore unmentioned in previous films – although a common thread is the explanation of how the 'System' works, through showing information being received from radar, then being transmitted by landline to the Filter Room at Fighter Command HQ. Unlike other films this is not conveyed to the viewer via narration, but by visual images.

At 0.03.26 we are in the 11 Group 'Hole', the underground bunker at Uxbridge, with WAAFs plotting the incoming raids on the huge map table and passing information by telephone – a hive of activity. In a scene well-familiar to the actor concerned, we then see the 'Group Controller' (Ronald Adam) bringing 'Raid 24' to the attention via landline of the Sector Controller at 'RAF Neethley', which is 'after "Tango" convoy, passing Dover'. The 'Neethley Controller', 'Squadron Leader Peter Moon' (Michael Denison), reassures his superior that 'Red Section of 2270 Squadron' were patrolling over 'Tango' but nearing the end of their fuel endurance 'if they have to mix it' – fortunately, though, 'White Section' is already en route to relieve, and the decision is made to 'get 1320 Squadron off'. 'Moon' then tells his assistant 'Bonzo' (Norman Pierce) to 'Get "Pimpernel" Red and Yellow Sections in the air, Dover, 15,000 feet.' …

The scramble order is communicated by landline to 'Pimpernel' Squadron, the telephone ringing at the pilots' dispersal hut (0.04.09), a pilot, 'Jacko' (John Barry), rushing to answer the phone while demanding that another pilot, 'Pilot Officer Dennis Falk' (Terence Longdon) switches the gramophone off. Having received orders, 'Jacko' shouts 'Scramble Red and Yellow Sections,

Dover, Angels-One-Five!' – leading to the 'chaps' rushing from all directions to their waiting Hurricanes. 'Falk' departs via the CO's office, repeating the order to the CO, 'Squadron Leader Bill Ponsford' (Andrew Osborn), who joins the rush, awaking from his slumber in an armchair Flight Lieutenant 'Batchy' Salter (Humphrey Lestocq) who likewise rushes to his fighter.

This is, however, a film primarily produced for entertainment, not a documentary, so let us not get too hung up on the later pattern lifejackets and roundels on the Hurricanes. Outside, the groundcrews already have the Hurricanes' engines running, the fighters prepared for flight. Parachutes and flying helmets are positioned to be swiftly donned. 'Batchy' jumps into his machine and at 0.4.45 we cut to the Hurricanes, now with more appropriate fuselage roundels, taxiing across grass, before meeting the decorated Station Commander, 'Group Captain "Tiger" Small' (Jack Hawkins, who had ended up a colonel in the Welch Regiment during the war and therefore had personal experience of the services and being a commanding officer) watching the aircraft taxi by – now on a tarmac runway.

'Tiger' then makes his way to the adjacent Operations Room – which was, in fact, the actual building in use as such at RAF Kenley during the Battle of Britain (unceremoniously demolished in 1980). The entrance is guarded by an RAF sentry, 'Thompson' (Peter Jones), who, in a mild Black Country accent strangely out of place amid the upper-class drawls dominating the film, stubbornly denies the Station Commander entry until 'Tiger' has provided him both his identity card and the day's password.

At 0.06.10, 'Tiger' then enters the busy Sector Operations Room – the authentic-looking interior of which, unlike the external scene is a studio recreation. 'Squadron Leader Moon' is 'Sapper Control', talking to 'Pimpernel Squadron', instructing Red Section to 'pancake' (land).

A good shot of Hurricanes in flight follows, the closest aircraft being the studio cockpit (with the later, square, reflector gunsight of the Hurricane Mk II), occupied by 'Beeswax Red One', 'Jacko'. 'Tiger' watches the air battle over convoy 'Tango' unfold on the plotting table, 'Squadron Leader Ponsford', 'Pimpernel Leader', confirms that the squadron is at 'Angels-One-Five' and 'In position', when 'Moon', in response to incoming radar information, orders the Hurricanes to steer a course (vector) towards 'bandits' ahead, over the Channel and at the same height. Somewhat pessimistically, 'Tiger' prophesies that the time is coming when the enemy, now '3,000 aircraft' strong, will not just attack convoys (as per the Battle of Britain's opening phase) but will bomb Fighter Command airfields. 'Moon' calculates the odds as '5:1', but 'Tiger' rightly points out that the odds are actually more, in terms of the south-east, because it is Fighter Command's strength in the main battle area that matters, so statistically the strength of squadrons based elsewhere is irrelevant. This is correct.

Although the two air forces were fairly evenly matched on paper, it was Fighter Command's strength in southern England, and the south-east especially, that directly mattered – and the majority of the German strength would be made available for the aerial assault on Britain. 'Moon' adjusts his calculation to '6:1', adding that 'We can cope with that.' And thus, in the film's first eight minutes, the traditional Battle of Britain narrative is outlined.

At 0.8.06, the pilots sight the enemy and shout 'Tally Ho!', the scene brought to life through vapour trails among the clouds, synonymous with the summer of 1940, and the chatter of machine-guns. On the ground, 'Tiger' quizzes 'Moon' about his recent flying experience, which clearly amounts to little, and advises him to get himself up in a Hurricane soonest – which 'Moon' is reluctant to do because the flying hours are needed more for operational flying. This alludes to aircraft being in short supply.

Precious they certainly were, but in reality, the aircraft factories and repair facilities maintained a steady flow of machines, which Fighter Command was never short of; what it was short of was operational pilots, especially those with combat experience. Nonetheless, aircraft, and pilots of whatever experience, were invaluable assets. This conversation between 'Tiger' and 'Moon', however, both pre-war, professional officers with a Cranwell background, prepares the way for the next event: three replacement aircraft being delivered that afternoon, the pilot of one of which, 'Baird', a 'volunteer reservist', will be joining 'Pimpernel Squadron'.

Before the Second World War, the RAF was a comparatively small peacetime service not dissimilar to an elite flying club, in which everyone pretty much knew everyone else. The war changed that, when the amateur airmen of the Auxiliary Air Force and Volunteer Reserve were called to full-time service. While the socially elite auxiliary squadrons were locally raised units in their own right, the 'VR' was intended to appeal to 'young men without any class distinctions' – and there was no shortage of volunteers: by 1 September 1939, 6,646 reservists were trained pilots, many of whom went on to fight in the Battle of Britain and serve with distinction on all fronts throughout the war.

Before leaving the building, the 'Tiger' subtly makes it crystal clear that he is unimpressed with 'Moon's' reluctance, on the excuse of being too busy on the ground, to get airborne in a Hurricane and update his flying experience, telling him to let 'Clinton' share some of the workload – this referring to 'Squadron Leader Barry Clinton' (Cyril Raymond). 'Clinton', who lives with his wife in a bungalow at the end of Neethley's runway, is then shown gardening (0.09.20) in a somewhat idyllic scene, while a Harvard aircraft taxies past beyond the perimeter fence; his presence is requested within by his wife, 'Nadine Clinton' (Dulcie Gray).

Inside is a rather portly, middle-aged police constable (Philip Stainton), allegedly 'bullying' 'Mrs Clinton' about infringing the blackout through leaving a 40-watt light on in the 'top landing window' – which is to act as an unofficial homing beacon, with the blessing of the 'Tiger', for returning aircraft at night. 'Mrs Clinton' has explained all this to the obstinate constable, who 'won't take it' from her, as she complains to husband 'Barry' – wearing an observer's flying brevet on his uniform tunic. The 'Squadron Leader' reiterates the defence as outlined, but the constable continues pointing out that it is 'against regulations'. This is actually an interesting scene. The 'Clintons' are clearly upper-class, and somehow nauseatingly smug, while the policeman is shown as dull and clearly of a lower social standing. The constable, somewhat stupidly, as is the director's intention, suggests the alternative expedient of hanging out a 'red light' instead – this causing further and even more nauseatingly smug knowing winks from 'Barry' to 'Nadine' – the red light, of course, being the age-old sign indicating a brothel open for business. It is a pathetic and completely unnecessary scene and put-down.

At 0.10.31, the policeman having been ridiculed, the scene changes to superb aerial footage of one of the three anticipated new Hurricanes (coded P2619) heading towards 'Neethley' over the Essex coast and Thames Estuary. Interestingly, the aircraft, which has yet to have squadron codes applied, as a new delivery, has neither rear-view mirror or radio mast. The new aircraft, call-sign 'Elfin 1', shows up on 'Squadron Leader Moon's' Neethley plotting table, but not at the best time, given that 'Pimpernel Squadron' will imminently be returning from combat. 'Elfin 1', 'Pilot Officer T.B. Baird' (John Gregson) calls up and identifies his presence and intention, requesting permission to land as per the training manual – much to the amusement of the controllers.

At 0.12.14 we have what is supposedly 'Pilot Officer Baird's' forward view from his cockpit, of 'Neethley' – really RAF Kenley. Coming in to land, 'Baird' has just touched down when suddenly, from his left, another Hurricane appears, landing cross-wind, the two aircraft on a collision course. Looking aghast, 'Baird' pulls up and roars over the top of the offending Hurricane, contacting it but avoiding a serious collision. 'P2619', now being the studio cockpit with a curious-looking radio-mast, is damaged however, and 'Baird's' flaps are inoperable – causing the new replacement pilot and aircraft to hurtle through the perimeter fence and crash into the 'Clintons'' garden, disrupting afternoon tea which the 'Clintons' are taking with the disgruntled constable. The aircraft, its wooden propellers shattered, comes to rest on its nose just outside the living room window. 'Squadron Leader Clinton' rushes out to assist (0.13.00).

Outside, 'Clinton' finds 'Pilot Officer Baird' climbing down from his aircraft: 'Hello, old man, dropped in for tea?' 'Baird' is largely unhurt, except self-diagnosing a strained *'ligamentum nuchae'*, the supraspinal ligaments of the lower vertebrae. Very formal introductions ensue, although when 'Baird' explains that he is posted to 'Neethley' and was delivering a new aircraft, 'Clinton' predicts that the hapless pilot 'won't be very popular'. Starting as he means to go on, however, 'Baird' retorts that the collision was not his fault, but caused by the other Hurricane, which cut across in front of him after he had received permission to land. Then (0.13.56) the 'Medical Officer' (Ewan Roberts) arrives, to whom 'Baird' explains that he was previously a medical student (leading to another knowing look exchanged between the 'Clintons') and hence his knowledge of the *'ligamentum nuchae'*. Nonetheless, the doctor insists upon a second opinion and whisks 'Baird' off to sick quarters.

At 0.14.52 the camera switches to two Hurricanes (US-H and US-B) returning from their recent combat. At 0.15.11 we re-enter the 'Pimpernel Squadron' pilots' hut at dispersal, where 'Batchy' reposes, smoking, in his armchair, awaiting his comrades' return. 'Squadron Leader Ponsford' arrives with other pilots, delighted to see their friend, whom they thought had 'bought it'. 'Batchy' explains that he destroyed a Me 110 but got shot-up himself, so returned to base – where 'Baird's Hurricane suddenly appeared on a collision course before pulling up and leaping over him. This leads to a spontaneous outbreak of a ribald song by the five pilots clustered around listening to the tale – which is even more cringeworthy than the 'Clintons'' nauseating smugness. Moreover, the 'pilots' are too old. In reality, most were in their late teens to mid-twenties; even Lestocq, playing 'Batchy', the only authentic one-time RAF pilot among them, was 32 when the film was made, and Andrew Osborn, 'Squadron Leader Ponsford', although 31 in 1951, looks much older.

'Ponsford', however, does not find 'Batchy's' tale amusing, especially upon discovering that the wrecked aircraft was one of his badly-needed replacement machines. Nearly bursting fifty blood vessels, and refusing to accept 'Batchy's' defence of the other pilot, who, he says, 'must have had his finger out' to avoid the collision, 'Ponsford' gets on the 'blower' to 'Moon' at 'Sapper Control', for a good old rant about the 'ferry pilot's' incompetence, which could have 'slaughtered an experienced pilot' and 'written-off a valuable aircraft: God, how we need them!'. 'Ponsford', however, gets rather shot down when 'Moon', although conceding that '"Batchy" is more valuable than a thousand non-operational types', points out that it was not a ferry pilot involved but a new replacement assigned to 'Pimpernel Squadron'. At this, 'Ponsford' nearly has an embolism, refusing to have the new pilot in his 'outfit'. 'I sympathise old man', says 'Moon', but wryly tells 'Ponsford' to tell the 'Tiger' himself.

At 0.17.40 the 'Tiger' pulls up outside the Officers' Mess and upon entering, orders a pint from the waiter (Sam Kydd). 'Clinton' finds 'Baird' looking a little lost, his neck bandaged, but toddles off home when the latter declines a drink, and goes off looking for his new CO, 'Ponsford', instead. Steeling himself for the encounter, upon entering the Annex, 'Baird' is shocked to see the sofas being used as jumps in a roly-poly game by tunic-less pilots, including 'Batchy', urged on by other, drinking, officers.

At the end of the line is a somewhat rough and tumble pile-on – involving both the 'Tiger' and 'Ponsford'. 'Baird' is introduced to his new CO after 'Ponsford' extricates himself from the bottom of the pile. Introducing himself as 'Pilot Officer T.B. Baird', 'Batchy' exclaims 'TB? Sounds a bit septic to me!' – and so the nickname sticks to 'Pilot Officer "Septic" Baird'. 'Ponsford', however, takes issue with the fact that 'Baird' 'nearly pranged' his best flight commander and wrote off a replacement aircraft. The somewhat pompous and humourless 'Baird' points out that the collision was not his fault.

An argument ensues, 'Ponsford' accusing 'Baird' of 'barging around like a bull in a china shop', but fortunately the hapless new recruit is rescued by the 'Tiger', who introduces himself as the 'Station Commander', puts 'Baird' at his ease and takes him off for a drink, remarking that 'You're a "Volunteer Reserve", I see, something of a novelty in these parts.' 'Baird' explains that he joined his 'University Air Squadron at the time of Munich' (referring to the crisis over the Sudetenland in September 1938), abandoning his medical studies because 'wars are won by pilots, not doctors'. In conversation, the 'Tiger' mentions that he is a 'professional fighter'. All of this requires explanation.

Firstly, howsoever irresponsible and immature it appears, such 'high-jinx' in the Mess did happen, as a means of relieving stress – and injuries arising were no respecters of rank. For example, Wing Commander A.B. 'Woody' Woodhall, Duxford's Station Commander during the Battle of Britain, described a similar 'scrum down' in which his arm had come into sharp contact with the tin leg of 242 Squadron's legless commander, Squadron Leader Douglas Bader – causing a hairline fracture and some embarrassment to 'Woody' during a subsequent formal interview with his Group Commander.

Secondly, we must examine the 'Tiger's' observation that VR pilots were 'a novelty' during the summer of 1940 – which was not, in fact, the case. The 'Tiger' is a career officer, trained at Cranwell, the film giving the impression of a service still virtually exclusively populated by such professional officer-pilots. In reality, by the summer of 1940 the small peacetime air force had substantially expanded, and its identity significantly changed through mobilisation of the hitherto part-time auxiliary squadrons, while amateur volunteer reservists, including pilots like 'Baird' from the University Air Squadrons (UAS), were absorbed into existing RAF squadrons. VR pilots were automatically made sergeants, although some were commissioned upon completion of training. While 324 VR officer pilots fought in the Battle of Britain, the majority were sergeants. UAS pilots, however, among the Few numbered twenty, so in that respect 'Baird' was 'a rarity'.

By August 1940, though, pilots from the occupied lands, continuing the fight, were reaching fighter squadrons, so that a squadron's pilots were not just professional officers, as 'Pimpernel' had supposedly been until 'Baird' arrived, but a mixture of auxiliaries, reservists, officers with Short Service Commissions, and both foreign nationals and sergeants. To put the 'Tiger's' comment into accurate perspective, therefore, of the 2,408 pilots among the 2,927 aircrew comprising the Few, only 1,162 were officers, of which just eighty-four were Cranwell-commissioned professionals, and 419 held Short Service Commissions (SSC) – many of the latter from the Commonwealth. So, to portray the composition of 'Pimpernel' as exclusively professional British officer pilots until 'Baird's' arrival is a nonsense, although the film does emphasise the gulf of difference between the professional officers and attitudes to their amateur counterparts. Another observation is that for someone hitherto at university, 'Baird' must have been a somewhat mature student, given that John Gregson, who had served aboard a Royal Navy minesweeper during the war, was 32 during the making of the film.

Moving on, the following morning sees 'Baird' report for a formal interview with the 'Tiger'. While awaiting his turn, an airman on a charge, 'AC2 Wailes' (Harold Goodwin), is marched in to be admonished by the 'Station Commander'. Meanwhile, 'Baird' hears from 'Squadron Leader Moon' that he will be spending a period in the 'Hole', as a controller – which fails to impress the keen young pilot with shiny bright brass 'VR' lapel badges. At 0.23.41, we see 'Tiger' disciplining 'Wailes' for using a crib sheet in a technical test, this being our first experience of a working-class airman 'type' – who appears uneducated and, frankly, pretty stupid.

The 'Tiger's' lecture, however, emphasises that everyone is part of a team and has to depend upon each other – before the hapless airman is marched out, and even gets that wrong. Then 'Baird', with his neck bandaged, has his turn, during which interview he argues that his injury should not prevent him from flying operationally. 'Tiger', however, explains that operational flying is very different to simply 'aviating around the sky', and that with an injured neck, 'Baird' would find 'Messerschmitt Twitch' – the need to twist the head and search the sky for enemy aircraft – too difficult in his current condition, and hence he has been allocated a period of duty with 'Moon' in the 'Hole'. 'Baird' continues to disagree, and is firmly put in his place by 'Tiger' who again emphasises that 'Pimpernel' is a team, in which everyone depends upon everyone else in what is a life or death scenario, meaning that 100 per cent fitness is required to ensure that all play their part and are not in danger of falling short, letting others down. Suitably advised, 'Baird' is sent off to the 'Hole', with a little fatherly advice from the 'Tiger': 'Don't rush your fences.'

This entire scene is all about the team – not the individual, a lesson 'Baird' clearly has to learn. As 'Baird' leaves, 'Squadron Leader Ponsford' enters to discuss 'Baird' with the 'Tiger', unhappy about having him in 'Pimpernel' on account of his 'black'. The 'Tiger' is more sympathetic, however, pointing out that 'Baird' has good reports and should be fine once he understands what *squadron espirit* is all about'.

'Baird' is next shown reporting to 'Clinton' in the 'Hole' and being introduced to his assistant, 'Ops B' (Gordon Bell, another 'VR type'), and 'Ops A' (Rosemary Lomax), and other personnel (0.27.22). Although a studio set, this is an authentic reconstruction of a sector operations room, and what goes on in it, all of which is explained to the newcomer. Around the table sit the WAAF plotters, the 'Beauty Chorus', currently unoccupied by any aerial action, one of which breaks the monotony by knitting – which surprises the somewhat formal and priggish 'Baird'. In response, the ever-pompous 'Clinton' observes that females are only able to relax by 'being busy'. 'Ops B' then notifies 'Clinton', the duty sector controller, that 'Group' are on the phone regarding an incoming raid.

The operations room immediately becomes a hive of activity as squadrons are scrambled in response to several new threats, and at 0.28.35 'Batchy' enters the 'Hole' and approaches 'Baird' with 'Wotcha "Septic", me old assassin, so this is where you hide', stinging 'Baird's' pride – who then learns that it was 'Batchy' with whom he nearly collided, the good airmanship of whom he takes issue with until learning that 'Batchy' had been shot-up and was landing a damaged Hurricane. Previously unaware of this, 'Baird' immediately apologises and is taken off by the decorated flight lieutenant to meet the 'boys' at dispersal.

Walking past the Hurricanes, 'Batchy' and 'Baird' discuss their 'shaky do', and 'Batchy' advises the new pilot not to take 'Ponsford's' outburst 'to heart' because 'he's a desperately keen type, wizard squadron CO and all that kind of thing'. At 0.30.15, 'Batchy' stops to look over his Hurricane, 'Jemima', in the cockpit of which his somewhat dim and working-class rigger, 'AC2 Wailes', is working. The conversation turns to the rigger's recent admonishment: 'You're a clot, Wailes.' 'Batchy' then imparts operational safety advice to 'Baird' (which ultimately transpires to be prophetic), as the pair continue towards dispersal. As they approach, a passing sergeant-pilot, 'Pete' (actor unknown) – who 'Batchy' assures 'Baird' is a 'good type' – tells 'Batchy' that the Flight is now on 'readiness'. 'Batchy' then introduces 'Pilot Officer T.B. "Septic" Baird, the celebrated leap-frog man', with inevitable banter.

Within the 'A' Flight pilots' hut, 'Batchy' shows 'Baird' the squadron's 'homework', a wall of scantily clad pin-up girls, introducing resting pilots, including the squadron's 'Tail-end Charlie, Pilot Officer Mortimer' (Harold Siddons), and 'Jacko' (John Barry). 'Baird' is more interested, however, in the squadron's war trophies, items salvaged from German aircraft destroyed, displayed on an adjacent wall. 'Baird' identifies a 'bombsight from a Junkers 87', which 'Batchy' enthuses is 'Bang on!', before pointing out the 'rudder off a Ju 87', which is actually one from an Me 109; considering Lestocq's apparent wartime RAF background, it is difficult to imagine how such a mistake could be made.

Other trophies are examined until reaching the 'Most highly derogatory order of the irremovable digit', a large wooden hand with raised finger. 'What's it for?', inquires the ever-humourless 'Baird', and is told that it is for examples of poor airmanship or anything else which 'blackens the fair record of the squadron'. 'Baird' cuts a stern glance at the laughing pilots watching nearby: 'No doubt you all think it is I who should be wearing it now.' Immediately, the smiles drop as the assembly realises that this is a completely humourless and personality free zone, and eye the newcomer with concern. 'Baird' is then saved from further embarrassment by the bell, as the telephone rings: 'Squadron scramble, chaps, Hastings, Angels One Five!', setting the pilots running out to their Hurricanes and leaving 'Baird', who is currently non-operational, alone.

The scene then changes to a conference held that night by the 'Tiger' with his squadron commanders and other key officers (0.33.12). With his top button undone in traditional fighter pilot's style, 'Tiger' shares what he has learned from the 'AOC' regarding how the battle is going and predictions for the future. The news is grim. That the Germans having just been probing defences to date is explained, along with the fact that Fighter Command has fifty squadrons with which to defend the whole country, the disposition and strategy illustrated on a large wall map. The stakes are high, the 'Few' outnumbered, considering that 'The Jerries have 120 squadrons of bombers and eighty of fighters from Brest to Amsterdam.'

The 'Tiger' emphasises three advantages over the enemy: 'Better aircraft, better pilots, and, most important of all, radio location and ground control.' As for 'Jerry's next move', 'Tiger' tells his officers that 'You can bet your shirts' he's got intelligence regarding all key bases and other targets, including fighter airfields and other defences, which are expected to be attacked next. If these can be neutralised, a seaborne invasion would be 'a piece of cake'. With such attacks imminently anticipated, much as the 'Tiger' regrets it, the Station will have to 'curtail its social activities', on account of not wanting to 'risk the lives of wives, sweethearts and also rans', meaning that 'next Sunday's cocktail party will have to be the last', and so will have to be 'memorable'.

We next join Neethley's officers and ladies in the aforementioned cocktail party, held in the Ladies Room of Neethley's Officers' Mess, where the socially awkward and solitary 'Baird' is, on the 'Tiger's' instruction, fetched from the anteroom, where he is sat alone, reading 'one of the Sunday heavies'. Meanwhile, more 'Beeswax' Hurricanes are scrambled, there being, according to 'Moon', 'Quite a flap on'. 'Tiger' tells the 'Controller types' to 'stop talking shop' and breaks the news in private to 'Mrs Clinton' that he wants her to leave the bungalow, given that bombing is expected – which the plucky service wife refuses to do. 'Baird' is then produced by 'Batchy' and introduced by 'Mrs Clinton' to 'Betty Carfax' (Veronica Hurst), the sister of 'Groucho Fairfax' (a 'Beeswax Squadron' pilot not present as on readiness), initially escorted by 'Pilot Officer Raines' (Russell Hunter). According to 'Mrs Clinton', 'Baird', 'being a "VR", probably has a wider range of conversation than us "regular types"'. The pair are left alone and Baird's social awkwardness but love of flying is evident.

At 0.39.40 we join 'Ponsford, 'Moon' and 'Batchy', the former pointing out to 'Moon' that while he, holder of a Short Service Commission, may well have command of a fighter squadron, 'all the pukka plum jobs go to you Cranwell types'. Interestingly, during the Battle of Britain, seventy-seven of the Few commanded fighter squadrons at some stage or another between 10 July – 31 October 1940. Of these, the type of commission held by twenty-three is unknown, but of the remainder, twenty-five were Cranwellians, four were auxiliaries, nineteen held SSCs, four were Direct Entrants, and one had come up from the ranks; all but one were public schoolboys.

At 0.39.56, 'Squadron Leader Clinton', controlling, speaks over the Tannoy, calling 'Pimpernel to readiness'. 'Baird' has to content himself with 'seeing them off' with 'Miss Carfax'. What follows is beyond cringeworthy. The pilots, hurrying down pints of beer, rush off and pile into their waiting transport, the atmosphere being one of a public school sports day and a jolly adventure. 'Baird' appears, against the odds, to have hit it off with 'Miss Carfax', with whom he returns to the Mess to listen to the radio traffic between 'Clinton' and the airborne squadrons, while the 'Mess Waiter' (Sam Kydd) helps himself to the sherry left behind by 'Squadron Leader Ponsford'.

By 0.42.40 we are back in 'Tiger's' office, and he has called in 'Squadron Leader Moon'. 'Squadron Leader Ponsford' has apparently 'bought it' ('rotten luck') and 'Moon' is to take over 'Pimpernel' – he protests that he has 'no operational experience'. This was not untypical, although not entirely accurate. Many squadron commanders who lacked combat experience were elevated to such positions owing to casualties during the Battle of Britain. Those officers, however, had spent a few days at least on an operational squadron as supernumerary, and had already converted to Spitfires or Hurricanes. From earlier conversations we know that 'Moon' has never even flown a Hurricane, so 'Moon's' appointment as 'Pimpernel' CO is a little exaggerated. What is accurate is the 'Tiger's' instruction that the combat-experienced 'Batchy' can lead in the air until 'Moon' gains experience.

This was not an uncommon scenario. On the first day of air-fighting at Dunkirk, for example, the CO of Duxford's 19 Squadron was captured, after which the squadron was successfully led throughout Operation *Dynamo* by the 23-year old commander of 'A' Flight, Flight Lieutenant Brian Lane. Although Lane received a DFC for his good leadership of the squadron in difficult circumstances, command of the unit went to an outsider, more senior on the Air Force List,

Squadron Leader Phillip Pinkham. With an AFC for meteorological flying and an experienced pilot, Pinkham had no combat experience and was killed in action on his first engagement – at which point Lane was, at last, promoted and led 19 with distinction throughout the remainder of the Battle of Britain.

Similarly, Squadron Leader G.A.L. 'Minnie' Manton was promoted to command 56 Squadron during the Battle of Britain, but lacking personal combat experience sensibly allowed either of his flight commanders to lead in the air until he felt sufficiently confident to do so. A more sensible approach perhaps would have been to give command of these squadrons to pilots within who did have combat experience, rather than simply seniority on the promotional list. Nonetheless, no getting out of it for 'Moon', who will be handing over his duties as Sector Controller to 'Clinton' and taking over command of 'Pimpernel' – in time for the long-awaited mass attacks on 11 Group's fighter bases.

With the action hotting up, at 0.43.20 the film switches to what is supposedly such an incoming mass raid – but it is a terrible graphic (even by 1951 standards), supposedly of German bombers based upon the Ju 88, but which, well, just look odd – all set to rousing Teutonic martial music and singing.

With 'Baird' now working in the Operations Room, super-imposed over his image we see Hurricanes starting up, scrambling, and some returning with combat damage – including 'Batchy', whose fuselage fabric is in tatters, the dim-witted rigger 'Wailes' enquiring 'Any luck, Sir?' 'Batchy' explains that 'There were thousands of the blighters', but following an attack admits he owes his life to the intervention of 'Squadron Leader Moon' (doubtless the pedantic will take issue with the incorrect lifejacket, flying helmet, goggles and oxygen mask worn by 'Batchy'). 'Moon' and 'Batchy' then walk over to dispersal, the latter saying how uncomfortable he feels with the senior officer 'flying as me Red 2', whereas 'Moon' acknowledges that 'Batchy' is 'teaching me a lot'.

The next scene is surplus to requirements. At 0.45.30 two airmen are considering the building of a tower on the airfield, one telling the other, to his amazement, that so short of aircraft are Fighter Command that the tower is so that the 'Tiger' can 'punch the Jerry pilots on the nose'. What makes this scene ridiculous – and an insult to the intelligence of 'Other Ranks' – is that the response of the other airman suggests he believes it: 'Cor, chase me round the 'angar.'

We then re-join the 'Clintons' for quickly grabbed tea and sandwiches at home (0.45.45) between raids. After dark, one section of 'Beeswax' remains aloft, but the bungalow's landing light bulb has gone and needs changing. I am really not sure why this equally pointless scene is included.

At 0.46.22 we enter a busy pub with 'Baird', where the 'operational types' are letting off steam. The licensee, 'Aunt Tabatha' (Amy Veness), knows the airmen well and is introduced to 'Septic' – who orders a Drambuie. The sole bottle, however, is preserved for 'Mr Mortimer', a 'Pimpernel' pilot (Harold Siddons), but the news is broken that he too has 'bought it'; 'Aunt Tabatha' insists upon keeping the bottle aside 'just in case Mr Mortimer calls in' – the bottle symbolically and solemnly placed on a shelf behind the bar.

Pubs were, in reality, great places for personnel to relax, not being subject to the social segregation of station messes. In this scene, for example, we see men – and women – of various ranks socialising together. Cases in point are The Chequers at Fowlmere, adopted by 19 Squadron during the Battle of Britain, and the White Hart at Brasted, known to many Biggin Hill-based pilots throughout the war. The importance of this scene, however, is to show that 'Baird's' standoffishness is now thawing.

At 0.47.20, 'Moon' – clearly having risen positively to the challenges of both operational flying and commanding a fighter squadron in action – is seen looking over his damaged Hurricane, 'Daisy', with the 'Tiger', who expresses concern not over aircraft shortages but a lack of pilots. Certainly the number of replacements coming through was a problem, their numbers swelled by volunteers from other commands and the Fleet Air Arm, but as previously explained the big issue was that these new pilots lacked combat experience. 'Moon' can expect one more pilot in a couple days, though, as 'Baird', the 'walking textbook', will be fit for operational duty.

At 0.48.26 we join 'Baird' and 'Miss Carfax' as the 'Clintons'' dinner guests in their bungalow. A speech is demanded ('No funking') from 'Septic', in which he acknowledges having 'made an arse of himself all over the Station'. Humbled by the 'Clintons'' friendship and hospitality despite his difficult behaviour, it turns out 'Septic', two days away from becoming operational, is 'being launched', and might just be a frightfully good type after all. After dinner, 'Baird' and 'Miss Carfax' watch the searchlights probing the night sky and are getting along splendidly, agreeing on a dinner date in Maidstone when operational commitments permit: 'You're a grand girl.'

We are returned to the 'Hole' at 0.51.56, with another incoming raid – '100 aircraft at 16,000'. 'Baird' is on the rostrum with 'Clinton', on duty as 'Ops B', conveying and receiving telephone messages from Group HQ, and passing instructions to airborne squadrons, 'Beeswax' and 'Nutmeg'. Meanwhile a WAAF, 'Ops A', passes instruction to the 'Beauty Chorus' working around the plotting table. This is a big raid, however, and 'Baird' brings 'Pimpernel' to readiness. We then see newsreel footage of Spitfires taking off, watched by the lookout on the aforementioned tower.

With raids being plotted all over south-east England, 'Clinton' predicts that 'This could be quite a party.' 'Baird' exclaims that there are just two Hurricane squadrons against '200 Jerries', which Clinton opines 'Doesn't make much sense.' Air Vice-Marshal Park, however, the commander of 11 Group, defending London and the south-east, had the difficult task of executing as much damage on the enemy as possible while preserving his limited resources – a difficult balancing act. History has confirmed that Park's chosen tactics of using small, flexible, formations, and using Spitfires, with superior performance as a high-altitude protective umbrella, were exactly right.

At 0.53.52, 'Clinton' and 'Baird' are joined by 'Bob', a squadron leader (actor unknown), an 'auxiliary type', with the Auxiliary Air Force's brass 'A' on his lapels – which some say stood for 'Argue and answer back', indicating the auxiliaries irreverent view of service discipline. The raids develop, 'Pimpernel' is scrambled – twelve Hurricanes taking off in an admirable 'three minutes dead'. As things intensify further still, 'Baird' is relieved by 'Bonzo', but decides to 'hang around, this looks like the biggest show yet'. 'Nutmeg' is engaged while 'Clinton' vectors 'Pimpernel' to the south-west of Beachy Head.

At 0.55.53 there is a switch to an 'in-flight' cockpit shot of 'Moon' receiving instructions. Confirming that the Battle of Britain was a very visible aerial battle, we then see a farm-worker looking up at the vapour-trail criss-crossed sky, standing near a Kentish oast house while seeing to his cattle. At 0.56.22, 'Moon' gives the 'Tally Ho!' – but is warned by 'Sapper' to watch out for 'hawks' – German fighters. With all three Neethley squadrons engaged, 'Raid 132' then becomes a concern – heading straight for the airfield. 'Clinton' seeks advice from the 'Group Controller' (Ronald Adam) who is despatching squadrons to intercept and trying to find reinforcements, in the meantime advising 'Clinton' to 'Do whatever you can', concluding, discouragingly, with 'Nice to have known you.' Permission is then refused for 'Nutmeg' to return and rearm, and the 'Tiger' orders 'Anything that flies' to get into the air 'quick'.

Grabbing his own flying kit, the Station Commander runs outside to find a Hurricane. 'Clinton', however, orders 'Every available pilot to report to Practice Flight and take 'orf' independently.' 'Baird' seizes his chance and joins the rush to find an aircraft. As the airfield is brought to 'Action Stations', we again see the un-cowled Spitfire, with another adjacent, while two silver Harvard trainers taxi past.

Both the 'Tiger' and 'Baird' espy the same waiting Hurricane, 'P2617', and sprint towards it; the younger man – unaware of his Station Commander's presence – winning the race. 'Baird' then takes off with a multitude of aircraft 'of all shapes and sizes', while 'Battle Bowlers' are donned by 'Sapper Control' personnel and the Operations Room's blast-proof doors closed – and all station personnel not engaged on operational duty are advised to take shelter, and 'Guns', the Army Liaison anti-aircraft officer in 'Sapper' (Neil Wilson) is requested not to 'pop off' at returning aircraft.

At 1.00.18, 'Clinton' is bemused by an incoming radio transmission: '"Septic" calling' – having been unaware that 'Baird' had taken-off. Told to 'Make Angels as fast as you can' (but not how many!), callsign 'Septic' answers in textbook style from the in-studio cockpit. Meanwhile as the sirens wail, the 'Tiger' takes a last look around his intact Station. A Bofors anti-aircraft gun is made ready by army personnel, while 'Septic' calls 'Tally Ho!', having sighted and about to attack a 'bandit' – actually another curious and unrealistic graphic of a rather stumpy Me 110. With a shout of 'Here I come!', 'Septic' attacks from the blind spot, below and behind.

The action then returns to Neethley, where (1.01.23) we see another improvised graphic of twenty-five German bombers approaching the airfield from the south-east, while being engaged by 'Ack-Ack'. Tension mounts in 'Sapper Control', 'Clinton' observing that 'This is when we learn how to take it.' Neethley's squadrons are ordered not to return to base – but 'Sapper's' transmitter fails, meaning that the order cannot be passed to the three airborne squadrons. 'Clinton' explodes that 'Some blithering idiot has left his transmitter on!' – thereby preventing any radio messages being passed by other callers on the same frequency.

Again we see the (terrible!) 'Ju 88s' in formation, bombs falling from them exploding on the airfield. One bomber attacks from low-level – in a scene not dissimilar, perhaps, to KG76's Do 17s' famous attack on Kenley during 18 August 1940. A moving lorry is hit and

Neethley's personnel run for cover. Aircraft and buildings are hit – but the 'Look Out' (Harry Locke) provokes a giggle in 'Sapper' when announcing that 'Enemy bombers are bombing the airfield!' The 'Tiger', having been unable to get up a 'kite', is furious, and pushes a machine-gunner aside, taking control of his twin Lewis guns and letting fly at the bombers, while bombs explode all around. We then see an aerial shot of a (real) distant Spitfire pursuing a Ju 88, while the 'Look Out' keeps up a spirited running commentary on the action in his working-class Cockney accent.

An explosion shakes 'Sapper', however, but the (mostly female) personnel within continue stoically working on until the ceiling caves in – causing casualties, fortunately none fatal. With all landlines dead, 'Clinton' decides to evacuate the damaged building and relocate to the Emergency Operations Room, prepared for such an eventuality – but the blast door is jammed and no way out of the battered 'Sapper Control'. The problem is, it is believed that an unexploded bomb is nearby. Nonetheless, 'Clinton' and staff have no option but to await rescue. However, when a WAAF, 'Foster' (Freda Bamford), hands 'Clinton' a mug of tea, he finds it a morale-boosting tonic.

Outside, Neethley's personnel battle with fires (1.05.46) and other damage, while the 'All Clear' sounds and we see 'Nadine Clinton' and working-class housekeeper (Joan Hickson, later well-known as 'Miss Marple' on 1980s television) emerge unscathed from the Anderson shelter in the bungalow garden. The 'Clintons' home, however, is flattened.

Neethley's aircraft can be seen returning to land at 1.06.08. 'Batchy' and pilots are told by the Intelligence Officer (Hugh Moxey) that the 'Jerries didn't have it all their own way' as the Station scrambled an 'Odds and Sods Section'. Indeed, one Me 110 was shot down and crashed 'just outside the perimeter', and 'a couple of probables'. 'Batchy' then reports that 'Pimpernel' attacked 'about fifty Dorniers', destroying seven. 'All confirmed?', inquired the IO: 'Absolutely, old boy.' Well, how can a chap's word be doubted?

The fact is, however, that owing to the fast-moving and confusing nature of aerial combat, claims are virtually always exaggerated, albeit unintentionally; sometimes, the record now shows, by as much as 7:1. Unfortunately, 'Pimpernel' was then attacked by Me 109s, three pilots consequently being missing, 'Although Matthews may have got down at Hawkinge.'

This was a frequent after-action occurrence, as news filtered through about missing pilots, some of whom may have baled out, others forced-landed or perhaps touched down at alternative aerodromes. Sadly, on occasion, there was no news. The IO tells the pilots that a shelter was hit on the airfield, and the 'Ops Room bought it', although everyone 'got out alive'. Upon learning that the crashed Me 110 is in a nearby field, however, the pilots dash off to inspect the vanquished foe, leaving the IO, another 'VR type', complaining that he has to fill out an after-action report. This was the case. Upon landing pilots would complete the Fighter Command Form 'F' – or individual combat report – from which the IO would reconstruct events and forward to Group HQ.

At 1.07.36 we arrive at the Me 110's crash site, in advance of 'Batchy' and friends – with a rather smug 'Baird', responsible for its destruction. This is, in fact, an incredible historic artefact in itself, loaned by the Air Ministry and brought out of storage: Me 110G (WN 180850), the aircraft of the German night-fighter ace Heinz-Wolfgang Schnaufer, which had been captured intact in 1945 (but unceremoniously scrapped after *Angels One Five* was made!). 'Baird' looks over his prize, while admiring civilians look on from a distance, proudly telling an officer examining the wreck that he was responsible for the enemy's demise. 'Baird' takes an altimeter as a trophy for the 'Pimpernel' gallery, as 'Batchy' and pals abruptly and noisily arrive on the scene – and are mighty impressed with 'Baird's' achievement. Indeed, 'Batchy' is 'Transbuggerified'! Chairing 'Baird' and carrying him aloft on the tailfin of Schnaufer's 110, the 'Pimpernels' cart the pilot off back to dispersal, singing an irreverent

RAF song, culminating in the rousing '"Septics's"' got a Jerry in the field, "Septic's" got a Jerry, the "Pimpernels" are merry, "Septic's" got a Jerry in the field!'

Back at 'A' Flight's dispersal hut, however, 'Squadron Leader Moon' is in no mood for a party (1.10.11), summoning 'Baird' to his office – 'Shut the door' (always a bad sign!). A delighted 'Baird' explains that he has been 'inspecting my kill, Sir', proudly showing the trophy. 'Moon' has not called 'Baird' in for congratulations – but to tear him off a strip for failing to first report to Intelligence, and worse, leaving his radio on transmit and blocking the channel throughout the bombing of Neethley. 'Baird', the 'textbook pilot who knows all the answers', has the consequence of his stupidity spelled out to him by his angry CO: that other pilots, perhaps shot-up, wounded, 'short of juice', were unable to communicate with 'Sapper'. 'Baird' is mortified. Fortunately, all Neethley's pilots returned safely, otherwise, 'Moon' tells 'Baird': 'I'd run you off the Station with my own bare hands' – a sharp lesson that training manuals are one thing, but operational flying requires experience.

To preserve the squadron's reputation and dignity, though, 'Moon' makes clear that this latest 'black won't be published outside these four walls'. Dismissed, the crestfallen 'Baird' declines to hang his trophy on the wall, instead leaving it on the CO's desk. Outside the CO's office, 'Baird' comes clean with the other pilots, admitting to his mistake. Then (1.13.04), 'Baird' is ordered to report to the 'Tiger' 'immediately'. Another ticking off follows, this time in the Station Commander's bomb-damaged office, the 'Tiger' again emphasising the need for teamwork with everyone working together, abiding by rules and regulations.

Dismissed, the formal interview over, the 'Tiger' removes his hat and invites 'Baird' to be seated and have a cigarette. In a fatherly chat, the 'Tiger' admits that he too ignored his service training that day in order to hit back at the raiders, when he took over the machine-guns. The 'Tiger' also points out that 'Baird' had not noticed him also running for the same Hurricane – but he, the Station Commander, stopped and let 'Baird' win – leading to another display of stupidity from 'Baird', who disputes that the older man could have beaten him in a sprint. Nonetheless, the chat ends in smiles and hopefully a lesson learned.

In the Officer's Mess (1.15.27) we join Neethley's pilots and ground officers relaxing after quite a day, a sign over bomb damage declaring 'Jerry has been here'. Power is out and 'Baird' appears bearing a lit candle, to be told by 'Jacko' that 'Squadron Leader Moon' was looking for him. Not good news, considering the latest 'black'. 'Moon' is found 'nattering with the 'Tiger'. 'Baird' is as surprised as he is delighted to learn that at first light the following morning he is to be on readiness and will be flying as 'Moon's' 'Yellow 2'.

The next scene shows five Hurricanes flying in line abreast formation, and 'Baird' jumping in his cockpit, taking-off, with various subsequent in-cockpit and in-flight footage. After action, 'Baird' lands to find Neethley bombed again. This kind of scene was all too common, in fact, at 11 Group sector stations during the latter half of August 1940, when the Luftwaffe pounded Air Vice-Marshal Park's airfields. Again (1.17.02) a couple of working-class airmen with a southern twang are shown repairing damage and discussing the merits of even bothering: 'After a couple of days of this, there won't be a Station left to tidy. Got a fag?'

This may be a slight exaggeration, but things certainly did get critical, with airfields cratered, facilities disrupted and operations rooms forced to set up in civilian buildings. 'Nadine Clinton' (who is actually a civilian but who apparently has free-run of RAF Neethley) is seen escorting a heavily bandaged casualty to a waiting 'ARP Ambulance', driven by 'Baird's' love interest, 'Betty Carfax' – who is, she tells her friend, 'thrilled' about the prospect of dinner with him in Maidstone that night. The 'Tiger' then arrives as the ambulance leaves, acknowledging 'Mrs Clinton's' help with the wounded – whereas our 'Lady of the Lamp' brushes this aside, paying her own tribute to the fighter pilots' bravery and efforts, day after day. 'We keep going because we've got to' responds the 'Tiger'. 'Mrs Clinton' expresses concern regarding the strain her husband is under, the 'Tiger' actually being on his way to see 'Barry Clinton' at 'Emergency Ops'.

At dispersal (1.18.55) the pilots await the next call to scramble, exchanging good-humoured banter, which focuses on the bashful 'Baird's' love life. 'Moon' enters and plays chess with 'Baird' – who, after flying five sorties that day, 'Batchy' describes as a 'Wonder child'. The atmosphere, however, is very relaxed, and 'Baird' has clearly dropped his previously priggish mantle and become an accepted and popular member of 'Pimpernel'.

We then see the 'Tiger' pull up outside a shoe-shop, inside which is actually 'Emergency Ops'. Things are quiet. Then more raids appear incoming. 'Pimpernel' is scrambled, but can only now muster six aircraft, which, according to 'Clinton', have already collectively flown forty-nine sorties that day. Nevertheless, what remains of 'Pimpernel' is off to patrol Dover at 'Angels One-Eight', with 'Baird' flying as 'Moon's' 'Black 2'.

Great footage again of the Hurricanes taxiing out and taking off – and the terrible graphic of the oddly shaped Ju 88s. Once more we go through the routine of 'Clinton' controlling 'Pimpernel' with a little light-hearted banter between himself and the airborne 'Moon': 'You funny little man!' (1.22). With two swastikas painted on his Hurricane, indicating aerial victories, 'Moon' climbs his formation as 'Sapper' warns of 'bandits' above and behind. 'Baird' then sights '109s above', which 'Moon' correctly identifies as a formation of 'Spitties' (1.23.19). More information from 'Sapper' regarding the bandits' location, and now a graphic from directly above of the formation of curiously shaped 'Ju 88s' (which look more, perhaps, like a He 111/Ju 88 hybrid). 'Pimpernel' then peel off and attack in a vertical dive, in line astern.

Unfortunately this is all achieved by strange graphics superimposed over aerial views on the ground, seen from the in-studio cockpit – it being fair to say that the film-makers dismally failed to take advantage of assembling so many Hurricanes in one place for filming purposes. 'Baird' attacks and destroys a bomber, which falls in flames.

More raids, however, are incoming on the plotting table at 'Sapper' (1.25.09) – a fighter sweep – 'Clinton' warning 'Pimpernel Leader' of 'Hawks in the sun'. 'Moon' and 'Baird', however, are still engaging enemy bombers when (1.25.41) a Me 109 (a model looking like a 109E/G hybrid) ambushes and attacks 'Baird'. Again, strange graphics simulate the two Hurricanes twisting and turning with a *Rotte* (fighting pair) of Me 109s, one of which 'Baird' shoots off 'Moon's' tail – but then the other enemy fighter attacks 'Baird' from behind, damaging the Hurricane and wounding the pilot, whose aircraft falls away. The groggy 'Baird' recovers control but finds his canopy jammed. 'Moon' then instructs his 'Black 2', who is unable to bale out, to 'Put down at Manston', a coastal airfield, and prepares to escort 'Baird' down. With 'Sapper' anxiously monitoring events, with 'Tiger' looking on, the two Hurricanes descend, using 'Button 'B'', the emergency radio channel.

Curiously, 'Mrs Clinton' then arrives and speaks with a WAAF outside the Emergency Operations Room, saying that the 'stragglers will be returning in the dark', so hurries off to illuminate her landing light beacon. Given that this appears to be a bright sunny morning or afternoon, for a Hurricane to be landing after dark, the endurance of a Vulcan bomber would be required! Another unnecessary and ridiculous scene.

At 1.28.28, the Hurricanes of 'Pimpernel' are shown in flight returning from the engagement. 'Batchy' (Red 1) is told to maintain radio silence, so that all ears are on 'Baird' and 'Moon'. The atmosphere is tense. With 'Baird's engine power failing, 'Clinton' hopes that on this occasion the pilot remembers to 'switch over to receive' – a lesson the 'Tiger' is confident he has now learned.

'Betty Carfax' then cycles around the Neethley perimeter track past two parked Spitfires (1.30.00), bumping into 'Mrs Clinton', who is 'Just 'orf to the bungalow.' 'Betty' explains that she is 'dashing off to change', on account of having the dinner date that evening with 'Septic'.

We are returned to an even more tense 'Sapper' at 1.30.28, where all personnel anxiously await the outcome of 'Baird's' forced-landing at Manston. 'Baird's' voice comes over the air, faltering, the wounded pilot regressing to using his original callsign of 'Elfin 1'. Finally calling up as 'Septic', the last message is to tell the 'Tiger' that their sprinting race 'will have to be postponed ... indefinitely'. Nothing more is heard from 'Baird', a silence descending over 'Sapper Control' – the consequence of 'Baird's' final message being obvious. During the Battle of Britain, 544 of the Few were either killed or reported missing in action – having now sadly made the ultimate, heroic, sacrifice, 'Septic' joined their ranks.

At 1.32.00 there is an elevated view of the 'Clinton's' bombed bungalow and adjacent airfield, with 'Mrs Clinton' hanging up a lantern – a symbolic homing beacon. The camera then pans out and above, the *RAF March Past* being played in slow time for dramatic effect, the bungalow's twinkling lantern seen through the bombed roof, undoubtedly a visual metaphor for the country refusing to give in and fighting on alone, no matter the odds or cost – achieving an almost spiritual dignity in the process. Finally, Churchill's words appear: 'Never in the field of human conflict was so much owed by so many to so few', as the music's tempo increases and becomes more upbeat as the credits roll.

So ends the stories of 'Pilot Officer T.B. "Septic" Baird', who turned out not such a bad 'type' after all, 'RAF Neethley', 'Pimpernel Squadron' and 'Sapper Control' during the Battle of Britain's most desperate days.

Conclusion

Angels One Five was intended as a tribute to the Few, and upon release was appraised by Group Captain Douglas Bader, who attended the premiere: 'I can't fault it in any detail ... depicts life on any fighter station in the South of England during the Battle.'

While the gutter press shared this positive view, the more upmarket newspapers and magazines were less enthusiastic, arguing that the film lacked real drama, excitement and tension. Rightly, Thomas Spencer, of the albeit communist newspaper the *Daily Worker*, complained at how the working-classes were portrayed in the film. Indeed, the whole production was arguably a romp for public school boys and girls rallying round and seeing off the jolly old Hun, backed up by some pretty dim and uncultured lower ranks.

The only glimmer of hope, in fact, is at 0.30.52, when 'Batchy' assures 'Baird' that 'Pete', the only sergeant-pilot seen throughout the entire film, and just for a second at that, is a 'good type'. *Angels One Five* may have been intended as a tribute to the Few – but the end result was a very selective one, there being no foreign pilots at all, and just that one fleeting glimpse of the lone sergeant-pilot.

While the film is undoubtedly of its time, and not dissimilar in approach to other British war films of the period, it fails to actually tell the Battle of Britain story in any detail, and would have benefited from a narration, providing context. Admittedly, the Battle of Britain is a very difficult and expensive story to translate to cinema, not least because accuracy involves using large numbers of aircraft, and these were simply unavailable. Nonetheless, the Hurricanes and Spitfires assembled provided for some excellent ground and aerial footage – but *First of the Few* proved that a realistic impression of combat could be achieved through splicing newsreel and cine-gun footage. Surprisingly, *Angels One Five* made no attempt to do this, relying instead on graphics primitive even by the standards of 1951.

THE BATTLE OF BRITAIN ON THE BIG SCREEN

Watching the film today, seventy-years after it was screened, I personally find it quite the worst kind of film, with its class distinction, and a massive let-down in terms of having been the first post-war project to attempt to tell the Battle of Britain story. How I would have felt had I watched it in 1951, and had lived through the times portrayed, we will never know, but personally I doubt my view would have been much different.

All of that said, the film's legacy – in addition to the aircraft and flying scenes – is some important footage of RAF Kenley as it appeared in 1951, just eleven years after the Battle and while still an operational station, and it especially recreates the workings and atmosphere of a sector operations room during the summer of 1940. Sight of Schnaufer's Me 110 is also a treat, but equally a sad reminder of how so many similarly historically important airframes survived the war only to be unceremoniously scrapped in peacetime.

Overall, then, *Angels One Five* gets a very definite 'no' from me. To coin Trevor Howard's words from *The Way to the Stars*: 'Bad show, I think.'

Chapter 4

Reach for the Sky

So far, films either revolving around the Battle of Britain, or at least referring to it, had focused upon the story of an individual, *The First of the Few* being a distinct case in point, while *Angels One Five* had majored on the importance of team-work, not individualism, through the story of 'Septic' Baird and 'Pimpernel Squadron'.

The next relevant film, Daniel Angel's 1956 biopic *Reach for the Sky*, focused on that one, larger than life, personality: Douglas Bader – whose life, of course, defied fiction. Bader had become a household name during the Second World War, the legless Battle of Britain fighter ace who ended up an unappeasable prisoner in the notorious Colditz Castle. Beyond doubt, even today, Bader remains the most famous of the Few, and in conquering his double-amputation, personified determination and courage at a superhuman level – which is what was required in wartime and, moreover, something post-war Britain needed reminding of.

A gifted sportsman and pre-war RAF aerobatic display pilot, the headstrong young Pilot Officer Bader had lost both legs performing low-level, unauthorised, aerobatics at Woodley in 1931. A lesser man might have died, but the indomitable Bader overcame his crushing disability, learning to walk on artificial legs, and even subsequently passed a flying test at the Central Flying School. Unfortunately, King's Regulations back then failed to cater for pilots with physical disabilities, and so Pilot Officer Bader was offered a return to duty in a ground-based role. Finding the idea of flying a desk intolerable, Bader left the service he loved so dearly in 1933, spending years in the wilderness.

War, however, was Bader's salvation, and, with strings pulled internally by fellow Cranwellians, the Air Ministry agreed to reinstate the determined former airman in a flying capacity *if* war broke out and providing he passed both a medical and further flying test. The storm broke on 3 September 1939, and Bader got the chance he craved. His flying test was taken by another Cranwellian, who considered Bader a 'God', and who operated the footbrakes for the legless pilot on the American aircraft involved. The brakes on British aircraft – which Bader would fly operationally – were operated via a lever on the pilot's control column, so being unable to use footbrakes on American machines was not, in fairness, an issue. It was, however, another example of Cranwellians looking after their own – and consequently Douglas Bader, now a married man (having wed Thelma Edwards in 1933), returned to flying duties.

Bader was reinstated as a mere flying officer, but by this time his contemporaries had aspired to greater rank. By February 1940, for example, Geoffrey Stephenson, his great friend from Cranwell and 23 Squadron days at pre-war Kenley, was a squadron leader and commanding the RAF's first Spitfire squadron, 19, based at Duxford.

As Flying Officer Bader neared completion of his operational training, Squadron Leader Stephenson arranged for his old chum to visit Duxford when the 12 Group AOC, Air Vice-Marshal Trafford Leigh-Mallory, was lunching with the Station Commander, Wing Commander A.B. 'Woody' Woodhall. Arriving at zero feet – inverted – in a Hurricane, Bader put on a show, as a result of which Stephenson had no trouble persuading Leigh-Mallory and Woodhall to approve the legless pilot's posting to 19 Squadron.

The biplanes flown by Flying Officer Bader pre-war, however, were very different to the new modern Spitfire and Hurricane fighters now in service, and initially Bader had difficulty getting to grips with the Spitfire, damaging several aircraft in blameworthy, careless, accidents. It was also clear that Bader was only a team-player if leader of it, and he had difficulty serving under his friend and Cranwell contemporary Stephenson. Indeed, although the oldest pilot on the squadron at 30, Flying Officer Bader was also the least experienced on the Spitfire. Taking orders from younger men and his old friend did not appeal, and so the unhappy Bader sought out Squadron Leader 'Tubby' Mermagen – another Cranwellian commanding Duxford's other Spitfire squadron, 222, and persuaded Mermagen to take him as a flight commander. Now a team leader and flight lieutenant, Bader was delighted with his elevation and new posting – and it is equally fair to say that neither Stephenson – with whom he had argued over tactics – or most of 19 Squadron's pilots were sorry to see him go.

It was on 1 June 1940, during the air operation covering the Dunkirk evacuation, that Flight Lieutenant Bader recorded his first victory, claiming a Me 109 destroyed and sharing a He 111. By this time, although Air Ministry policy was not to identify individual pilots for fear of creating an elite, the legless pilot was already attracting publicity – and was clearly a Godsend for the propagandists. Bader had also become a favourite of both Leigh-Mallory and Woodhall, for which reason, just in time for the Battle of Britain, he was promoted to acting squadron leader and given command of 242 Squadron – a Canadian Hurricane outfit in poor shape after a bad time during the Fall of France.

It was a meteoric rise, considering Bader had only reported to 19 Squadron five months previously. Arriving at Coltishall, Squadron Leader Bader gave immediate reassurance to his morose pilots that he was no legless passenger, delivering a daredevil performance of low-level aerobatics – impressing both seasoned veterans like the tough Canadian Stan Turner, and impressionable young English pilot, Denis Crowley-Milling. By 10 July 1940 – the official start-date of the Battle of Britain – 242 Squadron was fully operational again – and the following day its CO destroyed a Do 17 off Yarmouth. Bader rapidly inspired his new team – who would follow him anywhere – which is exactly why he was appointed to command. Indeed, he had never been happier.

While the epic air battle increased in ferocity over southern England, 242 Squadron found itself far from the action, in East Anglia, flying monotonous convoy protection patrols and chasing lone German reconnaissance bombers. 12 Group's job was to defend the industrial Midlands and North, which could be subjected to a heavy attack at any time, and defend Air Vice-Marshal Park's airfields, when 11 Group requested assistance and Air Vice-Marshal Park's fighters were engaged further forward. At the time, operational training had focused upon the flight of six aircraft, rather than a squadron flying together as a cohesive unit, and the limitations of aerial radio communications only provided for the pilots of one squadron to speak to each other and their ground controller.

With all of this in mind and considering Park's brief of executing maximum damage on the enemy while preserving his limited resources, he rightly decided to concentrate on reacting with small, flexible, formations, although squadrons were also used in pairs. 12 Group's fighter pilots watched the Battle of Britain develop further South, envious of the action being had by 11 Group, and anxiously awaited the call to scramble – which never seemed to come.

Bader, however, found it intolerable to play second fiddle while 11 Group's squadrons got all the action. He sulked and stormed, berating 'Woody', the Duxford Station Commander and Sector Controller, to let 242 Squadron sally forth over south-east England. This, however, Woodhall was unable to authorise unless requested by 11 Group. On 30 August 1940, Bader at last got his wish when 11 Group called for 12's assistance in dealing with raids heading for aircraft factories north-west of London.

Intercepting German bombers unescorted by Me 109s, in what was 242 Squadron's first experience of a mass enemy raid, Bader and his pilots claimed the destruction of seven Me 110s, with three probables, and five He 111s destroyed – generating congratulatory signals from far and wide, including the Chief of the Air Staff and Under-Secretary of State for Air. Enthused, Squadron Leader Bader subsequently submitted a report outlining his firm belief that had more fighters been under his command, greater damage would have been inflicted upon the enemy. Following rigorous post-war analysis, we now know the reality of that significant action of 30 August 1940 is that a total of fifty RAF fighters, including the fourteen of 242 Squadron, were actually engaged – immediately disproving Squadron Leader Bader's theory. Moreover, in total the Germans only lost nine Me 110s and He 111s in this action, of which only two can definitely be attributed to 242 Squadron. Nonetheless, these claims were accepted and so on paper 242 Squadron had scored a resounding victory.

Air Vice-Marshal Leigh-Mallory saw his subordinate's idea as a means of getting 12 Group into the Battle, and Wing Commander Woodhall agreed. So it was that the relatively inexperienced commander of 242 Squadron found himself at Duxford, leading a 'Wing' initially comprising the Hurricanes of 242 and 310 (Czech) Squadrons, and the Fowlmere-based Spitfires of 19, the idea being for 12 Group to arrive over the combat area in strength. The problem, however, is that Bader's thinking was flawed from the outset, owing to the amount of early warning provided, the speed of all aircraft involved, time and distance.

It was also contrary to the System of Fighter Control developed over time by two highly experienced officers of air rank, namely Air Chief Marshal Dowding and Air Vice-Marshal Park. Nonetheless, the 'Duxford Wing' first went into action on 7 September 1940, the first day London was subjected to round-the-clock bombing, but, caught by German fighters on the climb, it was not a resounding success. It was nevertheless agreed to add two further squadrons, and so Bader now found himself at the head of sixty fighters – a 'Big Wing' indeed.

As 12 Group's confidence grew, Bader increasingly led his formation on what were essentially free-ranging fighter sweeps over the 11 Group area – throwing the Observer Corps and defences generally into disarray. On 'Battle of Britain Day', 15 September 1940, it is often claimed that the sight of the 'Big Wing' arriving over London demoralised the German bomber crews, who had been led to believe that Fighter Command was finished. No evidence, however, has been found in German sources to confirm this, the issue not being the arrival of a single large formation but consternation at the numbers of RAF fighters generally.

What the 'Big Wing' did do that day, beyond doubt, was put hope and heart into 11 Group's hard-pressed pilots when the legless squadron commander arrived over the capital at the head of five 12 Group squadrons. On paper, the 'Big Wing' appeared enormously successful, claiming the destruction of far more enemy aircraft than 11 Group squadrons and giving the impression that mass fighter formations were the way forward. We know today that the 'Big Wing' actually continued to overclaim by as much as 7:1, but these figures were eagerly accepted at the time, leading senior figures at the Air Ministry and Westminster to question the penny-packet formations used by 11 Group, and Air Chief Marshal Dowding's overall strategy and tactics.

Cutting a long story short, this disagreement became a heated row between the two group commanders, involving politicians, and, once the Battle was won, ultimately played no small part in Dowding and Park being ignominiously replaced by Air Marshal Douglas and Air Vice-Marshal Leigh-Mallory respectively. The record proves, however, that Dowding and Park were, in fact, right, and 11 Group's combat claims were far more accurate than those of the 'Big Wing'. Indeed, it is inconceivable that an acting squadron leader should have considered himself such an expert in air fighting, having only met one massed raid, that he knew better than his Air Officer Commander-in-Chief, and perhaps even more astonishing that his Group Commander, Air Vice-Marshal Leigh-Mallory, supported this. But … there was a lot more to this, behind the scenes, old animosities and jealousies playing out between high commanders, and what has since become known as the 'Big Wing Controversy' is a dirty blemish on Fighter Command's Battle of Britain history.

Moving on, mass formations were pushed through by Fighter Command and 11 Group's new chiefs as standard in both attack and defence. In March 1941, the Command was reorganised with sector stations accommodating wings of three fighter squadrons, commanded by a 'Wing Commander (Flying)', a new post allowing the wing leader to concentrate on leading his wing in the air. Unsurprisingly, Wing Commander Bader – by now decorated with both the DSO and DFC – was among the first wing leaders appointed, and was even given his choice of stations. He chose Tangmere, on the south coast, near Chichester, from where his wing would participate in Fighter Command's 'Non-stop Offensive' of 1941.

Less than a year after the Battle of Britain, the intention was to adopt an aggressive posture, 'reaching out' and taking the war to the Germans in north-west France. The 'season' of 1941 was, therefore, a truly intensive period of offensive operations, including low-level nuisance raids by pairs of Spitfires, fighter sweeps, and complex 'Circus' operations involving hundreds of Spitfires escorting a small number of bombers attacking enemy airfields and other installations. Losses, however, were heavy, many irreplaceable and highly experienced combat pilots and leaders being lost – Bader among them.

By August 1941, it was obvious to all that the legless dynamo was tired, but Wing Commander Bader refused rest; 9 August 1941 should have been a routine operation for the Tangmere Wing, but everything went wrong from the outset, and, again cutting a long story short, the Wing Leader was brought down over St Omer and captured. Even so, throughout his years behind the wire, the press continued to share stories of the man, who was now a household name and made numerous attempts to escape, the first from St Omer's Clinique Sterin, assisted by brave locals. Not all, however, shared the positive view of Tangmere's swashbuckling Wing Leader, many fellow prisoners resenting Bader's relentless trouble-making, leading to the retraction of Red Cross parcels and other essentials.

THE BATTLE OF BRITAIN ON THE BIG SCREEN

In April 1945, Wing Commander Bader was released from Colditz – where, coincidentally he had joined his pre-war 23 Squadron flight commander and aerobatic team leader Harry Day, and Squadron Leader Geoffrey Stephenson – and returned home to his wife. Who else but Group Captain Bader, as he became, could possibly lead the RAF victory flypast over London on 'Battle of Britain Day' that year? The post-war service, however, was not to his liking, and our legless hero left the service for the second time, returning to work as an executive in the aviation section of Shell.

Times, however, were changing. The Conservative-dominated Britain of the 1930s, for example, was disappearing. In 1945, in spite of Churchill's enormous popularity as Britain's war leader, Clement Attlee's Labour Party won the General Election. The socialists immediately set about creating the welfare state, providing more educational equality and nationalising key industries, public transport and the Bank of England. The truth was that although Britain had emerged victorious from those long years of struggle, it was financially exhausted.

The immediate post-war period saw a shortage of food and clothing, meaning that rationing and 'austerity' continued into the 1950s. Nonetheless, that decade saw virtually full employment and the majority of Britons had never been so well off. On the wider stage, though, while Britain remained a leading European power, America had emerged leader of the Free World, and the Soviets had retired behind the 'Iron Curtain' – heralding the Cold War between democracy and communism. Moreover, Britain's Empire was now rapidly waning: in 1947, India won independence, and British influence in Africa was in decline; large-scale immigration transformed post-war Britain into an ethnically diverse and multi-cultural society. It was in many ways a difficult time for Britain.

The British contribution to victory in the Second World War, however, was – and is – the supreme moment in the modern national story and identity, providing a declining post-war Britain with a mythic reminder of the country's great past. Against this backdrop, Douglas Bader's story was screaming out to be told. It had all the ingredients for a book and film to 'stir a glow in English hearts', as the *Daily Mail* later wrote of the story – which was very much needed in austerity Britain at the time. So far as Group Captain Bader was concerned, however, there was only one man to write his story: Paul Brickhill.

Reach for the Sky

Paul Chester Jerome Brickhill was an Australian journalist in Sydney who joined the Royal Australian Air Force when war broke out. After training, Brickhill flew Spitfires with 92 Squadron in the Western Desert, but was shot down over Tunisia and captured in 1943. The following year saw the Australian incarcerated in *Stalag Luft* III, Sagan, and was behind the wire there when the 'Great Escape' took place.

After the war, given his journalistic ability and first-hand experience of the services, Brickhill spotted an opportunity to produce popular narratives of inspirational wartime stories. His first book, *Escape to Danger*, co-authored with Conrad Norton, appeared in 1946, and four years later came his first best-seller: *The Great Escape*. A year later came *The Dam Busters*, chronicling Operation *Chastise*, the famous raid on three German dams led by Wing Commander Guy Gibson of 617 Squadron, which was another huge success. Indeed, it was *The Dam Busters* which paved the way for Brickhill's next project, a colossal money-maker, and a seminal text of romantic exaggeration.

Noting the plethora of wartime memoirs being published, Douglas Bader had started writing his own, working with an unnamed author whose idea of a film was rejected by Rank, after which the project foundered. After his collaborator walked away, Bader kept the

100,000-word manuscript and pondered how to progress getting it into print. After reading *The Dam Busters*, both Douglas and Thelma Bader were convinced that Brickhill was the man to tell their story.

The Baders reached out, inviting the best-selling author to dinner in London and putting the prospect to him. Brickhill, however, was aware that while everyone had nothing but respect and admiration for how he had conquered his disability, inspiring in the process people the world over, Bader was in other respects very much a 'marmite' character. While his inner-sanctum of close friends and cronies worshipped the man, others found him arrogant, rude, opinionated, unreasonable and imperious. Over dinner, Brickhill decided that Bader's huge personality 'hits you like a bolting steamroller' – and, with full access to the original manuscript and Bader's personal records and papers, he agreed to take the job on. Soon, Brickhill's agent, David Higham, lined up Collins to publish the Douglas Bader story: *Reach for the Sky*. Published in 1954 – the year Britain's austerity measures ended – the book was an overnight success.

In the same year that saw *Reach for the Sky* become an international publishing phenomenon, Brickhill's *The Dam Busters* was made into a film, which became a box office hit in 1955. The film rights to *Reach for the Sky* were actually purchased by independent film-maker Danny Angel for £15,000 – even before he had read Brickhill's book. Angel, a former army major, was a producer, the director he worked with being Lewis Gilbert. The pair had previously collaborated to make two films concerning the wartime Royal Navy, *Albert RN* (1953), a story about naval officers in a German prison camp, and *The Sea Shall Not Have Them*, telling the story of an RAF High Speed Launch's daring rescue of a downed RAF bomber crew from beneath the Germans' noses.

With *Reach for the Sky*, Angel was to produce the film while Gilbert both directed and wrote a screenplay based upon Brickhill's book. Clearly, the story's key points were the devastating crash at Woodley followed by Bader's astonishing survival and relentless determination to walk – and fly – again, his war service confirming his incomparable courage and personal victory over the loss of both legs. There was never any question that a film based upon Bader's incredible life story and Brickhill's latest best-seller could be anything other than a massive success.

Richard Burton was preferred to play Bader in the film but turned the role down. Instead, Kenneth More was chosen, who desperately wanted the part:

> I admired Douglas Bader. He was to me a Rudyard Kipling figure; you don't find them anymore. I understood him. He was a harder man than I am. To me he represented everything that every Englishman wants to be: courageous, honest, determined – but knows he hasn't the nerve or capacity to be. He has got his faults – who hasn't? He was difficult, impulsive, strong-headed; he was all these things. But I felt that someone had to give him to the world.

And give him to the world More certainly did. During his research for the part, More met Bader twice – first over lunch before golfing at Gleneagles. The pair got on, and most importantly Bader trusted the actor. Naturally, Bader wanted the film of his life to be as accurate as possible, so some of his friends became involved, advising the film-makers. Group Captain Harry Day, for example, became official Technical Advisor. It was a good job, as Air Marshal Sir Denis Crowley-Milling remembered:

> When Angel discovered that I had been shot down and was hiding in St Omer at the same time Douglas was in hospital there, he immediately came up with the ridiculous idea that the story should be changed to show me leading an attempt with the French Resistance to break Douglas out. We swiftly put a stop to that nonsense!

Bader was adamant that everyone who had played a part in his life story should be faithfully represented – which was impossible in a film of 136 minutes, dictating the need for composite characters and the 'telescoping' of certain events. For example, Cambridge graduate Lyndon Brook, who had already starred alongside Gregory Peck in *The Purple Plain* (1954), became 'Johnny Sanderson' – a composite character based upon Geoffrey Stephenson; 'Sanderson' was also used as the narrator. After the Woodley crash, the film did not portray Australian Jack Cruttenden lifting Douglas from the wreckage, as in fact had happened, because this would have dictated introducing and explaining another character.

This was a great worry to Douglas. Some of his RAF friends were included by name, however: Harry Day was represented by Michael Warre, Stan Turner by Lee Patterson, 'Woody' Woodhall by Howard Marion Crawford, and Crowley-Milling by Basil Appleby. 242 Squadron's Engineering Officer, Warrant Officer West (Michael Ripper) also appeared, as did Air Chief Marshal Dowding (Charles Carson) and, of course, Air Vice-Marshal Leigh-Mallory (ironically, given the 'Big Wing' dispute between 11 and 12 Groups, played by former 11 Group Battle of Britain Controller Ronald Adam). Certain medical staff were also included: Nurse Brace (Dorothy Alison), the surgeon Mr Joyce (Alexander Knox), and consultant Robert Desoutter (Sydney Tafler). Naturally, a crucial character was Thelma Bader – played by former Royal Shakespeare Company and ENSA actress Muriel Pavlow (who in 1953 had starred alongside Alec Guinness in *Malta Story*).

The film was shot at Pinewood Studios, Denham Aerodrome (which became Woodley), and RAF Kenley, the latter providing a setting for multiple locations, including pre-war Cranwell and Kenley itself, Duxford, North Weald and Tangmere. As always, finding authentic aircraft was an issue. Permission was granted by the Science Museum for use of the sole surviving Bristol Bulldog (the type Bader was flying when he crashed at Woodley), while the Shuttleworth Collection of historic aircraft provided a Bristol Fighter, Avro 504 and Hucks Starter. Only one airworthy Hurricane, the RAF's LF363, was available, along with two static aircraft and the replica built by the film's art department. More Spitfires were available, but these Mk XVIs were visibly very different to the Mk Is, IIs and Vs Bader had flown in wartime, with a pointed rudder, cannons, tear-drop canopy, razor-back fuselage and a four-bladed propeller. The American-powered Mk XVI's nose, like the IX, was also eighteen inches longer than the earlier Spitfires, to accommodate its more powerful engine's two-stage supercharger, which also required twin under-wing radiators. Nonetheless, they *were* Spitfires – and airworthy – eight Mk XVIs and a Griffon-engine powered F.22. Unsurprisingly, no airworthy German wartime aircraft were available, and so Gilbert would rely upon newsreel footage, gun camera film, studio close-ups and models to recreate combat scenes. As usual, flying kit was also improvised, using whatever surplus was readily available – none of it authentic.

And so, in October 1955, the cameras were ready to roll.

Reach for the Sky: A Reading.

The film's opening scene is of an Avro 504 biplane taking off, a moment of pure nostalgia harking back to the halcyon days of vintage flight. At 0.1.04 a text card appears over a backdrop of clouds, telling us that 'Douglas Bader has become a legend in his own lifetime. His courage was not only an example to those in War but is now a source of inspiration to many in Peace.' From the outset, then, we are clear that this is a sympathetic approach to the story. Another card then explains that for 'dramatic purposes' it has been necessary to 'transpose in time certain events' and 'reshape some of the characters involved'. The producers apologise to those possibly affected by these 'changes or omissions' – something that we know troubled Bader himself.

After the cast and credits, we return to the airborne Avro 504, flown by 'Flying Instructor Pearson' (Michael Gough) of the RAF College Cranwell, who spots and 'buzzes' a motorcyclist, who ends up in a ditch: enter 'Douglas Bader' (Kenneth More, 0.02.10), en route to fulfil his ambition of becoming a Cranwell Flight Cadet. Bader had actually reported to Cranwell in 1928, aged 18; More was considerably older, at 41.

The new flight cadet's journey to Cranwell in 1928 was, however, inauspicious, a cow wandering out in from of his motorcycle on the Ankaster Straight, spilling the rider into a ditch and bursting the crown of his bowler hat, balanced on the front headlamp. Although the cow is replaced by the aeroplane in the film, the end result is identical: Flight Cadet Bader's bowler is damaged and he soon cuts a ridiculous figure on the drill square, incurring the wrath of the 'Flight Sergeant' (Eddie Byrne) and admiration of certain fellow students, among them 'Johnny Sanderson' (Lyndon Brook), in equal measure. At 0.04.56 the new cadets are marched off, 'Sanderson' and 'Bader' instant 'chums', and 'Sanderson' begins his narration.

While the film cuts to the airborne 504, and 'Pearson' instructing 'Bader', the narration explains that 'Douglas' was an excellent pilot. Having first made a hash of landing, however, the following day 'Bader' lands safely and successfully solos (0.07.03). Immature and irresponsible behaviour on the ground, however, earns 'Bader' and chums a dressing down from the Commandant, 'Air Vice-Marshal Halahan' (Walter Hudd). Then we see 'Bader' the talented sportsman, playing cricket, obviously superbly, when 'Sanderson' brings the great news that both, now pilot officers, are posted to 23 (Fighter) Squadron at Kenley.

The scene now shifts to Kenley in '1930' (0.10.59), where at 0.11.49, 'Flight Lieutenant Harry Day' (Michael Warre), their Flight Commander, advises Pilot Officers 'Sanderson' and 'Bader' regarding the perils of unauthorised low-level aerobatics, cautioning them that in the last month two pilots have been killed. 'Bader', naturally, knows best, and, having been, according to 'Day' 'the worst offender of all since selected for the Hendon Air Pageant' comes in for the bulk of his Flight Commander's attention.

This is true: Day did advise Pilot Officer Bader after the latter dropped out of formation during a flight to Cramlington and hedge-hopped all the way. Here we see some of what drives Bader: 'Day' advises 'Bader' that 'a really good pilot shouldn't have to prove it all the time'. Next (0.12.22), we are transported to a dance at the Kenley Officers' Mess, 'Bader' dancing ably with a girlfriend, 'Sally' (Beverley Brooks), where, informally, 'Day' reiterates his advice.

The next scenes are significant. At 0.13.46, three 'RAF chaps', 'Bader', 'Sanderson' and 'Richardson' (Alexander Harris) are shown visiting the 'Reading Aero Club' at 'Woodley'. There, although at first declining civilian flying members' request for a 'show', 'Bader' is stung into action by an acerbic comment, suggesting that 'These boys only perform when there's a crowd.' Consequently, 'Bader' purposefully strides out to takes off in his Bulldog biplane and beats up the airfield at zero feet – the display recreated using studio close-ups and a model.

At 0.15.19, shocked spectators watch in horror as the aircraft's wing touches the ground, the machine crashes and breaks up (superbly recreated). Within the tangled wreckage lies the dreadfully injured pilot, who, as previously mentioned, is lifted out of the wreckage by 'Sanderson'. 'Bader', however, observes that he is unable to feel his legs – and symbolically we see his shoes on the ground, removed from his shattered limbs.

'Bader' is then given a life-saving operation, although first one, then the other, leg is amputated in the process, while family and friends gather at the hospital. As 'Day' says, considering that 'Bader' was poised to play rugby on the international stage, it was a 'Hell of a thing to happen to a man like Douglas'. Hovering somewhere between life and death, the young pilot overhears a passing nurse remark that he is dying – awaking inside him the superhuman will to win, and in this case beat death, which, of course he does.

A recovering 'Bader' is seen in a wheelchair, outdoors, with his nurse, 'Brace' (Dorothy Allison), enthusing about 'Sally' – who dumps him by letter – and exhausting himself trying to walk on crutches. 'Brace' sets her patient, understandably depressed, straight and informs him that the Court of Inquiry had decided to take no action against him for the accident – giving 'Bader' hope that he may be allowed to fly again. Although on crutches but back in uniform, after fond farewells to hospital staff, at 0.38.48, 'Pilot Officer Bader' is picked up by a corporal and is driven away for the next stage of his recovery at the RAF Hospital, Uxbridge.

At 0.39.03, we rejoin 'Bader' and other injured pilots in their ward, spirits high. Soon, the legless and bored pilot gets his thrills and spills driving the Bentley of a fellow patient, 'Peel' (Jack Watling), with another patient, 'Vic Streatfield' (Nigel Green), joining the high-jinx. Surviving many a near-miss with innocent and legitimate road users, the daredevil threesome end up taking tea at the 'Pantiles', near Bagshot, where 'Bader' lays eyes on his future wife, 'Thelma' (Muriel Pavlow), for the first time, who is working as a waitress – and resolves to one day ask her out, when he has his artificial legs. The next scenes are the guts of the film, really, from 0.43.56, we see 'Bader' learning – with that superhuman courage and determination – to master walking on 'tin' legs.

It is an agonising process, not least because of the patient's refusal to walk with a stick. More really brings these scenes to life, and ultimately 'Bader' walks out of the hospital unaided, later driving to do as he promised himself and ask 'Thelma Edwards' out. The pair have dinner, during which 'Bader' learns that 'Thelma' knows all about him on account of her father having been a wing commander and her cousins all RAF pilots (the Donaldson brothers). The couple get on famously and even dance. Romance blossoms.

In 1942, Lesley Howard's film *First of The Few*, a somewhat romanticised version of the R.J. Mitchell and creation of the Spitfire stories, was premiered and became one of the Second World War's biggest grossing films. Staring Howard as Mitchell, and David Niven as Supermarine test pilot 'Geoffrey Crisp', 118 Squadron supplied the Spitfires for flying scenes, which were filmed at RAF Ibsley in Hampshire. Amongst the pilots involved was Flight Lieutenant Peter Howard-Williams DFC, one of The Few, who was a keen photographer and whose snapshots we see here. This picture of Lesley Howard, who also produced and directed the film, was taken by another pilot using Peter's camera; Peter can be seen at right in the background with his friend Flying Officer John Robson DFC, who also flew for the cameras.

Flight Lieutenant Peter Howard-Williams in conversation with Lesley Howard at Ibsley during the filming of *First of The Few*.

Above: Lesley Howard in conversation with Flying Officer Robson (left) and Flight Lieutenant Peter Howard-Williams.

Below: Lesley Howard enjoying some banter with pilots of 118 and possibly 501 Squadron during the filming of *First of The Few*.

The opening scenes of *First of The Few* include actual Ibsley Spitfire pilots discussing the R.J. Mitchell and Spitfire story. Some of those present were members of The Few. Here, Lesley Howard directs Flying Officer David Fulford DFC (left), who had flown with 19 Squadron during the Battle of Britain, and a most distinguished veteran of the air battles in 1940, namely Squadron Leader Christopher 'Bunny' Currant DFC, who was commanding 501 Squadron at Ibsley when the film was made.

Lesley Howard directing the scene in *First of The Few* wherein a shot-up squadron commander crash-lands his Spitfire. David Niven is in civilian dress with sun-glasses, standing with the pilot concerned, another distinguished member of The Few, Wing Commander Frank Howell DFC – who would survive years of deprivation as a prisoner of the Japanese, only to die in a tragic flying related accident in 1948. The aircraft is another presentation Spitfire, Mk VB P8789, named *Borough of Wanstead and Woodford*, which was on charge with 118 Squadron, but had suffered an undercarriage collapse on 26 September 1941. After use in the film and repair, the Spitfire resumed operational flying, but was lost on 1 June 1942 when its engine failed, causing Flight Sergeant Ron Stillwell of 65 Squadron (who appears elsewhere in this book) to bale out into the sea – fortunately the pilot was rescued two hours later.

Left: Hurricanes return to RAF Tangmere. Aircraft and pilots from a Hurricane-equipped Portuguese Air Force squadron are pictured being welcomed by RAF officers following their arrival at Tangmere for the filming of *Angels One Five*. On the left of the picture is Group Captain T. Pritchett, Tangmere's CO. The aircraft were all painted in the colours of 56 Squadron and were based at RAF Kenley during the filming. (Historic Military Press)

Below: Air Vice-Marshal Johnnie Johnson, the official top-scoring RAF fighter pilot of the Second World War and a protégé and close friend of Group Captain Sir Douglas Bader, in conversation with Kenneth More during the making of *Reach for the Sky*.

Above: A number of the aircraft used in the filing of *Reach for the Sky* can still be seen. One of the survivors is Hurricane Mk IIC LF363 – one of two Hurricanes operated by the RAF's Battle of Britain Memorial Flight. First flown on 1 January 1944, LF363 is believed to be the last Hurricane to enter service with the RAF. (Courtesy of Adrian Pingstone)

Right: A pair of aces: Squadron Leader James 'Ginger' Lacey, one of the highest scoring RAF fighter pilots in the Battle of Britain (left), and Group Captain Peter Townsend examine a Spitfire whilst both were advisors on the 1969 film *Battle of Britain*. Ironically, both flew Hurricanes during the summer of 1940.

Above: Another aircraft that appeared in one of the films featured in this book, in this case the *Battle of Britain*, is Supermarine Spitfire Mk IIa P7350. Also operated by the Battle of Britain Memorial Flight, this aircraft was restored to flying condition for use in the film. P7350 was actually shot down during the Battle of Britain on 25 October 1940, its pilot, Pilot Officer Ludwik Martel, being forced to land in a field near Hastings. (© MoD/Crown Copyright 2020)

Below: An RAF legend during the filming of the *Battle of Britain*. The original caption states: 'This is what it was like. During the filming of the *Battle of Britain* at Duxford airfield in England, the legless flying ace Group Captain Douglas Bader visited the set and made friends with some of the children of RAF personnel there.' (Historic Military Press)

Above: Two of The Few during the making of *Battle of Britain*. Seen here on the set are Group Captain Peter Townsend CVO, DSO, DFC & Bar, in the cockpit, and Ginger Lacey, standing. (Historic Military Press)

Right: Spitfires in formation – an image taken during the making of the blockbuster movie *Battle of Britain*. (Historic Military Press)

Above: On 14 September 2010, BBC2 broadcast Matthew Whiteman's docudrama *First Light*, based upon Squadron Leader Geoffrey Wellum's best-selling memoir of the same name. Here actors Ben Aldridge (left), playing Flight Lieutenant Brian Kingcome, and Sam Heughan, portraying 'Boy' Wellum, are pictured during filming. (Courtesy Etienne Bol)

Below: 'Pilot Officer "Boy" Wellum' exits his Spitfire after a fierce action – Sam Heughan felt privileged to pay the part and has since found great success and fame as 'Jamie Fraser' in the blockbuster Netflix series *Outlander*. (Courtesy Etienne Bol)

At 1.02.05, 'Bader' returns to duty at Kenley and a poignant scene where he spots his rugby boots, his aspirations to play for England crushed. Persuading 'Day' to take him flying in an Avro 504, 'Day' feigns 'cramp' so that 'Bader' has to take the controls, which, naturally, he does with aplomb, even flying aerobatics. This flight increases the latter's confidence that he will be allowed to continue flying, as, of course, does passing a test at the Central Flying School – but is devastated when told otherwise in an interview with 'Wing Commander Hargreaves' (Raymond Francis) at the Air Ministry (1.05.12). Later, 'Bader' tells 'Thelma' that if he cannot fly he will leave the RAF, which he does, returning to civilian life. Going to work for Shell, 'Bader's' brusque manner is not well-received, and he learns to be slightly less forthright, at least in correspondence. Finding a new challenge in golf, which he pursues relentlessly, 'Bader' marries 'Thelma', and so is not alone in the wilderness.

While golf provides a focus and a game 'Bader' can play on equal terms with the able-bodied, at 1.13.13 the narration explains that war came in 1939, and we see scenes of civilians entering air raid shelters and observe a warning siren whirring away. At 1.13.25, 'Bader' is back at the Air Ministry, badgering his old Commandant, 'Air Vice-Marshal Halahan' – whose assistant is none other than 'Sanderson' – to let him return to the service and fly again. Passing a medical and further flying test, with the support of Cranwell chums, 'Flying Officer Bader' returns, at last, to operational flying. So far, the film has actually followed Brickhill's book remarkably closely.

The film now skips 'Flying Officer Bader's' actual return to the service, training, and return to operational flying with 'Squadron Leader Johnny Sanderson's' Duxford-based 19 Squadron. Naturally, the film passes over the difficulties Bader experienced when converting to the Spitfire, and, indeed, the blameworthy accidents involved.

At 1.16.33, we see a Spitfire hurtling towards the camera at zero feet, presumably flown by 'Bader', before a pair of Spitfires taxi into dispersal after landing. Then we see 'Sanderson' discussing fighter tactics with 'Bader', the latter having all kinds of bright ideas and naturally knowing best in spite of only recently returning to the service and having little experience on the new monoplane fighters. The film also fails to mention Bader's unhappiness on 19 Squadron and difficulties serving under his old friend Stephenson. Instead, 'Sanderson' simply gives 'Bader' the good news that 'Tubby' Mermagen wants him as a flight commander in 222 Squadron, which the AOC has approved. At 1.17.39 excited pilots appear, celebrating the fact that the 'Phoney War' is over, Germany has attacked the West, and action is at last imminent. Naturally, 'Bader' is delighted.

Evocative dawn shots of Hurricanes follow, and at 1.18.10 'Flight Lieutenant Bader', now a flight commander on 222 Squadron, is roused by his batman (Ian Whittaker) before first light on account of there being a 'flap on, so the squadron is taking off at four'. This, of course, is what 'Bader' has been waiting for – action this day – and the Dunkirk evacuation. 'Bader' and 'Sanderson' wish each other good luck. This is far from factual. On 22 May 1940, while the battle raged in France, 222 Squadron had been sent not south, towards the action, but east – to patrol shipping off the coast from Kirton-on-Lindsay. Bader was exasperated.

On 25 May 1940 however, Squadron Leader Stephenson led 19 Squadron from Duxford to Hornchurch, from where the squadron was to patrol the French coast. The following day the decision was made for the British Expeditionary Force to retire on and evacuate from Dunkirk. Air Vice-Marshal Park was put in charge of organising Fighter Command's contribution to Operation *Dynamo*, as the evacuation was codenamed, and 11 Group was reinforced by various 12 Group units for the undertaking.

On that first day, 19 fought its first major engagement and attacked a formation of Stukas over Calais – but the Spitfires, throttled back to match their targets' speed, were ambushed by Me 109s. Pilot Officer Watson was shot down and killed while Squadron Leader Stephenson crash-landed near Calais and was captured. It was not until 28 May 1940, that 222 Squadron arrived at Martlesham Heath in 11 Group, to participate in *Dynamo* – which was already over a week old. Indeed, the original squadrons involved were by now comparatively highly experienced, having met the Luftwaffe in strength and, indeed, the Me 109.

Among these units was Biggin Hill's 92 Squadron, also operating from Martlesham, which, like 19 Squadron, had lost its CO, Squadron Leader Roger Bushell. Just as Flight Lieutenant Brian Lane had assumed command of 19 Squadron in the air after Stephenson's capture, Bushell's senior flight commander, Flight Lieutenant Robert Stanford Tuck, found himself in temporary command of 92. Upon landing at Martlesham, Flight Lieutenant Bader marched up to Tuck and demanded to know 'the score'. Tuck's response was to rebuke Bader for not having tucked the loose end of his silk scarf into his tunic – which, in the event of bailing out, could have snagged on something. Indeed, Tuck's first impression of the 'obstreperous man' was that he was 'too cocky' and 'ought to be taken down a few pegs'.

So in sum, Bader and Stephenson were not on the same station when *Dynamo* began, and nor was 222 Squadron involved from the off. It is also worth mentioning that Air Commodore Geoffrey Stephenson survived his years of captivity but was sadly killed on an exchange visit to the United States in 1954, flying a Super Sabre jet fighter; what he would have made of the film, therefore, we will never know.

At 1.18.45, we see 'Bader' in his cockpit amid a formation of Spitfires, heading for the French coast. A minor detail is that the camera zooms in on the Spitfire's 20mm cannon – but at this time the fighter was only armed with eight rifle-calibre machine-guns – a deficiency not rectified until after the Battle of Britain. Moving on, action follows, a combination of air-to-air footage of the Mk XVIs cut with newsreel and combat film, together with the usual in-studio cockpit close-ups. We peer through a square-lensed gyro gunsight, as opposed to the correct semi-circular reflector sight, and see a FW190 from later in the war go down in flames, these scenes depicting the air battle over Dunkirk. It was not, however, until 1 June 1940 that Flight Lieutenant Bader made his first and only combat claims during *Dynamo*, a 109 destroyed and He 111 probable, by which time the evacuation was nearly over. Back at base 'Bader' claims a '109' but receives news that 19 Squadron's CO, 'Johnny Sanderson' is missing.

We then join 'Bader' at 1.20.23 during an interview with 'Air Vice-Marshal Leigh-Mallory' (Ronald Adam), in which, accurately, 'Bader' admits to having damaged a Spitfire the previous night in a landing accident. This was the case. Air Commodore Mermagen remembered that: 'On that occasion Douglas came in far too high and far too fast. He went through a hedge. I drove over to pick him up and he was ranting, shouting that the flarepath was incorrectly laid out. I thought 'Well, look at that, what a total lack of humility, he's blaming someone else now!' Nonetheless, Leigh-Mallory promoted Bader to command the demoralised Canadian 242 Squadron – just in time for the Battle of Britain.

We are then, at 1.21.07, presented with what is supposed to be 242 Squadron's base at Coltishall, but is of course Kenley. Here we see Hurricanes on the ground, curiously not wearing the 'LE' fuselage codes of 242, but 'SD' of 501 Squadron. A second later and we are outside the pilots' dispersal hut, where we meet, among others, 'Crowley-Milling' (Basil Appleby), who alerts the pilots within, including the morose 'Stan Turner' (Lee Patterson) that their new CO has just arrived by car – and, incredulously, that he has no legs. 'Squadron Leader Bader' then enters with his Adjutant, 'Flight Lieutenant Peter MacDonald' (Peter Burton), those pilots seated making no effort to stand up and show respect. Many years later, Group Captain Bader recalled the actual event:

> I found myself … in conjunction with my adjutant, an elderly gentleman of the finest class who had been member

for the Isle of Wight for the past plus 500 years, and had fought in World War One, he took me into a dispersal hut where these chaps were lying about on beds, wearing Mae Wests and flying clothes, and all reading comic strips. He said 'Gentlemen, this is your new Squadron Commander, Squadron Leader Bader' – and for some extraordinary reason, because I had been trained at the RAF College Cranwell, I thought they might stand up. In fact some of them lowered their comics, looked over the top, obviously didn't care for what they saw, put the comics back up and went on reading! There was one chap lying with his back to me. He actually turned over, had a look, then turned back again and went on reading!

Naturally 'Bader' is unimpressed and gives 'Turner' a short, sharp, lesson in discipline – before grabbing a flying helmet and striding out to a waiting Hurricane, subsequently delivering a faultless performance of low-level aerobatics – inverted – confirming for the benefit of all that, legless or not, the new CO was no passenger. Afterwards, the new CO demanded the presence of all pilots in his office. Again, Group Captain Bader remembered that:

> They arrived and I gave them what I thought was a reasonable three-minute talk. When finished I said 'Has anybody got anything to say?' There was a long silence, then, from the back of the room a voice said 'Horseshit!' Again, they hadn't taught me at Cranwell what to do in such a situation. As I was getting rather red around the neck and face, and was about to make a bloody fool of myself, the same voice added 'Sir!'

A lively discussion then ensued, in which Bader was enlightened as to why morale was so poor: even the pilots' clothes, left behind in France, had yet to be replaced, and neither had they been paid for some time. Immediately recognising the urgent need for strong leadership in all aspects, Douglas firstly sent his pilots clothes-shopping in Norwich, personally guaranteeing payment, then established a new command team, bringing in friends from other squadrons. These scenes are well replicated in the film.

At 1.25.15, as the pilots' meeting with their super-charged new CO concludes, 'Crowley-Milling' points out that the Hurricanes lack essential spares and equipment. 'Bader' strides off to find the Squadron Engineering Officer, 'Warrant Officer West' (Michael Ripper), who confirms that despite repeated requests, replacement spares for those lost in France had still failed to materialise, compromising the squadron's operational efficiency. An angry 'Bader' stomps off to 'ruddy well unclog' the blocked administration channels.

There follows an argument with a pedantic stores officer, who is subjected to the full-force of the 'Bader' super-charger and left in no doubt that 242's CO wants his spares 'quick'. 'Bader' then visits the hangar, taking a paternal interest in the groundcrew. This is unlikely. The evidence from survivors confirms that Bader was frequently unnecessarily rude and unreasonable to those considered of inferior rank or social status – using offensive language in the process. This is a clear juxtaposition between certain officer pilots, particularly those with a pre-war or Cranwell background, being in awe of their legless leader, whereas to many in supporting roles he was disliked and feared. This is entirely contrary to the benevolent and overly charming character portrayed by Kenneth More.

Of this scene, many years later, George Reid, who had served under Wing Commander Bader as an undercarriage inspector at Tangmere, said quite simply 'I could not believe my ears. This was not the man I knew, he was ill-tempered and foul-mouthed.'

At 1.26.34, 'Bader' in conversation with Coltishall's Station Commander, 'Wing Commander Beiseigel' (Ernest Clark), commonly known as 'Bike', explaining that he had sent a signal to 12 Group and Fighter Command HQ declaring 242 Squadron non-operational until his spares arrive – by-passing in true Bader fashion the chain of command and to the Station Commander's astonishment. A minute later we see 'Bader' in his element, holding court with his pilots in the Officers' Mess and expounding his theories on fighter tactics. In reality, Bader was far from alone in realising that Fighter Command's pre-war book of tactics was actually unfit for purpose and irrelevant to modern fighter combat.

At the time, after hard lessons on the continent, squadron and flight commanders throughout the Command were experimenting with alternative tactical formations in particular – and it was highly experienced and successful squadron commanders such as the legendary South African commander of 74 'Tiger' Squadron, Squadron Leader A.G. 'Sailor' Malan, who not only worked things out but shared that knowledge. Nonetheless, the film gives the distinct impression that Bader, and he alone, is the man who really understands it all. The convivial gathering is then interrupted by a 'Squadron Leader Edwards' (George Rose) a wingless staff officer from Fighter Command HQ on the telephone for 'Bader'. A heated argument over the spares, and the signal, ensues between the two men, culminating in 'Edwards' assuring 'Bader' that the Commander-in-Chief of Fighter Command, Air Chief Marshal Sir Hugh Dowding is 'furious' – at which point 242's CO hangs up. Summonsed to Fighter Command HQ, at 1.28.27 'Squadron Leader Bader' is shown into 'Dowding's' (Charles Carson) office to explain himself. 'Dowding', however, is unhappy that 'Edwards' said he was 'furious' – and gave 'Bader' his way.

This did happen: the obstructive stores officer found himself removed from his cushy HQ post and 242 Squadron's much-needed equipment was soon arriving – which we see, by the truckload, at 1.29.44, enhancing the reputation of 242's new CO in the process, who signals HQ confirming that his Squadron was now operational. That was on 9 July 1940; the Battle of Britain officially began the following day.

The officer pilots of 242 Squadron are partying in the Mess at 1.30.32, while a benevolent CO looks on with 'Thelma', to whom he enthuses about them being 'a good bunch … coming along nicely'. The party is interrupted, however, by the Prime Minister's broadcast announcing that the Battle of Britain is about to begin, and making clear what is at stake and the consequences of defeat. Sobering stuff indeed.

The scene then switches to the Battle of Britain in progress, using models, graphics and newsreel footage to show enemy aircraft bombing southern England. At 1.32.38, 'Squadron Leader Bader' and 242 Squadron are at readiness, the news broadcast over the radio providing news of heavy fighting over the Channel and south coast. 'Woody' then cops an earful over the telephone from 'Bader', who demands that 242 Squadron be sent into action. This is accurate, although Woodhall was the Duxford Sector Controller, not at 242's base at Coltishall, so we must assume that this is an occasion when 242 have been sent forward to operate from Duxford – which was closer to the action. Arguing that 'they need all the fighters they can get in the south', 'Bader' gets nowhere and is advised by 'Woodhall' (Howard Marion Crawford) that if all fighters are concentrated there, that leaves other areas undefended. 'Bader' is exasperated.

There is a Mess dance at 1.33.50, during which the affable 'Bader' mingles with guests and is delighted to learn from 'Thelma' that 'Johnny Sanderson' is alive and a prisoner. The 242 Squadron CO is then once more shown as a benevolent patriarch shepherding his flock when two nervous young replacement pilots, 'Jones' and 'Nicholson' (actors unknown) introduce themselves and are warmly welcomed – with 'Bader' assuring 'Thelma' that he will 'look after them' – while assuring his wife that with an engine in front and 'tin legs' beneath him, 'how the devil can they get me?'

At 1.35.00 there is a return to the action and newsreel footage of Stukas. At 1.35.25 there comes what 'Bader' hopes is an order to scramble, but no, a routine order, and so 242's pilots continue sitting idly by. More newsreel footage shows a formation of enemy aircraft, and in the 'Ops Room', 'Woodhall' monitors the progress of a big incoming raid. Then at 1.36.07 comes what Duxford has been waiting for: a request for 12 Group to reinforce 11 Group. A delighted 'Woodhall' scrambles 242 Squadron, and an ecstatic 'Bader' stomps to his Hurricane, leading the equally excited pilots of 242 off.

There are actually some excellent shots of the film's sole airworthy Hurricane starting up and taking off, 'Bader's' aircraft correctly displaying his rank pennant. Although ordered by 'Woodhall' to patrol 'North Weald' (to protect the airfield while its squadrons are engaged), 'Bader' knows better and insists that he is instead turning west and 'climbing up-sun' – intercepting the raiders. Again, the combat is recreated in the usual way, 'Bader' leads 242 into the attack and, of course, German aircraft are apparently shot down in droves. This, of course, is supposed to be the action fought against the Hatfield raiders on 30 August 1940. Back at base (1.40.09) the victorious pilots are ecstatic, making their combat claims, the Intelligence Officer confirming that 'not one' raider 'got through the North Weald'.

This has no basis whatsoever in fact. 'Leigh-Mallory' then appears with 'Woodhall', congratulating 'Bader' and providing the latter an opportunity to opine to the AOC that had he more aircraft, the greater damage would have been inflicted. This is not what happened. As previously explained, Bader submitted a post-action report outlining his theories, and spoke to his AOC on the telephone, as the group captain himself recalled:

> When we were writing up our combat reports afterwards, Leigh-Mallory rang me up and said 'Congratulations, Bader, on the squadron's performance today.' I said 'Thank you very much, Sir, but if we'd had more aeroplanes then we would have shot down a whole lot more.' He asked what I meant and I explained that with

more fighters our results would have been even better. He said 'Look, I'd like to talk to you about this', so I flew over to 12 Group HQ at Hucknall and told the AOC what I thought. He agreed and created the 'Duxford Wing', under my leadership and comprising 19, 242 and 310 Squadrons. Leigh-Mallory said to try the idea and see what we could do.

In the film, however, the conversation takes place on the airfield, immediately after the action, and Leigh-Mallory agrees to 'Bader' leading a wing of three squadrons – and so the variously called 'Duxford Wing', '12 Group Wing' and/or 'Big Wing' found its way to the silver screen.

At 1.41.45, 'Squadron Leader Bader' returns from a sortie, his Hurricane battle-damaged. The Duxford Wing first saw action over the Thames Estuary on 7 September 1940, although poorly positioned height-wise the wing was attacked by German fighters, suffering casualties – and Bader's Hurricane was shot-up that afternoon; an explosive bullet came through the right-hand side of the fuselage, touched the map case and knocked off a corner of the undercarriage selector quadrant, finishing up against the petrol priming pump. 'Woodhall' then appears and discusses events, to whom 'Bader' enthuses that he needs two more squadrons – 'Woodhall' agrees and promises to arrange an interview with the AOC, who he is 'sure will agree'.

On 10 September 1940, Squadron Leader Bader flew to 12 Group HQ at Hucknall for an hour-long interview with Leigh-Mallory, and at which meeting the five squadron 'Big Wing' was agreed.

We return to action at 1.42.44 with models representing the 'Big Wing' patrolling, and 'Sanderson's' narration telling us that 'Douglas's tactics proved so successful that very soon he was leading a unique formation of five squadrons', the pilots of which 'looked on him as a superman ... [his] breezy confidence in the air so reassuring for young pilots'. At 1.42.53, we see the young replacement pilot 'Jones' clearly inspired by his legless leader's radio conversation with 'Woodhall' while heading for action over North Weald – booking a squash court. This kind of thing is true.

As Air Marshal Sir Denis Crowley-Milling remembered, 'Douglas maintained a constant stream of chatter over the radio', and certainly Pilot Officer (later Group Captain Sir) Hugh 'Cocky' Dundas, a 20-year-old Spitfire pilot in 616 Squadron, found his legless leader massively inspiring, after returning to operations with the 'Big Wing', his confidence shaken by having been shot down and wounded previously. The downside is that Bader's radio traffic blocked the air waves, causing communication issues, and his wandering around south-east England unannounced on what were essentially independent fighter sweeps, threw the defences into confusion. So, there is very much an alternative and more accurate perspective to the one provided by Brickhill's book and Angel's film.

Again, the film next recreates hectic aerial combat using the usual tools, and at 1.44.10, 'Sanderson' tells us that by 'the 12 October Hitler had postponed his invasion … Hitler the invincible had suffered his first defeat.' Operation *Seelöwe* was actually postponed indefinitely on 17 September 1940. Certainly, the Few had provided Hitler his first reverse and maintained Britain as a base from which war could be waged and, ultimately with American help, the liberation of enemy occupied Europe launched – but this was far from achieved just by Douglas Bader and his pilots, and his 'Big Wing' ideas, as the film perhaps implies. Indeed, as previously explained, we now know that the 'Big Wing' was nowhere near as successful as claimed, and that the entire concept was flawed – but it was certainly an effective and newsworthy means of getting Leigh-Mallory, Bader and 12 Group into the war.

At 1.44.23 there is an informal pow-wow in the Officers' Mess with 'Leigh-Mallory' congratulating 'Bader' on the Duxford Wing's great success in the Battle of Britain, 'Turner' confirming the number of enemy aircraft destroyed as '152'. The reality, as already discussed, was nothing like – but this paper success led to the film's next segment: the change in command, Fighter Command's new offensive strategy, the reorganisation into wings of three Spitfire squadrons based at each sector station, and the appointment of the first wing leaders. Indeed, this is the purpose of 'Leigh-Mallory's' visit, to tell 'Bader' of his promotion to Wing Commander (Flying) and appointment to lead the Tangmere Wing – much to the displeasure of 242 Squadron's pilots who are unhappy to see their swashbuckling leader move on. Again, this is not entirely accurate because although Bader was among the first wing leaders appointed, he was actually given his choice of stations; he chose Tangmere on the basis that it was far enough away from London's still vibrant social scene for it not to be a distraction to his pilots.

On the subject of pilots, it is also worth observing that at no time in this film is there a sergeant-pilot in sight – and, as discussed in previous chapters, there were many. An interesting observation is that in a world of surnames, 'Leigh-Mallory' refers to 'Bader' in conversation as 'Douglas' – this was indeed the case. Bader was a firm Leigh-Mallory favourite and had become a personal friend of both the AOC and Woodhall – the latter, promoted to command Tangmere as a Group Captain, welcomes the newly arrived 'Wing Commander Bader' (1.45.21) as 'Douggie', who responds to 'Woody'.

This was a close triumvirate of friendship, which had various consequences for the Command, and strategy, as a whole, given how much Bader's flawed ideas regarding wings had now been adopted as standard in both defence and attack. The scene, however, is incorrect, because when Bader arrived at Tangmere on 18 March 1941, the Station Commander was Group Captain Jack Boret. Woodhall did not arrive and take over as Station Commander and Sector Controller until 9 June 1941, on which date Bader's former

242 Squadron Adjutant, Flight Lieutenant Peter MacDonald MP, also arrived from Manston.

At 1.45.43, 'Wing Commander Bader' reaches his new office door, on which a sign has been fixed: 'Bader's Bus Company: Still Running.' This is incorrect. The Tangmere Wing did become known as 'Bader's Bus Company', on account of its radio callsign 'Greenline Bus', but the 'Still Running' was not added until after Bader was captured on 9 August 1941. Within are three former 242 Squadron pilots, 'Turner', 'Crowley-Milling' and an unidentified individual (but very likely supposed to be the tall and thin Flying Officer Hugh 'Cocky' Dundas), which is apparently a surprise to 'Bader', the three men having applied for the posting, to follow their popular leader. This is not entirely accurate.

Naturally, Bader was keen to import men he knew and trusted into his new wing, but Turner did not arrive until 16 April 1941, when he took over 145 Squadron on promotion, and Crowley-Milling not until 12 June 1941, when, also on promotion, 'Crow' became commander of 610 Squadron's 'B' Flight. At Tangmere, Bader had found 145 Squadron, which operated from the Merston satellite from 7 May 1941, and at nearby Westhampnett both 610 and 616 Squadrons. The latter he knew from Battle of Britain days, the unit having flown in the five-squadron 'Big Wing' – and its CO was a fellow Cranwellian, Squadron Leader H.F. 'Billy' Burton. For those reasons Bader chose to base himself at Westhampnett and virtually exclusively lead the Tangmere Wing at the head of Burton's Squadron, and consistently with the same pilots flying in his 'Dogsbody Section', namely Flying Officer Dundas, Pilot Officer Johnnie Johnson, and either Sergeants Alan Smith or Jeff West. This, however, created an elite within the wing. Other wing leaders, including Johnson when his time came, avoided this scenario by alternating the squadrons and wingmen they flew with.

At 1.46.01 there is an orderly clerk enter with a pile of paperwork for 'Bader's' attention – which ends up in the bin. This, of course, is a man of action – not a paper shuffler – and Group Captain Woodhall later recalled how 'Douglas was very apt to cut corners', an endeavour 'Woody' entirely supported – enabling Bader to 'get on with the war'.

An anxious 'Thelma', awaiting her husband's safe return from yet another sweep over France, can be seen at 1.46.27. The Baders had taken a house near Tangmere, the 'Bay House', where the wing commander entertained his inner-sanctum, and held court – but Bader slept in the Officers' Mess at Tangmere, 'Just to keep in touch.' The 'Wing Commander' arrives home (1.46.38) but laments the loss of three pilots, 'all first-class chaps'. The 'season' of 1941 was a relentless period of offensive operations over north-west France for sure, and Fighter Command's losses were heavy. Indeed, the German fighter pilots had everything in their favour, especially a superb aircraft in the Me 109F, which outclassed the Spitfire Mk II predominantly in service at this time, and equal to the newer Spitfire Mk V. The Germans only attacked the massed RAF formations when tactical conditions were favourable, and did so from on high in diving, high-speed, ambushes – fire and away.

'Thelma' implores her husband to rest on account of having 'flown more sweeps than anyone else in Fighter Command'. This is an unlikely claim. Other wing leaders were equally committed, not least the excellent Wing Commander 'Sailor' Malan at Biggin Hill. Indeed, Malan recognised that he was exhausted, and given the negative consequences this could have in the air for others, he agreed to be rested on 28 July 1941. By that time, Malan's personal score stood at twenty-seven enemy aircraft destroyed, seven more shared, as well as two unconfirmed destroyed and another shared, three probables and sixteen damaged. This made the South African Fighter Command's top-scorer, which he would remain until his record was exceeded only by Johnnie Johnson in 1944.

Malan, acting responsibly and thinking of others, went to pass his enormous knowledge on to new fighter pilots. Typically, however, Bader, driven by his thirst for action and desire to always be the best, refused to rest. On 8 August 1941, according to Brickhill, Peter MacDonald insisted that Bader took a few days off for a golfing break at St Andrew's as of 11 August 1941 – this, though, is unlikely, given that MacDonald had actually been posted away from Tangmere on 1 August 1941. As Air Vice-Marshal Johnnie Johnson later remarked, 'Douglas was very greedy, you know, and when he was shot down it really was his own fault' – but for now, much to his wife's concern, he pressed on, determined to 'finish the season', albeit promising a break 'next week'.

A return to some very poor graphics occurs again at 1.48.20. This scene represents the Tangmere Wing setting off across the Channel, bound for France. The wing would invariably rendezvous with bombers and the other fighter wings involved on these 'Circus' operations, over Beachy Head and the Seven Sisters cliffs, a questionable artistic impression of which provides the backdrop to this scene. 'Sanderson' then resumes his narration over a close-up of 'Bader' in his cockpit, leading the wing, explaining that 'everyone in the wing thought him invulnerable'.

Strangely, some of the subsequent graphics include formations of Hurricanes. At 1.48.42, 'Bader' sights enemy aircraft below, and we see a studio close-up of the German leader and his formation of Me 109s. This, however, is not what happened on 9 August 1941 – Bader's last operational flight. On that day his Air Speed Indicator had gone unserviceable almost immediately after take-off, as a result of which he should have handed over lead of the wing to another pilot and returned home. Characteristically, he did not. The lead was handed over to Flight Lieutenant (as he had become) Hugh Dundas, to adhere to timings, but once over the French coast Bader resumed the lead. Then, over St Omer, Squadron Leader Ken Holden, leading 610 Squadron, sighted enemy aircraft below, which, having lost the 'edge', Bader could not at first see.

What should have happened is that Holden, with the Germans in sight, should have been despatched to attack them first, but Bader, knowing that the wing was above and unseen by the enemy, waited until he could personally see them and attack – all being well increasing his personal score in the process. Unfortunately, this selfishness lost several vital seconds, by which time the large German fighter force in the area had seen the danger – and attacked. Chaos ensued, the subsequent combat involving upwards of seventy Spitfires and Me 109s, a whirling, confused, mass of aircraft at close-quarters. In the film, however, the combat is reconstructed in the usual way, the impression being that the Tangmere Wing, and its leader in particular, are knocking down Germans like nine pins.

Then, at 1.49.48, a German fighter collides with 'Bader's' Spitfire, chopping off its tail. Later, the Germans were unable to say with certainty who had shot the famous Tangmere Wing leader down. The reason for that, I discovered in 1995, was that Bader was actually the victim of friendly fire. In the confusion Flight Lieutenant L.H. 'Buck' Casson of 616 Squadron had inadvertently and unknowingly mistaken Bader's Spitfire for the similar-looking Me 109F – and shot its tail off. Casson later described in a post-war letter having watched the stricken machine's pilot bale out many thousands of feet below – which is exactly what happened to Bader, one of whose tin legs became stuck, trapping him in the cockpit.

As the only other aircraft actually destroyed in the engagement was a 109F, the tail of which was discovered at the crash site in more recent times, there can be no reasonable doubt that Casson accidentally shot the wing leader down (as it happened, Casson was himself shot down a few minutes later while returning to the French coast, also spending the rest of the war a prisoner). Bader, however, always believed that he had collided with a 109, such was the damage to his Spitfire and given that the enemy were later unable to confirm his victor; in any case, Bader never wanted to give credit to the Germans for actually shooting him down.

Moving on, Bader's ordeal – trapped and trying to bale out of his Spitfire – is well replicated in the film; 'Bader' eventually breaks the straps of the trapped leg and bales out, his empty right trouser leg flapping in the wind as he floats down by parachute, buzzed by a 109. At 1.50.58, 'Wing Commander Bader' alights in a French field – where a reception committee of German soldiers already await and take him into custody.

By 1.50.00 we are back at the 'Bat House', or 'Bag House', as Tangmere's inner sanctum called it , where 'Thelma', 'Turner', 'Crowley-Milling' and the Dundas-like unknown character, anxiously wait for news of 'Douglas', who is missing. Certainly, for 'Dogsbody Section' and friends, this was an anxious time indeed, such a despairing mood descending over the Tangmere Wing that Johnnie Johnson later remembered how he and 'Cocky' Dundas sank a good bottle of brandy that night. All, however, is reasonably well: 'Woody' calls with welcome news – 'Douglas is a prisoner', much to the delight of all at the 'Bay House'.

The rest of the film is really irrelevant for our purposes, following Wing Commander Bader's various escape attempts while in German custody, and his passage through various camps – and rekindling auld acquaintance with 'Johnny Sanderson' and 'Harry Day', ending up in Colditz. One failed escape was from St Omer's Clinique Sterin, with the help of local people – emphasising the perils and punishments these brave French patriots faced if caught harbouring and assisting Allied airmen. Many downed RAF airmen were helped in this way, making 'home runs' across the Pyrenees – including Air Marshal Sir Denis Crowley-Milling. Fighting over France was disadvantageous for the RAF in having to make two sea crossings, but the possibility of being assisted by the French Resistance if brought down was an advantage not enjoyed by the Germans when operating over England. One point about the prisoner of war minutes of the film is that the Germans are invariably portrayed as buffoons, in common with all but one film of the time – more of which later.

Upon repatriation, 'Bader' returns to 'Thelma' at the 'Bay House' (where, in reality, she no longer lived) but, incredibly, wants to find more action in the Far East, where the war against Japan remained ongoing! It was not to be, however, and the film's conclusion begins at 2.07.46 with preparations for Group Captain Bader to lead the massed flypast over London to commemorate the first post-war anniversary of 'Battle of Britain Day': 15 September 1945. It is a triumphal conclusion in all respects, for the nation and 'Bader' personally, but, as 'Sanderson' tells us, the story has no end, 'because courage has no end ... the victory of a man's own spirit creating victory out of disaster' – and that, above all else, way beyond his service and war record, is what made *Reach for the Sky* a film people took to their hearts and made it a box office giant.

Conclusion

Reach for the Sky was released in July 1956, the film's premier attended by the Duke of Edinburgh – but not Group Captain Douglas Bader, who, in fact, only watched the film on television some years later and declared it 'Rather good'. It was certainly an entirely sympathetic depiction – which became the biggest box office success of 1956. Indeed, the *Daily Mirror* considered Gilbert and Angel's work to be 'one of the greatest British films ever made and one of the most inspiring'.

Like the fateful crash in 1931, the film was also a defining moment in Douglas's life. Millions of people watched the film worldwide in 1956 and when re-released in 1959, and have since done so on television and at their leisure since videos, DVDs and online streaming became available. The book and film super-charged the Bader story and presented it to countless people globally, making Bader a household name the world over – enabling him to do great work, it must be said, for the disabled community, to whom he was an obvious source of inspiration. While, according to film industry chronicler Josh Billings, the film was a 'colossal money maker', it was not for Bader himself. Having agreed to a one-off payment, the Baders received no royalties.

A massive success though *Reach for the Sky* was, it had focused upon one hero, providing a somewhat inaccurate view of the 'Big Wing', making no mention of the controversy and row surrounding it, and made no attempt to tell the Battle of Britain's overall story. That was yet to come …

Chapter 5

Battle of Britain

While *Reach for the Sky* was another film focused on an individual's story framed by wider events, it was evident from its success that aviation-related war films were lucrative business. Surprisingly, it was still some time before the overall Battle of Britain story would be told.

One notable thing about 1950s British war films, and *Angels One Five* and *Reach for the Sky* are no exceptions, is that it remained unthinkable to show the Germans in any kind of positive or sympathetic light. Bravely, Roy Ward Baker had directed *The One That Got Away*, released in 1957, based on the book of that name by James Leasor and Kendal Burt, telling the story of Oberleutnant Franz von Werra – an enemy fighter pilot shot down and captured during the Battle of Britain and who infamously became the only German prisoner of war to escape from Allied custody and return home.

Baker was heavily criticised for heroicising a German airman (nonetheless his film was popular in both Britain and West Germany, making a profit of £3 million). Moreover, in 1956, a former Luftwaffe fighter ace currently serving in an RAF squadron on an exchange visit through NATO, was not allowed to take part in that year's annual Battle of Britain flypast over London. That same year, the Foreign Office had expressed concerns that the German war trophies displayed annually at Horse Guards could offend the democratic West Germans, who were a valued Cold War ally. Four years later, this commemoration was discontinued, and in 1961, the annual RAF flypast was scaled right back. Clearly, things were changing, the old 'triumphal mood', as the *Daily Express* put it, evaporating – and with it, potentially, the opportunity to translate the Battle of Britain's big story to the silver screen.

By the 1960s, times had very much changed in post-war Britain. The domestic television was making a significant impact, a negative one so far as British cinemas were concerned, the population increasingly watching the 'box' at home, rather than go to the 'flicks'. With reduced cinema attendance, the British film industry suffered financially. Indeed, from now on, the world of film would be dominated by America, and in Hollywood there was little or no interest in Britain's Finest Hour.

Moreover, by 1960, twenty years after the event and fifteen after the Second World War ended, there were generations of young people with no personal experience of what was seen as their parents' war, with which most modern teenagers had little or no affinity. Indeed, they actively sought to distance themselves from their parents' world and values, and, owing to the fear of nuclear weapons and America's controversial war in Vietnam, the decade saw a growing and vocal peace movement. The world and internal order had also changed – and many did not now see the Battle of Britain as a big story to trumpet, but one best buried and forgotten.

Fortunately, the former RAF pilot and successful Polish film producer Ben Fisz was not among them. Fisz, together with his Director, Guy Hamilton, was determined to 'tell it how it was' and produce 'a tribute to the Few'. Both were aware of their self-set task's enormity – an even greater undertaking than most realise, perhaps, against the backdrop of the 'Swinging Sixties'.

In more recent times, however, various academic historians, not least among them Clive Ponting (*The Myth of 1940*) and Angus Calder (*The Myth of the Blitz*), have argued that the 'Finest Hour' was nothing of the sort and little more than a manufactured myth, something explored in detail by Malcolm Smith in his excellent study *Britain and 1940: History, Myth and Popular Memory*, and who wrote that 1940 and the Battle of Britain seems 'to have been the one genuinely heroic moment in twentieth-century British history. Britain was fighting alone against something which simply had to be stopped if any kind of acceptable values were to survive in Europe.' Guy Hamilton certainly acknowledged that 1940 was undoubtedly heavily myth-laden – but took a very different tack, one which this author wholeheartedly supports – proclaiming that his intention was 'to destroy the myth, only to create a greater myth, because it's a *fantastic* story'.

Battle of Britain: A Reading.

00:28/2:12

In the opening few minutes, we have a clear message: the Fall of France is underway, Allied forces in full retreat. British soldiers in a (post-war) armoured car ponderously make their way West, towards the Channel coast, in a long, rag-tag column of dejected French civilians – now refugees. Overhead, an RAF Hawker Hurricane performs a victory roll before landing at an adjacent airfield. There we meet 'Harvey' (Christopher Plummer), a flight lieutenant and flight commander now leading his squadron after the CO, 'Jumbo', was reported missing. Harvey, however, takes issue with the victory roll just performed by 'Jamie', the latter having naively considered the low-level aerobatics a morale-boosting gesture for the refugees' benefit. Harvey is unmoved, making clear the value of both aircraft – and pilot.

01:44/2:12

Then, as a section of Hurricanes arrives, enter Robert Shaw's character, a comparatively elderly, bullish, no-nonsense squadron commander called 'Skipper'. According to Leonard Mosley in his

1969 book *Battle of Britain*, which accompanied the film's release, Shaw was apparently inspired by, and researched, the story of the legendary South African, A.G. 'Sailor' Malan, basing 'Skipper' on him. If this truly was Shaw's aim, it was a failure.

Having written Malan's most recent biography, Malan, a pre-war pilot on 74 'Tiger' Squadron, who commanded that unit during the Battle of Britain, was a quiet, reserved and almost shy individual. A consummate professional, yes, presented as a cold-hearted killer on occasions by the propagandists, a loud-mouthed bullying martinet like 'Skipper', definitely not. The Malan family remain unhappy with the portrayal for these reasons, and Shaw's character appears more aligned to the irascible, swashbuckling, Douglas Bader than Malan.

02:30/2:12

Also, while in France, we have a clear indication of how society and the services were hierarchical and delineated by class and rank. At the time, only those with a public school background, a School Certificate 'A' and a letter of recommendation signed by at least a colonel, were eligible to be commissioned. So, here we have the clearly 'posh' 'Pilot Officer Archie' (Edward Fox), sneeringly translating French for his companion, 'Sergeant-Pilot Andy' (Ian McShane, whose surname we learn later is 'Moore') who, by virtue of rank, has not the benefit of a private education, which in those days was the key to the primary professions.

Nonetheless, 'Andy', with at least a grammar school education, throws the light-hearted put-down right back by translating himself 'Archam can't believe Sedan has fallen. I can.' 'Archam' being a French NCO on the telephone (André Maranne). After the disconcerting news from a French pilot that the Germans 'Will be 'ere in 'arf an hour', the Hurricanes hurriedly take-off, leaving the groundcrew to destroy the 'lame ducks' – just in time, as a formation of 'Me 109s' streaks across the airfield at zero-feet, strafing as they go. Interestingly, one of the Hurricane pilots (Stuart Hoyle), anonymous but wearing a 'New Zealand' shoulder flash, beckons to a forlorn-looking Free French pilot, 'Jean Jacques' (Jean Waldon), and the pair take off together, crammed into the single-seater Hurricane. This scene was surely inspired by a very similar one in *Flemish Farm* (1943), when (at 0.13.08), during a bombing attack on their airfield in Belgium, Belgian Hurricane pilots take-off hurriedly – one pilot knocking out a comrade and bundling him into a Hurricane, in which they fly off to safety together.

05:57/2:12

The scene then abruptly changes to an Air Ministry corridor, where we meet Air Chief Marshal Dowding (Laurence Oliver), Air Officer Commanding-in-Chief of Fighter Command, making his way to a meeting with a 'Senior Civil Servant' (Harry Andrews). In the background, Olivier recites the text of Dowding's letter imploring the Prime Minister not to send any more Fighter Command squadrons to France, to be squandered away in a battle already lost, making clear the minimum number of squadrons required to defend Britain. This was surely among the most significant documents of the Twentieth Century, and from the film's outset, 'Stuffy' Dowding is upheld, rightly, as a man totally committed to the defence of Britain – bringeth the hour, bringeth the man.

07:47/2:12

We then hop across the Channel and see armour and infantry of the victorious German army (it must be said a somewhat slovenly and scruffy lot of extras from the Spanish army!) entering 'Dunkerque', watched by two elderly and despairing French civilians.

08:16/2:12

Then, we see the aftermath of the Dunkirk evacuation, the detritus of war scattered over the beaches and the French port's still-burning oil tanks, seen in the right distance. The evacuation from the beaches, however, occurred at Zuydcoote, Bray Dunes and De Panne, to the north-east of the actual port, so the burning oil tanks should really be to our left. The voiceover comes from Churchill's famous speech, in which he made clear that now France had fallen, ' … the Battle of Britain' was about to begin. In history, this is possibly unique, certainly in modern times, that a battle was named before even it had been fought.

08:53/2:12

The film's preamble now over, we have the opening titles to stirring martial music, Generalfeldmarschall Erhard Milch (Dietrich Frauboes), the Luftwaffe's Inspector General, arrives in France to inspect Luftflotte (Air Fleet) 2, commanded by Field Marshal Albert Kesselring (Peter Hager), and in particular the bombers commanded by Oberst Johannes Fink (Wolf Harnisch). Kesselring would be primarily responsible for the forthcoming daylight air assault on England. Fink commanded KG2 'Holzhammer', equipped with Do 17 bombers; the availability of serviceable aircraft for the film, however, dictated the use of Merlin-engine powered Spanish Air Force CASA 2111s, a design based upon the He 111, which we now see Fink's 'I/KG637' operating. These scenes provide a lasting impression of German aerial might, undefeated to date, and confidence.

13:06/2:12

We then see Milch leaving a conference with Hitler (whom we do not see) in Berlin, in company and conversation with Generalmajor Hans Jeschonnek (Karl-Otto Alberty), the Luftwaffe Chief of Staff. Interestingly, in this scene – contrary to those previous showing Milch, Kesselring and Fink – Milch observes wryly that the Führer did not consider Britain to be Germany's natural enemy, and that the plan to mount a seaborne invasion of southern England would be a catastrophe. Jeschonnek, conversely, opined that the British were already finished and that such an opportunity would never arise again.

This is a short but significant scene, indicating the divided opinion within the German High Command regarding the way forward.

A joint service amphibious landing is a vast undertaking, as evidenced by the preparation and resources required for the Allies to successfully return to France on 6 June 1944. The German air force, navy and army were not equipped or trained for such an operation, which was simply not foreseen. Indeed, no one, least of all Hitler, could have possibly predicted such a lightning advance to the Channel coast and collapse of the old European order. This scene acknowledges that, and also Jeschonnek's over-confidence. Throughout the Battle of Britain, Jeschonnek's staff would provide inaccurate intelligence, leading to poor target selection and a false impression of how the battle was going, the Germans consequently and repeatedly making the wrong strategic and tactical decisions.

13:42/2:12

The viewer is then transported to the British Embassy in Switzerland, for a meeting between the German Foreign Minister, 'Max, Baron von Richter' (Curt Jürgens), a character based upon Joachim von Ribbentropp, straight from a meeting with Hitler, and 'Sir David Kelly, British Ambassador to Switzerland' (Sir Ralph Richardson).

Again, the German confidence is emphasised, Von Richter insisting that 'London is ours' and referring to the unsuccessful requests Britain was making to neutral America for direct support – drawing a rousing stiff-upper-lip riposte from Sir David, causing the German to withdraw, offended. The scene concludes with Sir David painfully admitting the following to his wife, 'Lady Kelly' (Eileen Peel): 'It's unforgiveable. I lost my temper. The maddening thing is that he's right. We're not ready. We're on our own. We've been playing for time – and its running out!'

The scene leaves the viewer in no doubt as to Britain's perilous position – alone – and also pays due acknowledgement, perhaps surprisingly, that behind the scenes, diplomatic negotiations remained ongoing between Britain and Germany to try to reach a peaceful solution – something the British Prime Minister, Winston Churchill, found abhorrent and made this clear in his famous 'fight them on the beaches' speech, which is also referred to. What we learn from this scene is that a diplomatic solution is not an option – and everyone involved knows that sooner, rather than later, the storm will break.

16:49/2:12

We are now transported to an RAF fighter base 'somewhere in England', in June 1940. This is 'Skipper's' squadron, which has exchanged its Hurricanes for Spitfires. It is worth noting that during the actual Battle of Britain, there were two-thirds more Hurricanes than Spitfires, so most Fighter Command squadrons were equipped with the former type.

The following year, however, the superior Spitfire, with better all-important high-altitude performance, replaced the Hurricane as the RAF's front-line day fighter, and, after engine and many other upgrades, was ultimately developed through twenty-four marques and remained in production until 1947, and in service until 1954. Some 14,000 Hurricanes were built until the type was discontinued in 1944, whereas 22,000 Spitfires rolled off production lines.

Consequently, this is why comparatively few airworthy Hurricanes were available when *Battle of Britain* was made, and why the impression given by the film is that the Spitfire was the RAF's predominant fighter. On the subject of the film's Spitfires, only one, Mk IIA, P7350, had flown in the Battle of Britain, the others being later Merlin-engine powered marques and even including Griffon-engine powered types. To the general viewer, none of this detail matters.

17:13/2:12

In this scene, a Spitfire appears, flown by a new pilot, 'Simon' (Nicholas Pennell), who forgets to put his wheels down, and is reminded in the nick of time by a warning flare. The scene implies that Fighter Command already was already suffering a severe shortage of pilots, and that operational training was being drastically reduced to ensure a flow of replacements for the squadrons. Certainly, after the Fall of France, during which Fighter Command lost some 300 pilots, and on 1 June 1940, Dowding's operational strength was 1,200 pilots – of which only 906 were combat ready, most of these lacking actual combat experience.

19.13/2:12

Unimpressed with Simon's performance, the unsympathetic Skipper has the youngster airborne again immediately, practising dogfighting and impressing upon him the golden rules of air fighting, 'Before Jerry has you for breakfast.' In truth, after being rested from operations in July 1941, at his own request, Sailor Malan went into training, imparting his wealth of knowledge for the benefit of young pilots such as Simon; it was, in fact, something the great South African ace felt strongly about.

20:40/2:12

Next, we see 'Group Captain Hope' (Nigel Patrick) briefing a group of fighter controllers as to how Fighter Command is organised and how the 'System' works. Again, this is another important scene, providing the viewer clarity as to how Britain will be defended in the battle ahead. Interestingly, one of the 'controllers', is 'Squadron Leader Evans', played by Bill Foxley, an RAF navigator disfigured by burns suffered when his bomber crashed in 1944.

22:00/2:12

Again, we return across the Channel – this time focusing on a fine al fresco coastal dinner with General Theo Osterkamp's (Wilfred von Aacken) fighter pilots, including Majors 'Falke' (Manfred Reddeman) and Föhn (Paul Neuhaus), entertaining Generalfeldmarshall Milch.

The cigar-smoking Falke was based upon none other than Adolf Galland, the film's often difficult German technical advisor.

An ace and veteran of the Spanish Civil War, during the Battle of Britain Galland was elevated to command JG26, a twelve-squadron-strong fighter group, and went on to succeed his friend Werner Mölders as the fighter pilots' General. Föhn was based upon Mölders, the Kommodore of JG51 and so-called 'Father of Modern Air Fighting', ultimately killed in a flying accident. In this scene exemplifying the total confidence of the Luftwaffe and keenness to 'set about England', we are also introduced to Falke's brother, 'Hans' (Dagobert Walter) – Galland himself was actually one of four brothers, all fighter pilots, two of which, Wilhem-Ferdinand and Paul, were killed in action.

22:52/2:12

Also, in this scene we are introduced to radar, the Inspector General viewing the Chain Home Low Radio Direction Finding (RDF) masts near Dover – just twenty-two miles across the Channel. RDF was a key advantage to the British, providing early warning of German formations assembling over France, and their time, strength and direction of travel towards England. This information was communicated to Fighter Command HQ at Bentley Priory (Stanmore), and thence to the relevant sector airfield operations rooms, which would scramble fighter squadrons accordingly. While in this scene we are introduced to unnamed Stuka aircrew, who will 'deal with' the English 'secret weapon', the reality is that had Luftwaffe intelligence fully appreciated the crucial significance of RDF, infinitely more effort would have been invested in its destruction.

23:37/2:12

Now, we are returned to London, and an informal meeting between Dowding and the 'Minister' (Anthony Nicholls), this being the Liberal Party Leader, Sir Archibald Sinclair, who served as Air Minister in

THE BATTLE OF BRITAIN ON THE BIG SCREEN

Churchill's coalition war government. The conversation revolves around what was a fortuitous lull between the Fall of France and the Battle of Britain starting, providing the defenders much-needed breathing space to regroup after the continental disaster. The Minister refers to 'Beaverbrook', the Minister for Aircraft Production (whose son, Max, was one of the Few), and his optimism regarding the flow of aircraft from the factories to Dowding's squadrons.

Dowding, however, points out that it is not a lack of aircraft that concerns him – but a potential deficiency in pilots. In terms of fighter aircraft, the two sides were, in fact, fairly evenly matched. Two-thirds of the RAF strength were Hurricanes, however, whereas the majority of enemy fighters were the superior Me 109E – which also had certain technical advantages over the Spitfire too. In terms of aircrew, as the battle progressed, training courses were foreshortened, but it is important to understand how Fighter Command was deployed. 11 Group, covering London and the south-east, was the front-line; 12 Group, defending the industrial Midlands and the North, the second-line.

Covering the south-west was 10 Group, and Scotland and Northern Ireland was the responsibility of 13 Group. Clearly, the hot combat zone was the 11 Group area, but far from concentrating his strength there, Dowding cleverly dispersed squadrons around the country, carefully considering the respective defensive responsibilities of each group. Consequently, after tours of duty in the front line, decimated squadrons were withdrawn to rebuild in quieter sectors, before relieving a similarly depleted unit and returning to the front line.

By shepherding resources in this way, there would never be a shortage of aircraft, pilots or operational squadrons in the battle ahead. Fighter Command casualties were certainly critical by the first week of September 1940, but never dropped to an unmanageable level. For this, Dowding deserves great credit – but the facts, of course, do not provide the myth-making film-maker much ammunition.

BATTLE OF BRITAIN

25:16/2:12

Now we leave Whitehall's corridors of power and return to a fighter squadron in southern England. In this scene, we also see how equally keen RAF fighter pilots were to engage the enemy, with 'Pilot Officer Charlie Lambert' (Alan Tucker) requesting permission from Squadron Leader Canfield (Michael Caine) for 'an instrument check', and hurrying off to get airborne.

25:29/2:12

We see Harvey, promoted to squadron leader, complete with 'Canada' shoulder-flash, having handed over command of '188 Squadron', also now Spitfire-equipped, to Squadron Leader Canfield, leaving for a new posting in Scotland. 'Sergeant-Pilot Chris' (David Griffin) request permission for a test flight, but, wiser now after some advice from Harvey, Canfield refuses this.

26:37/2:12

Squadron Leader Harvey arrives at and parks his green MG outside 'The Jackdaw' (at Denton, near the Kent Battle of Britain Museum at Hawkinge, both essential locations for the enthusiast to visit). We are now given a glimpse of the difficulties experienced by wartime marriages, and some male attitudes towards women serving. Inside the quintessential English pub, 'Section Officer Maggie Harvey' (Susannah York) of the WAAF, patiently awaits her fighter pilot husband's arrival. Unfortunately, a domestic storm brews when Maggie, who (we later discover) is serving at a busy southern fighter station, is reluctant to comply with her husband's insistence that she should apply for a posting and join him in Scotland. Unable to talk his wife around, Harvey exits, just as Local Defence Volunteers (Home Guard), armed with shotguns and pitchforks, finish their drill in the car park, leaving behind his watery-eyed and beautiful wife (complete with 1960s hair-do).

28:53/2:12

Back at Canfield's airfield, Charlie is overdue, causing grave concern. Suddenly, a Hurricane, 'out of juice very likely', lands unexpectedly – the pilots at dispersal disconcerted to see that the pilot is their Air Officer Commanding (AOC), Air Vice-Marshal Keith Park (Trevor Howard). Interestingly, as the AOC enters the dispersal hut, we see displayed on the wall next to the Orderly Clerk Sailor Malan's famous 'Ten Rules of Air Fighting' – which were not published, in fact, until 1942.

In this turn of events, however, we learn that this is a coastal airfield and of the AOC's concern about losing pilots unnecessarily over the Channel. Unfortunately, Lambert had flown over the sea, looking for trouble – and found it: he was ambushed, out of the sun by Major Falke and shot down. Baling out into the water, Lambert was not rescued – and at this stage RAF Air Sea Rescue, unlike the German set-up, was as embryonic as it was ad hoc.

31:12/2:12

We now return across the Channel to see the cocky and arrogant Falke preparing to celebrate his latest aerial victory by having dinner in Boulogne with his friend Föhn, who, while awaiting Falk, is entertained by Hans and other officers. Again, the Germans' high-morale and total confidence is emphasised. The revelry is cut short, however, when both Kommodoren are urgently called to a conference at Osterkamp's Wissant HQ. En route, the officers are held up by a great column of barges being moved by road to Calais and Boulogne in preparation for Operation *Seelöwe* – the seaborne invasion of England. The impression given is that German preparations and resources for this colossal undertaking were up to the challenge – in reality they were not, although barges were converted and assembled in the Channel ports for this purpose.

34:02/2:12

We now jump to 'Eagle Day', which, the caption tells us, is 10 August 1940. It was not. Although originally planned for that day, bad weather delayed this major attack until three days later. This, however, loses a whole month of the Battle of Britain. So far as the British were later concerned, the Battle started on 10 July 1940, this opening phase featuring the Luftwaffe cautiously probing coastal defences, and especially attacking shipping in the Channel.

Apart from the isolated loss of Pilot Officer Lambert on a test flight, this period – the 'Kanal Kampf' (Channel battle) – is ignored by the film-makers. This is a pity, notwithstanding that the fighting actually began on 4 July 1940, because this ignores the loss of life suffered by Fighter Command and merchant seamen. Nonetheless, we do know that on 10 August 1940, Dowding had at his disposal 1,100 serviceable fighters – but only 750 combat-ready pilots. Returning to 'Eagle Day', we see Fink briefing his bomber crews, using a pointer to indicate target airfields – although where his stick lands on the map bears no semblance to the reality of these geographic locations.

34:30/2:12

In the briefings on their respective fighter airfields, Falke and Föhn emphasise the importance of height – and the need to carefully monitor and conserve fuel. Like the British fighters, the Me 109, which Merlin-engine powered Spanish Air Force Hispano-Buchons masqueraded as in the film, was designed as a short-range defensive interceptor – not a long-range escort or offensive fighter. What the German fighter pilots were now being asked to do, escorting bombers to a distant strategic target, was contrary to the designer's intention – more of which later. The Germans would also have to make two sea-crossings per sortie on a single-engine – a nervous undertaking for any pilot at the best of times – hence the emphasis on fuel states. Indeed, the 109s only had sufficient fuel for twenty minutes of combat flying over south-east England.

36:58/2:12

The subsequent aerial combat sequence features Stukas dive-bombing, with a degree of success, radar installations at Ventnor on the Isle of Wight, and Dover. Interestingly, the young WAAF radar operator at Ventnor – 'I'm afraid the raid is entering my ground-range, Stanmore' – is a 22-year-old Dame Maureen Lipman. The Stukas are intercepted by Canfield's Spitfires; 'Pinetree Squadron'.

Over the white cliffs of Sussex's iconic Seven Sisters and Beachy Head, the Spitfires pounce – although with formation and other flying best-suited to camera angles than the Fighter Command Book of Tactics. The unescorted and hapless dive-bombers are soon knocked about however, indicating the Stukas vulnerability, the type suffering such heavy losses that it was withdrawn from the actual battle. In this scene, German aircraft, on being hit, invariably burst into flame and blow up – which many of the Few confirmed to me never happened in their actual experience.

42:43/2:12

We then see the 'He 111s' escorted by 'Me 109s', their formations' course plotted from the ground by the Observer Corps (OC). Once the enemy had crossed the coast, RDF at this time was of no use – hence the importance of the OC, which is not emphasised sufficiently.

43:07/2:12

The information from radar and the OC having been received by Fighter Command HQ Operations Room and 'filtered' out to the relevant Sector Airfield Operations Room, the Clerk, 'LAC Arnold' (David McKail), answers the telephone at Squadron Leader Skipper's 'Rabbit Squadron' dispersal: Arnold's cry of 'Two Section: *SCRAMBLE*!' sets the pilots running for their Spitfires, which take-off just as the 'Look-out' sounds the hand-cranked air-raid siren – which the complacent station personnel assume to be a practice.

Fighter squadrons were actually divided into two flights of six machines each, 'A' and 'B', which were sub-divided into two sections of three. Each section was colour-coded, and each pilot in every section numbered one to three (hence, for example, Blue 2,

Red 1 etc). Correctly, then, Arnold should have shouted for whatever flight or colour-coded section was an immediate readiness.

44:21/2:12
Now, we have a glimpse of wider life on the same RAF fighter airfield, the Station Commander, 'Group Captain Baker' (Kenneth More) rebuking 'Warrant Officer Warwick' (Michael Bates) for there being 'muck and filth everywhere', standards having slipped, apparently, on account of long hours being worked. Section Officer Maggie Harvey is also in Baker's sights on account of some WAAFs having been noted using the 'men's trenches' during air raid practice – an indication of how the sexes were segregated at the time. The 'Groupie' also complains that WAAFs are using gas mask cases as handbags – all very petty – when bombs start exploding across the airfield, and Group Captain Baker rushes to the nearest slit trench – which, ironically, is a female shelter …

46.38/2:12
The confused Arnold then takes another call: a squadron scramble. Squadron Leader Skipper, having only just landed, is unimpressed and demands to speak to the 'Duty Controller' – just as bombs start exploding on the airfield and, there being no further doubt, sending Skipper and his remaining pilots sprinting for their aircraft. The still bewildered Simon is unsure what to do, as Skipper barks 'Don't just stand there – get one up!' Without delay, with bombs exploding all around, the Spitfires are off – although at least one is destroyed while taxiing.

This happened. On 31 August 1940, 11 Group's sector airfields were being truly hammered, the Spitfires of 54 Squadron scrambled during a heavy raid on Hornchurch; eight Spitfires scrambled safely while one section of three were completely wrecked by exploding bombs while taking off – although miraculously all three pilots, including the tough Kiwi ace Flight Lieutenant Al Deere, survived.

48:44/2:12

Rabbit Squadron assembles in the air, the bad-tempered Skipper taking issue with the tardy ground controller, and the inexperienced Simon's poor formation flying. Inevitably, the high-flying 109s bounce and kill the bewildered 'Red 2' in their usual high-speed diving pass.

50:32/2:12

Back at Group Captain Baker's airfield, the damage is extensive. Section Officer Harvey is stunned by a line of dead, blanket-covered, WAAFs. Shocked, the young officer goes to light a cigarette when the experienced and professional airman Warwick cannot believe his eyes, shouting, regardless of rank 'Put that cigarette out! The mains have gone! Can't you smell gas?!'

In that superb moment of highly emotional cinema, Warwick becomes the focus of all Maggie's fear and rage: 'Don't you yell at me, Mr Warwick!' In that instance she snaps out of her shell-shocked state and gets on with it. It is a great and fondly remembered scene – but, in reality, just three WAAFs lost their lives during the actual Battle of Britain: one died of injuries sustained when Detling was bombed, another at Biggin Hill, and the last, who was pregnant, was tragically killed while off-duty and shielding her mother-in-law from shrapnel during a raid on Eastbourne, where the pair were enjoying a shopping trip. Nonetheless, the scene gets the point across, that 'they' also served – and, of course, a number of WAAFs were decorated for their bravery during the battle.

52:31/2:12

As the raid withdraws, we now join Air Vice-Marshal Park in his 11 Group underground Operations Room at Uxbridge (now open to the public, the 'Battle of Britain Bunker'), as two controllers, 'Wing Commander Willoughby' (Robert Flemyng) and his assistant (Tom Chatto) lament damage to the airfields and suggest that the fighter squadrons should be moved north of the Thames – which Park is rightly having none of.

52:52/2:12

We now see Group Captain Baker surveying the colossal damage to his airfield, this scene leaving us in no doubt as to how badly the airfields were damaged and disrupted, with even some sector operations rooms having to be set up in civilian properties off the station.

53:51/2:12

The next scene shows Jeschonnek providing intelligence for a major raid being planned on north-east England, by bombers based in Norway. 'Even a Spitfire', he gloats, 'can't be in two places at once'. This tells us two things: first, that the Germans failed to understand how Dowding rotated his squadrons around the Command, and maintained sufficient fighters in all sectors to meet their geographic defensive responsibilities, and second, that the Spitfire was an especially respected opponent.

55:40/2:12

Squadron Leader Harvey's northern-based Spitfires subsequently intercept the unescorted 'Heinkels', which immediately break formation upon being attacked. This would not happen. German bomber tactics relied upon carefully practised and rehearsed formations providing mutual protection. To break formation was suicide – leaving the individual aircraft wide-open to attack – but it made for good cinema.

The actual attack, on 15 August 1940, was made by seventy-two He 111s escorted by twenty-one twin-engine Me 110s, and met by various squadrons of Spitfires and Hurricanes. It was a disastrous day for Luftflotte 5, which lost a total of eighty-one aircrew, and indicated the folly of sending bombers to England unprotected by the Me 109.

These are, however, terrific aerial combat sequences – set to Ron Goodwin's rousing *Battle of Britain Theme* score.

58:57/2:12
Back at base, Harvey's pilots make out their combat reports to the Intelligence Officer (Basil Dignam), and 'Peter' (Myles Hoyle) is disappointed to learn that the He 111 he has destroyed has to be shared with two other pilots, who also attacked the same enemy aircraft – as so often happened.

59:33/2:12
Squadron Leader Harvey, however, takes issue with Peter for victory-rolling over 'his' airfield before landing. To be fair, Harvey had a point: on 10 April 1941, Pilot Officer Peter Chesters of 74 Squadron destroyed an Me 109 over Kent, then jubilantly victory-rolled over Manston airfield, badly misjudging things and crashing into the parade ground – killing himself.

1:00/2:12
We then switch to Fighter Command HQ, Bentley Priory, and a staff officer (John Savident) excitedly sharing with a colleague (John Tatham) the claim figures arising from the northern raid, keen to share these with 'Stuffy' Dowding. While pleased, Dowding voices more concerns over pilot shortages to his Senior Air Staff Officer (SASO), Air Vice-Marshal Evill (Michael Redgrave), although in fact Fighter Command had by now been reinforced by pilots from other commands and the Fleet Air Arm – but these men had to be converted to modern fighters and lacked combat experience. And therein lies the rub: Dowding's concern was not the overall number of pilots, but the number of experienced pilots being lost.

By this time, in fact, Fighter Command's establishment had risen from 1,482 in June 1940, to 1,558 by 17 August 1940, of which 1,379 were operational – how many were combat ready at that time is unrecorded, but we do know that the figure had dropped from 906 on 1 June 1940 to 735 by 1 September, and on 1 November 1940 – the day after the Battle of Britain officially ended – this reached an all-time low of 673. In the scene, Dowding rejects a proposal to make the new Polish and Czechoslovak squadrons operational on the grounds that they could still not understand English sufficiently well to be anything other than a 'menace to themselves and everyone else' in the air.

By this stage of the battle, however, this is not strictly true – there were already a number of Polish and Czech pilots serving in RAF squadrons (alongside men from Britain, the Commonwealth, and those from other occupied lands, including French and Belgians – not to mention a small number of volunteers from neutral America). On 10 July 1940, the Czech 310 Squadron was formed at Duxford, and 302 (Polish) at Leconfield, both in 12 Group. On 29 July 1940, the Czechs were made operational, and were a component part of the 12 Group 'Big Wing', led by Squadron Leader Bader and based at Duxford (of which more later).

By 15 August 1940, 302 Squadron was also declared operational, becoming the first Polish squadron to be so; the unit also subsequently participated in 12 Group Wing operations. The second Polish squadron, 303 at Northolt in 11 Group, however, was not formed until 2 August 1940 – and this unit was not operational by mid-August, when the scene in question is supposed to have taken place. These new squadrons of foreign nationals had British squadron and flight commanders, to ease their passage into RAF operational and other procedures, who were shadowed by their Polish and Czech counterparts, and everything was being done, in fact, to resolve the language issue and get them into the line.

At Duxford, for example, the Station Commander, Group Captain A.B. 'Woody' Woodhall garnered help from the BBC, which cut an LP record for him translating aerial commands in English into

Polish and Czech. Indeed, it was to everyone's benefit to get the Poles in particular into action, as some of their number had experienced combat over their homeland and in France. This scene therefore, does neither Dowding or Fighter Command justice, simply helping fuel a myth (as we will see).

1:01/2:12
We then see a major raid developing in the Fighter Command Operations Room. Skipper's Rabbit Squadron, already airborne, intercepts a formation of bombers – but the Spitfires are bounced from above by a large force of Me 109s. The following action is superb, and these aerial scenes are the film's real tour de force. Off Eastbourne, at which point a modern high-rise building is clearly visible, Sergeant-Pilot Andy is shot down and takes to his parachute. Interestingly, and purely as an aside, in a number of combat sequences we, the viewer, are placed in a Spitfire cockpit – only to actually be peering out of a Hurricane's windscreen …

1:05/2:12
Back at base, Skipper pays full acknowledgement to the squadron's groundcrews, working tirelessly to keep the Spitfires flying. Sergeant-Pilot Andy's reappearance after being rescued from the Channel provokes rebuke for getting bounced – followed by the Skipper adopting a more paternalistic attitude and giving the cold and wet sergeant a lift back to his accommodation.

1:07/2:12
We are next exposed to Canfield's anger and frustration at his airfield having been wrecked by German bombs, and dissatisfaction at being dispersed to operate from a former civilian flying club. All sector stations had satellite airfields, some of which had primitive facilities and only tented accommodation, such as Fowlmere – Duxford's satellite. Others, such as Gravesend for example, had previously

been civilian airfields. Cranfield makes an acerbic observation, that unless 'someone' protects the airfields while 11 Group's fighters are airborne, the destruction will continue.

1:08/2:12
At Canfield's new airfield, he and 'Pinetree Squadron' are at cockpit readiness, propellers turning: 'How much longer, Ops? The engine's overheating and so am I. We either stand-down or blow up. Which do you want?' Then, up goes a flare and the Spitfires scramble.

1:09/2:12
In the next sequence we see Air Vice-Marshal Park, a man under pressure if ever there was one, considering the battering his airfields were getting, insists that the controller reminds 12 Group fighters that their task is essential: to protect 11 Group's airfields while his fighters are engaged further forward. In reality, by this time, a row had broken out over 12 Group's apparent inability to effectively provide the cover required and as demanded by the System.

On 15 August 1940, for example, 12 Group's Fowlmere-based 19 Squadron's Spitfires arrived too late over Martlesham Heath to prevent it being badly damaged. 12 Group, commanded by Air Vice-Marshal Trafford Leigh-Mallory, however, argued that it was being requested too late to have any realistic chance of intercepting the enemy, and also accused 11 Group of 'hogging' the battle. The problem was the limitations of RDF in use at that time, the comparatively limited warning time it gave offset against the speed of the aircraft involved, both in terms of those attacking and defending. 11 Group, however, was fighting the battle exactly as per Dowding's wishes, intercepting the enemy using small, flexible, formations, in order to carefully preserve resources. That said, Park was not averse to using wings of two or more squadrons when the occasion demanded, and would soon use Spitfire squadrons in pairs as a high-flying protective umbrella.

1:10/2:12

In the ensuing action, Pinetree Squadron is bounced by 109s (another superb aerial combat scene) and Canfield is killed: 'He just … Blew up!', and an airfield operations room is bomb-damaged, indicating that the Germans reached their target.

1:14/2:12

A furious Air Vice-Marshal Park is then seen having flown to a meeting with Dowding, bitterly complaining to a Fighter Command staff officer, a group captain (Jack Gwillim) that 'God knows how many aircraft we'll have in the morning – all because 12 Group didn't do their stuff. Leigh-Mallory's so-called 'Big Wings' might as well stay on the ground for all the good they are.' This leads perfectly into the next scene, which in many ways is a significant one.

1:14.27/2:12

We now join Air Vice-Marshal Park, and Air Vice-Marshal Leigh-Mallory (Patrick Wymark) at a meeting with Air Chief Marshal Dowding at Fighter Command HQ, Bentley Priory. This room has, in fact, been preserved as part of the excellent Bentley Priory Museum, and is open to visitors. In this meeting, the two group commanders argue about the effectiveness or otherwise of Leigh-Mallory's 'Big Wing'. This requires explanation. Among Leigh-Mallory's squadron commanders was the swashbuckling dynamo Douglas Bader, who, as discussed earlier, was unable to tolerate playing a secondary role in 12 Group and not being at the sharp end.

Bader was continually exasperated that 11 Group did not call for (or need!) his help. On 30 August 1940 (again, of which more later), 11 Group did request 12 Group's assistance, and Bader's 242 Squadron caught its first sight of a mass German raid, which it intercepted over Hatfield, with some success. A euphoric Bader reported that had he more fighters at his disposal, greater damage to the enemy could have been effected, and that, contrary to the

System and Dowding's well-thought out strategy, which balanced conserving resources against the needs of defending targets before they were bombed, while achieving the greatest enemy losses, several 12 Group squadrons should operate together, as a 'wing', under his overall leadership, heading straight for the action or patrolling over the combat area in readiness for an attack.

The concept was flawed from the outset, however. In their excitement, Bader's pilots had failed to notice that 11 Group squadrons, among them the highly experienced Nos 1 and 222, were also engaged and recorded successes. Indeed, we now know that 242 Squadron overclaimed that day by at least 4:1, so the results were actually nothing like as successful as they first appeared. Both the ambitious Leigh-Mallory, and Duxford's Station Commander and Sector Controller, Group Captain Woodhall, agreed with Bader. It was decided that 242 would fly with 310 Squadron, both from Duxford, while the Fowlmere-based Spitfires of 19 Squadron provided top cover. Bader first led the Wing into action on 7 September 1940, claiming more successes, and so it went on – the overclaiming ratio reaching an all-time high of 7:1.

These figures, however, were accepted and two more squadrons were added to the 'Big Wing'. There was a long history of hostility on Leigh-Mallory's behalf towards both Dowding, who he had vowed to see 'replaced', and Park, of whom he was jealous, and, supported by the Deputy Chief of the Air Staff, Air Vice-Marshal Sholto Douglas, the 12 Group commander initiated a 'dirty little intrigue', involving even Churchill himself, arguing that mass fighter formations should be adopted as standard, and that the tactics employed by Dowding and Park were comparatively ineffective.

We know today, from rigorous analysis, that 11 Group's claims were infinitely more accurate than 12's, and that the Big Wing concept simply did not, and could not, work. Because the claims were accepted with little question, however, there was a very different impression at the time. Ultimately, Dowding and Park were called to a meeting at the Air Ministry in October 1940, at which, to their surprise, they were called upon by the Air Staff to justify their tactics, and at which the Big Wing protagonists advanced support of their theory. Cutting a very long story short, there is little doubt that this controversy led to the replacement of Dowding and Park by Douglas and Leigh-Mallory respectively, almost immediately after the Battle of Britain had been won. Both men remained bitter about their treatment, and were concerned at how both they and the controversy would be treated by the film.

Returning to the actual scene, the main point is that it never happened. Dowding was a hands-off Commander-in-Chief, who set out his instructions and left his group commanders to carry them out. Indeed, he was not a politician and only realised the danger from the Big Wing camp too late. After the war, he admitted that not having intervened in the dispute between Leigh-Mallory and Park was his one big command failing. Indeed, at no time during the Battle of Britain did Dowding call his group commanders together for a conference; had he done so after the issue over Martlesham on 15 August 1940, the Big Wing Controversy may have been avoided.

In the event, Lord Dowding and Air Chief Marshal Sir Keith Park, as they had become, were sympathetically treated in *Battle of Britain*, which, unlike *Reach for the Sky*, indicated antipathy over tactics between the two group commanders behind the scenes. When Lord Dowding visited the film set at Pinewood Studios, Group Captain Sir Douglas Bader – who Dowding actually held responsible for 'much of the trouble' – insisted on pushing the old man's wheelchair.

1:15/2:12

Leaving behind arguments over 'Big Wings' and 'Small Wings', we move to London's Savoy Hotel and a bedroom scene with Colin and Maggie Harvey – which again draws into the big story issues besetting wartime marriages. The night, however, is shattered by German bombs exploding – this being the first time the capital was bombed, on 24 August 1940, an accidental occurrence as Hitler had placed London off limits while still reluctant to commit to an all-out air offensive against the British civilian population.

Churchill, however, immediately ordered a retaliatory raid on Berlin the following night, made by eighty-one Wellingtons and Hampdens, although only half found and bombed the cloud-obscured target, causing the death of just one elephant at the city's zoo. The bombing of Berlin in the film, however, indicates the peacetime atmosphere and lack of air raid precautions, a direct contrast to the blackout of British cities – another indication of German over-confidence.

1:22/2:12

RAF Bomber Command's raid on Berlin incensed Hitler, who we see in the film (Rolf Stiefel) addressing the Bund Deutscher Mädel (BDM), the League of German Girls, and promising to flatten British cities in retribution. This was a turning point in the Battle of Britain – because Hitler now ordered a turn away from the bombing of airfields, which was actually increasingly successful, and instead prioritised the destruction of London.

1:24/2:12

Frustrated at his Luftwaffe's inability to achieve the required decision over England, and with new orders from Hitler, we see Reichsmarschall Herman Göring (Hein Reiss), the Luftwaffe chief himself, arriving by special train in the 'Pas-de-Calais' – which is essentially a flat landscape, whereas the Spanish station used for the scene is overlooked by a mountain. The Reichsmarschall is met by a reception committee of senior officers, including Kesselring and Osterkamp.

By now, the majority of Me 109 fighters had been moved into the Pas-de-Calais, ready to escort bombers to a new target: London. This was not, however, just because of the Berlin attack. To achieve aerial supremacy, the Germans needed to destroy Fighter Command. So far, however, thanks to the way Dowding had organised his Command and rotated squadrons, the Luftwaffe had failed to lure the defending fighters into the air for destruction en masse. London, however, was believed to be the one target that Dowding would commit his force in its entirety to defend.

1:26/2:12
The arrogant Göring and his staff are seen on the French cliffs at Cap-Gris-Nez, gleefully watching a huge aerial armada making its way overhead towards the British capital. This did happen, on 7 September 1940.

1:27/2:12
At a sector operations room in south-east England, the Controller (Eric Dodson) vectors Skipper's Rabbit Squadron in anticipation of another airfield raid – only for the vexed Skipper to find no enemy aircraft in sight. Meanwhile, the confused Controller telephones 11 Group HQ at Uxbridge – where it is realised that while squadrons are up over airfields, the Germans have stolen a march and are heading for the undefended city of London.

1.28/2:12
On the ground, East End 'mudlarks' watch the approaching phalanx of German aircraft, disputing whether they be 'Messerschmitts' or ''einkels'. This is the first big attack on the capital, starting on 7 September 1940, which went on around-the-clock, the German bombers flying a shuttle service back and forth, guided to the burning docklands like moths to a flame.

1:32/2:12
On the ground, amid the bombs that night we again meet Sergeant-Pilot Andy, on leave after having baled out into the Channel, and seeking his family – which his wife (Isla Sinclair, also complete

BATTLE OF BRITAIN

with 1960s hair-do) has brought back to London from safety in the country. Andy finds his wife and two young boys in a 'Rest Centre', but answers the call for volunteers to help rescue a family in 'Shaw Street'.

The devastation to the East End slums is apparent, the bombed family found dead – and upon return, Andy is devastated to find the Rest Centre destroyed and his family killed. These scenes emphasise the civilian loss of life, and that the East Enders suffered – and that servicemen also had to deal with personal tragedy.

1:35/2:12

Staying with Sergeant-Pilot Andy, we see him lodging with Squadron Leader Skipper and his family, and preparing to leave the house early doors to go on readiness. Considering the segregation of ranks on the ground at the time, NCOs and officers each in their respective messes or sharing accommodation with men of at least equal rank and status, this is a highly improbable scenario. As the pair leave the house, we see a 1960s doorbell – which enthusiasts delight in pointing out to this day!

1:37/2:12

We now come to some real myth-making. Air Vice-Marshal Park is portrayed watching the progress of a raid in his Uxbridge Bunker, at which point he is informed that plot 'T5' is 'A training squadron ... the Poles'. This led the Duty Controller, Wing Commander Willoughby (Robert Flemyng), to give the order, 'Get them out of it. Get them down.'

This implies that this particular unit is the only Polish squadron, which, as previously explained, was not the case, and other Polish pilots were operational and serving in RAF squadrons. This order is communicated by radio to 'Blackhawk Leader', the Hurricane-equipped unit's English CO, 'Squadron Leader Edwards' (Barry Foster). This character is based upon Squadron Leader Ronald Gustave

Kellett, a pre-war auxiliary who formed 303 (Polish) Squadron at Northolt on 2 August 1940. On 30 August 1940, 303 Squadron was up from Northolt on an affiliation exercise with Blenheim bombers, when the raid came in against Hatfield, intercepted by Bader's 242 Squadron and 11 Group units.

In the film, Blackhawk Leader gives his pilots a course to steer – away from the trouble – but one, 'Ox' (Andrezej Scibor), sights the enemy, leading to excited Polish chatter over the ether. Unable to contain himself, Ox responds 'Repeat please', feigning ignorance of the order, and peels off to engage the Germans – followed, one by one, by his comrades, while Squadron Leader Edwards flies on, momentarily oblivious, until out of the corner of his eye he catches sight of what is going on and, with a cry of 'Oh, Gawd, streuth!', makes after his errant Poles, by now successfully in action.

This is what really happened, as recalled by Wing Commander Kellett himself in 1978:

> On the last training occasion we had twelve Blenheims as 'targets' when we were warned that enemy aircraft were in the vicinity. We were to guard the bombers. I ordered the squadron to assemble above and behind the bombers and cease 'attacking'. It was, however, too much for Paskiewicz, who, having seen an enemy aircraft, attacked and shot it down. Fortunately, the Blenheims were not attacked, and I reported to Group Captain Vincent (Northolt's Station Commander) and Air Vice-Marshal Park, that we were ready for combat.

Flying Officer Ludwik Paskiewicz (Green 1) reported that:

> We took off in two flights, (A and B) for exercises in attacking Blenheims, at 1615 hrs. After climbing to 10,000ft, we flew northward. After a while we

noticed ahead a number of aircraft carrying out various evolutions. The centre of the commotion seemed to be about 1,000ft below us, to starboard. I reported it to the CO, Squadron Leader Kellett, by Radio Telephone, and, as he did not seem to reply, I opened up the throttle and went in the direction of the enemy. I saw the rest of the Flight some 300 yards behind me; behind me were the burning suburbs of some town and a Hurricane diving with smoke trailing behind it. Then I noticed, at my own altitude, a bomber with twin rudders – probably a Dornier – turning in my direction. When he noticed me, he dived sharply. I turned over and dived after him. When turning over I noticed the black crosses on the wings. Then I aimed at the fuselage and opened fire. When I drew very close, I pressed down for a new attack and then I saw another Hurricane attacking and a German baling out by parachute. The Dornier went into a steep turn, and then I gave him another burst. He dived and then hit the ground and burst into flames. I then approached the other Hurricane and saw its markings: VC I. I have been firing at an enemy aircraft for the first time in my life.

Paskiewicz was credited with a 'Do 17' destroyed near St Albans, shared with Pilot Officer J.B. Wicks of 56 Squadron. The enemy aircraft concerned was actually a Me 110 of 4/ZG76, however, the starboard engine of which was disabled by Paskiewicz before being attacked by Wicks and exploding at Barley Beans Farm, Kimperton.

According to *Destiny Can Wait: The History of the Polish Air Force in Great Britain* (1949): 'Squadron Leader Kellett neither restrained Paskiewicz nor allowed the other pilots to follow him. He continued the exercise, which consisted then of protecting, instead of "attacking", the Blenheims'.

THE BATTLE OF BRITAIN ON THE BIG SCREEN

Wing Commander Johnny Kent, Kellett's 'A' Flight Commander, wrote in his memoir, *One of the Few*, that over this first victory, 'the Poles were absolutely cock-a-hoop over it. Ronald Kellett was so pleased with the way they had behaved that he immediately asked permission to declare the squadron "operational".' Certainly, all of Kellett's pilots but one had obeyed his order, and there was clearly sympathy for Paskiewicz's ill-discipline. Nonetheless, what could have happened to the Blenheims, had all the Poles followed Paskiewicz, as in the film, bears no thinking about.

It is not widely appreciated that certain aircraft within a squadron at this time were fitted with a navigational device called 'Pip Squeak', which automatically blocked all transmissions for fourteen seconds of every minute while broadcasting a 'fix' on the aircraft's location. It is likely that a squadron commander's aircraft would be fitted with this device, which may explain Squadron Leader Kellett's lack of response to Paskiewicz. Either way, the actual circumstances involving 303 Squadron on 30 August 1940, were very different to the exaggerated but entertaining version in *Battle of Britain*.

1:39/2:12

In the next scene, we have an initially angry Squadron Leader Edwards delivering his Polish pilots a rocket via a translator, 'Pasco' (Mark Malicz), for their indiscipline, concluding with the good news that the squadron is 'operational'. Then, Park and Dowding discuss the development, Dowding stating that he was 'wrong about the Poles', and Park pointing out that there was a second Polish squadron, which Dowding then agreed to likewise make operational, along with the Czechs and Canadians.

As we have seen, the other Polish unit, 302, was already operational, and had scored its first victory on 20 August 1940 – ten days before 303 Squadron. The Czechs of 310 Squadron, operational since 29 July 1940, would make their first kill the day after 303.

Similarly, the Canadians of No 1 Squadron RCAF were also already operational, and scored their first victory against the Luftwaffe on 26 August 1940.

These facts, therefore, tell a different story to the film – which presents an exaggerated incident involving 303 Squadron, and that squadron's success, as sole catalyst for the other foreign squadrons also being made operational. Clearly this is not true. The reader may wonder why this point is being laboured. This is because, without detracting in any way from the squadron's achievements and courage, in recent years a substantial cult has built up around 303, not least inspired by *Battle of Britain* – and the historian must always strive to provide accurate context. To my mind, upholding 303 Squadron as the film-makers did in *Battle of Britain* was disrespectful to the achievements of the existing foreign squadrons – all three of which were fully operational by the time of Paskiewicz's unauthorised combat over St Albans. This is one example of the actual story being even more dramatic than the cinematic version – if only it had been possible to somehow show in the limited time available.

1:40/2:12

Dowding and Park then step out onto the terrace of Bentley Priory, watching the night-bombing of London, the former commenting that there is 'nothing we can do about it'. Unfortunately, this was largely true: Britain's night defences remained in their infancy, hence the Germans shifted their main bombing effort to the hours of darkness. Although less accurate than daylight bombing, the trade-off for the enemy was that nocturnal operations were safer, at least at that time, before the advent of Airborne Interception radar-equipped and dedicated night-fighting aircraft arrived.

In this scene, Park makes the point that the Germans' change of tack is permitting his airfields to recover – and Dowding remarks that if the enemy concentrates on London, the Luftwaffe has further to travel to the target and back – allowing more RAF fighters to be brought into action, including 12 Group and Leigh-Mallory's 'Big Wing'. This was all certainly the case.

1:42/2:12
We now approach the fighting's climax, with the Germans still targeting London. Echoing Dowding's prophecy, we watch various RAF squadrons being vectored to intercept the enemy, including the arrival of 'a friendly wing' – greeted by one Hurricane pilot with 'bloody marvellous'.

It has traditionally been written that the arrival of Douglas Bader at the head of five 12 Group squadrons over London on Battle of Britain Day, 15 September 1940, was a crushing blow to enemy morale. Having researched the 'Big Wing' in minute detail for many years, this author has found no specific evidence from the Luftwaffe side to support that claim. German aircrew certainly were demoralised by the overall numbers of RAF fighters in action that day, but nowhere is it recorded that this was caused specifically by the arrival of the Big Wing.

What Bader's appearance did undoubtedly do, however, was massively inspire and uplift the morale of 11 Group's outnumbered pilots that day – and this comment in the film acknowledges that. What is confusing, however, is that in these incredible scenes of fighter versus fighter combat, Canfield's voice is identifiable – who is supposedly already killed in action – and Harvey, who is still in Scotland!

1:44/2:12
What follows are absolutely superb scenes of aerial combat, and we hear Harvey's voice giving commands to his pilots over the radio. We see the Pole, 'Ox', shot down, baling out and amusingly mistaken for a German upon landing by a farmer (John Baskcomb).

1:47/2:12
With so many RAF fighters, the Germans are roughly handled, a badly damaged He 111 struggling back to France, trailing smoke and flying

low over German troops, giving them cause for concern regarding how the air assault on England was going, before crash-landing with badly wounded crewmen aboard. Clearly, the tide of battle has turned in the defenders' favour.

1:48/2:12

This turn of events, however, leads to a furious Göring berating his high and field commanders. Those assembled explain that the aircrew and their machines are tired, after weeks of fighting, and that the enemy is now attacking in greater strength. To a degree, this was true; the Big Wing, by now with political support, was virtually a law unto itself, roaming over London and Kent – although its impact was actually negligible. Göring rants that the fighter pilots are cowards and should be escorting the bombers more closely – ordering that this will from now on be the case – drawing fire from the fighter leader who argues that this deprives his pilots of the advantage of surprise. Then, Göring calms down and offers help, asking what his commanders need. Falke's response was 'A squadron of Spitfires!' This informal conference did indeed take place, as General Galland remembered:

> We received many more harsh words. Finally, as his time ran short, he grew more amiable and asked what were the requirements for our squadrons? 'I should like an outfit of Spitfires for my Group.' After blurting this out, I had rather a shock, because it was not really meant that way. Of course, fundamentally I preferred our Me 109 to the Spitfire, but I was unbelievably vexed at the lack of understanding and the stubbornness with which the command gave us orders we could not execute – or only incompletely – as a result many of the shortcomings for which we were not to blame. Such brazen-faced impudence made even Göring speechless. He stomped off, growling as he went.

1:49/2:12

We then return to the air and another great raid on London. In this sequence, Pilot Officer Archie (Edward Fox) attacks a He 111 but is shot-up by the rear-gunner; wheeling around, although trailing smoke, the Spitfire pilot returns to the attack, shooting down the enemy aircraft before taking to his parachute, while the stricken German narrowly misses Buckingham Palace and crashes on Victoria Station. There are various echoes of truth here.

On 16 August 1940, Flight Lieutenant James Brindley Nicolson of 249 Squadron was leading his section of Hurricanes over Southampton when they were jumped by enemy fighters, now believed to have been Me 109s. One of Nicolson's pilots, Pilot Officer Martyn Aurel King, the youngest of the Few at 18, was shot down and killed, and his No 3, Squadron Leader Eric King, was shot-up and crash-landed. Nicolson was hit and set on fire. As 'Nick' was preparing to bale out, he saw an enemy aircraft in front of him, so climbed back into the furnace-like cockpit and opened fire, before finally exiting his machine.

Badly burned and wounded by a cannon shell, Nicolson was awarded Fighter Command's sole Victoria Cross of the Second World War. Also, on 'Battle of Britain Day', a KG76 Do 17, having been attacked by a host of RAF fighters, was abandoned by the crew and did crash on Victoria Station; the pilot, Oberleutnant Robert Zehbe, landed by parachute at Kennington and was so roughly handled by a civilian mob that he subsequently died. The scene concludes with the charming Pilot Officer Archie landing by parachute on a suburban London greenhouse – the young schoolboy of the house (Steve Morley) immediately fetching and offering the pilot one of his father's cigarettes: 'Thanks awfully, old chap!'

1:52/2:12

Again, we return to the troubled Harvey marriage, Colin calling from his Scottish base, enquiring whether Maggie, on duty at a bombed-out operations room in 11 Group, has applied for the posting North he so insists upon. Maggie, however, is totally committed and preoccupied, during what is the climax of the Battle of Britain – which is no time for applying for postings to quieter sectors.

1:54/2:12

Although there is no narrative explaining this, Squadron Leader Harvey's 'Dogtail Squadron' then goes South, to relieve a depleted unit, the next scene cutting to another huge Luftwaffe attack – with Harvey in the thick of it. Again, more superb combat footage, in which Harvey gets a 109 but then becomes a 'flamer', only narrowly escaping from his Spitfire before it blows up.

After more combat and watching Harvey alight safely by parachute in a cornfield, the scene moves to Section Officer Maggie Harvey and her corporal, Seymour (Pat Heywood) giving orders to their flight of WAAFs – and Group Captain Baker appearing to give Maggie the news that Colin has been shot down and badly burned, while assuring her that 'They can do wonders these days', and, ironically, 'We'll get you a posting, so you can be near him.' Beyond doubt, fire was the fighter pilot's greatest fear, the main fuel tank in a Spitfire and Hurricane being immediately in front of the cockpit, underneath and behind the 109 pilot's seat.

The brilliant surgeon Archibald McIndoe and his team at East Grinstead Hospital did indeed 'work wonders' of pioneering plastic surgery on their so-called 'Guinea Pigs', those brave, disfigured, airmen of whose celebrated number Squadron Leader Harvey would soon be among.

1:57/2:12

With Harvey gone, a flight commander takes over the squadron and 'Peter' is elevated to Red Section Leader, his numbers two and three being 'a couple of new lads', two unidentified, anxious-looking and very young, inexperienced pilot officers: 'Stick to me like glue – and keep your eyes open.' Although usually pilots fresh from Operational Training Unit went to squadrons in quieter sectors, this did not always happen. One example springing readily to mind is 19-year-old Pilot Officer Robin Rafter, formerly an army cooperation pilot who answered Fighter Command's call for volunteers.

On 31 August 1940, whereas an experienced and older pilot who converted to Spitfires with Rafter was posted to 13 Group, Rafter arrived at Hornchurch, which was heavily bombed that day, to join 603 Squadron. He would not fly his first operational sortie until 5 September 1940 – when he was almost immediately shot down and wounded in a big engagement with German fighters over Kent. It was not a case, however, of these inexperienced pilots arriving on a squadron and being expected to jump into a Spitfire and Hurricane and 'get one up'.

This was neither practical nor safe for them or anyone else. Every effort was made to at least give 'sprogs' some local flying experience, even at the busiest sectors, before sending them into battle. This scene, therefore, is a little exaggerated but makes a point well – combat experienced pilots were now in short supply.

1:58/2:12

We move again to the underground operations room at 11 Group's Uxbridge HQ, a scene of great activity as we approach the film's climax. On this day, Churchill visited, enquiring of Air Vice-Marshal Park what reserves there were – he was told 'None'. Certainly, all of 11 Group's squadrons would soon be engaged over London, and those of 12 Group's 'Big Wing' along with other reinforcing squadrons from 10 Group, but this comment should not be interpreted as there being no reserves at all. There were, in 10, 12 and 13 Groups.

The next few minutes of aerial footage, supported by Sir William Walton's superb *Battle in the Air*, are so brilliant that they require little comment. By the end of this sequence, with German aircraft falling out of the sky in droves, there is no doubt that the Germans have suffered a major defeat.

BATTLE OF BRITAIN

2:03/2:12

Across the Channel, the Germans' exuberant and over-confident mood of a few weeks earlier has given way to depression. Falke dines in silence at a table with his officers – candles burning in the empty places of those killed or missing. By now, it was clear that the Luftwaffe was incapable, in spite of Göring's boastful assurances, of defeating Fighter Command, and the emphasis of their attack now shifted to the night Blitz on cities – implied by a section of He 111s taking off at dusk.

2:04/2:12

In a London Underground station, sheltering civilians are ecstatic at hearing the BBC's 9 pm news on the radio that 165 German aircraft have been destroyed, against thirty fighters lost with ten pilots safe. The British actually claimed 185 destroyed, the true figure being fifty-six; less, in fact, than on 15 August 1940 (seventy-five) and 18 August 1940 (sixty-nine), but clearly the enemy was unable to continue sustaining such heavy losses indefinitely.

Fighter Command losses were actually better than represented in this scene: twenty-six fighters lost and eleven pilots killed. At the time, everyone sensed that this was the turning point, and rightly so. This day, 15 September 1940, went down in history as 'Battle of Britain Day'.

Interestingly, the radio broadcast concludes by informing listeners that 'Buckingham Palace has again been bombed' – indicating that in this, the 'People's War', everyone was in it together, regardless of rank or status. It was actually to the King and Queen's great credit that they remained in London throughout the Battle of Britain and subsequent Blitz, winning much respect from the people.

2:05/2:12

Now back to Dowding's office and a call from the Air Minister, desperate to confirm the claims for the American press, Dowding's attitude being disinterest in propaganda, responding that 'if we are right, they'll give up; if we're wrong, they'll be in London in a week'. Dowding was a pragmatic man with a sound technical mind, not given to politics, which is the point of this scene, in addition to emphasising the importance of proving to neutral America that Britain was successfully holding and far from a lost cause.

2:06/2:12

We are then returned to Rabbit Squadron's base, with pilots, including Pilot Officer Archie and Sergeant-Pilot Andy, disembarking from a truck at dispersal for readiness. The telephone rings, just to say 'tea's up', causing a keyed-up pilot to vomit outside. Here then, is fear – an attempt to make these fabled knights of the air 'human'.

Unusually, given the intense fighting over recent weeks, there is no enemy air activity. Silence descends over the airfields and operations rooms. Then, we are shown the Germans abandoning invasion preparations, the impression being that the Battle of Britain has been won – and that the daylight fighting simply and abruptly *stopped*.

It did not. Indeed, from 20 September 1940 onwards, the Germans began using fighter-bombers in their high-altitude fighter sweeps, meaning that every incursion had to be intercepted by Fighter Command – a period many RAF pilots remembered as the most exhausting and one during which, arguably, the German fighters, no longer chained to the close escort role, achieved a degree of ascendancy. The two fighter forces, in fact, continued to clash by day until February 1941, when bad weather brought a stop to it.

2:09/2:12

By now, the outcome being clear, Göring is incandescent with rage at his Luftwaffe's failure, ranting from his train at Kesselring and Osterkamp about what he sees as a betrayal. As his train pulls away, Osterkamp gives the normal military salute – while Kesselring raises his right arm in the Nazi style. This scene had, in fact, infuriated General Galland, causing all kinds of arguments, but the film's producers refused to delete the Nazi salute – and Kesselring was, after all, a Party member.

Eventually, when Galland saw the scene he was mollified, as it is a dignified one not treating the Germans as figures of fun – although the general always maintained that the scene was unnecessary. It does, however, show a division in the military between Nazis and those simply fighting for Germany, although it was not the first time that the Nazi salute was used in the film: at 13:05, when Milch and Jeschonnek are seen entering Hitler's office, both give their Führer the Hitlergruß (or Hitler Greeting), as does Baron von Richter at 13:40, when also given an audience with Hitler.

2:10/2:12
The final scene is Dowding's triumph, the battle over, he leaves his office via the terrace, overlooking the formal gardens of Bentley Priory, towards London. Churchill's immortal phrase then appears over a blue sky: 'Never in the field of human conflict has so much been owed by so many to so Few' – leaving us in no doubt whatsoever of the enormity of Fighter Command's achievement.

Finally, the casualty statistics indicate the Finest Hour's human cost, nation by nation, demonstrating that it was a broad multi-national force which kept Britain free in 1940. True, neither side was decisively defeated at the end of this sixteen-week conflict, but Hitler's proposed invasion was off – and, indeed, would never happen. And that, of course, is what the Battle of Britain was all about.

Conclusion

Although upon release in 1969, the American-financed and British-made *Battle of Britain* failed to excite the critics or aspire to investors' box-office expectations, there is no doubt that Fisz and Hamilton tried their best, under often difficult wider circumstances, to tell this *'fantastic* story', and, for the first – and probably last – time, succeeded in telling the big story that the Battle of Britain most certainly is. Unlike previous films lauding individuals, Fisz and Hamilton showed the disparity between the politicians' agendas and Fighter Command's requirements, and touched upon the internal argument over strategy and tactics (more of which later).

The contribution of foreign aircrew was not ignored, and neither was the WAAF. The suffering of civilians, work of the emergency services and Observer Corps (OC), along with the contribution made by radar, is all included. Bravely, the Germans – twelve years after Baker was criticised for *The One That Got Away* – were shown as a brave and skilled adversary, although the portly and flamboyant Luftwaffe chief and Hitler's deputy, Hermann Göring, was, rightly, not portrayed so sympathetically.

To aviation enthusiasts the world over though, what made – and still makes – the film unique was the extensive use of actual aircraft, and brilliantly filmed and edited aerial sequences, married to a superb soundtrack by Sir William Walton and Ron Goodwin. Unlike *Angels One Five* and *Reach for the Sky*, it was also in full technicolour, making it more contemporary to modern audiences.

With regard to how historically accurate the film is, this is a complex question and not an easy one to answer. At the film's press conference, the Battle of Britain ace Squadron Leader James 'Ginger' Lacey, who had worked as a Technical Advisor on the project, claimed that *Battle of Britain* was a catalogue of no less than 193 errors. Some were unavoidable and dictated by the availability of aircraft types and flying kit, for example, but clearly an effort was made to align these things as closely as practically possible with the real deal.

These are, in any case, arguably micro-details which do not affect the overall story-telling and end result, and are noticed only by we enthusiasts. On the macro-stage there are also certain things not quite right, nor correctly interpreted and presented. Without question, though, the producers of *Battle of Britain* have left behind a rich legacy – and have done this big and *'fantastic* story' a great and lasting service.

Chapter 6

First Light

Battle of Britain, without doubt, succeeded in telling the big story, while taking some liberties, by necessity with micro-detail and concluding with the false impression of an abrupt and final defeat. The aerial scenes remain second to none and out-takes are film-makers' standard go-to source for such footage even today. The film was made over fifty years ago now, long before the digital age, and those aerial scenes, using largely real aircraft, are its strength. Today, flying Spitfires and Hurricanes are aplenty, and we still have a number of airworthy Buchon 'Me 109s' in addition to actual Me 109Es – but we have no airworthy Stuka or any of the twin-engine German bombers or fighters.

The other problem is that the numbers of aircraft required would be financially prohibitive. Computer Generated Images (CGI) provide a cost-effective alternative and compromise – but this technology is not yet sufficiently advanced, in my personal view, to be entirely convincing, and seems to be more a matter of providing a 'shock and awe' viewer experience.

So, the issues around using real vintage aircraft are a significant factor in why there has been no other film like *Battle of Britain* – and Guy Hamilton did such a good job in 1969 that another film is probably unnecessary anyway. Furthermore, whether there would be sufficient interest in today's world to make such a project commercially viable is a moot point, and, of course, the British film industry is not what once it was.

Although the Battle of Britain has not featured in British cinema since 1969, the subject has been visited by eastern and central

THE BATTLE OF BRITAIN ON THE BIG SCREEN

European cinema. In 2001, the Czechoslovak director Jan Sverák gave us *Dark Blue World*, a film about free Czech pilots fighting with the RAF. In the film, a Spitfire attacks a train – that scene alone costing more to film than the entire budget for the director's previous movie, the Oscar-winning *Koyla*. The reception to *Dark Blue World* was mixed, but nonetheless it grossed $2.3 million worldwide and won several international awards. In 2018, Polish director David Blair made *303 Squadron* (also released under the titles *Hurricane* and *Mission of Honour*), telling the story of the famous Polish squadron during the Battle of Britain, recreating combat scenes using CGI – the result being more spectacular than convincing. Blair's film only made $7,694,425, less than the reported $8 million budget, and there, for now, the Battle of Britain story in cinema ends. But what about television?

The advent of domestic television saw a burgeoning interest in producing programmes for broadcasting on the 'telly', while concurrently the British film industry declined. In 1988, Derek Robinson's irreverent novel *Piece of Cake*, following the fortunes of 'Hornet Squadron' during the early war period, including the Battle of Britain, appeared on our television screens as a six-part London Weekend Television series.

Like the book itself, reaction to the series was mixed, the highlight for aviation enthusiasts being some thrilling low-level flying by the late, great, Ray Hanna in Spitfire MH434, and the series failed to live up to expectations; 12.1 million watched episode one, but only 9.2 saw the series out. In 1991, the popular British actor Nigel Havers appeared as 'Hugh Fleming', a Battle of Britain Spitfire pilot recovering from horrific burns, in *A Perfect Hero*, loosely based upon a novel, *The Long-Haired Boy* by Christopher Matthew, which had been inspired and informed by Richard Hillary's classic memoir *The Last Enemy*. Unfortunately the series was bland at best and poorly received. Nearly twenty years would pass before the Battle of Britain again appeared dramatized on our home televisions.

FIRST LIGHT

During the Battle of Britain, Geoffrey Harry Augustus Wellum was an 18-year-old Spitfire pilot serving at Biggin Hill with 92 Squadron. Known as 'Boy', Wellum survived intensive action, earning the DFC, became an ace and later fought in the defence of Malta before suffering a breakdown. Although Wellum did not keep a diary, he did make some notes on his experiences while en route to Malta, and retained his personal pilot's flying log book. Thirty-five years after the war, partially as a means of exorcising the violent and traumatic past, he sat down with these aged references and started writing – and didn't stop until his story was committed to paper.

The book, though, would not be published for over twenty years, until produced and distributed by Viking Books, under the evocative title *First Light*, in 2002. The following year, Penguin distributed the title – which leaped onto the best-seller list and catapulted its very modest author into the public eye. The book was lauded as among the most honest, accurate and gripping memoirs to have emerged from the air war, with which assessment I would entirely agree. As the 70th anniversary of the Battle of Britain approached, Wellum's best-seller also inspired film producer and director Matthew Whiteman:

> In a way, this was a dream come true – getting the chance to dramatise *First Light* for BBC Two to mark the 70th anniversary. The book is Geoffrey Wellum's memoir of what it was like to be an 18-year-old Spitfire pilot, thrust into the gut-wrenching, life-and-death struggle of the most violent aerial combat ever. And it also deals with his mental disintegration in eighteen relentless months on the frontline.
>
> This was one film where we had to get not just the emotional thrust right, but also the historical detail. There are a lot of people out there for whom this really matters – and I am one of them. It's not a question of being 'nerdy' – I believe we all know when something

feels right; whether it is in the tone of a performance, costume, props, or whatever else clouds the mind of a director trying to truly evoke the time and place of a story.

The conversations started early about getting Spitfires airborne. But what is it they say? Never work with animals, children ... or, in my case, vintage aircraft! We were discussing a scene in which 'Boy' Wellum, the hero of our story, makes his first flight in a Spitfire, and our actor, Sam Heughan, couldn't wait to get into the air. The problem was how to convince the audience that he was actually at the controls of a Spitfire for the first time, rocketing through the clouds. The big snag was that there was no way we could get Sam airborne in a real Spitfire.

This scene was crucial to the story, appearing little more than ten minutes after the opening of the film. We had to produce a sequence breath-taking enough to make the audience believe that flying the Spitfire was love at first sight for 'Boy'. We had access to a real Spitfire – and the budget for maybe forty-five minutes flying time – but the Spit is a single-seater and there was no question of anybody but a very experienced pilot taking the controls of several million pounds' worth of vintage aeroplane. And we also had access to a replica Spitfire, which could be shoved about on the ground, but had no proper cockpit interior. We soon decided that rather than shooting costly air to air footage, we would use outtakes from the Battle of Britain movie – and enhance it with CGI.

This was a huge task in itself; viewing around fifty hours-worth of unused and unseen material, but it was great that we could give some of this footage the light of day at last! The old movie footage was lovely stuff, but the code letters and numbers on the side of Spits in the movie footage didn't begin to match our real or replica planes. One plane was brown and green, the other brown and grey. And the real one was based at Wycombe Air Park, while our replica was eighty miles away on the drama set outside Dunstable. Bringing the replica down would nuke what little was left of the budget, but if we didn't, Sam could be walking in the rain to the replica on one location, and then climbing into the cockpit (to shoot an authentic start-up sequence) in bright sunshine on the other. It was quite a headache! Somehow, we wangled it in the end. New codes and numbers were put on the replica – and the owner was persuaded to bring his baby to stand side-by-side with the real McCoy.

Then we found a friendly pilot, prepared to have the back cockpit of his two-seater Russian YAK trainer converted to look like a Spitfire cockpit interior. Sam leapt in, surrounded by high definition (HD) mini-cams, and took to the sky with his script taped to the instrument panel. Meantime, our real Spit took off with the pilot delivering 'Boy' Wellum's point of view (by way of a specially designed camera mounting on his flying helmet). When we got into the edit, the whole story came together. By combining Sam walking to the replica Spitfire, the real thing taxiing, Sam in close-up in the back seat of the YAK – and then cutting to his point of view, shot in the real Spit, we got the hair-raising images of 'his' first take-off. Once airborne, we started to inter-cut Sam in the cockpit with flying footage from the Battle of Britain movie.

… And that was the easiest of the flying sequences in the film!

Then we had to work out how to create a full-blooded dogfight, and a nightmare flight in torrential rain over the Channel – during which 'Boy' shoots down a German bomber. Looking back on it all now, I can't believe that we shot the whole drama, including the flying, in just nine days. We couldn't have done it without the orchestration of the first assistant director Chris Carreras, whose experience spans the *Bourne* movies, *United 93*, *Harry Potter* and many other big films. And Chris was dead right when he took one last long look at the schedule just before we began the shoot, and, having considered the weather and all the other infinitely frightening variables, commented dryly: 'We're going to have to be 100 per cent lucky on this one!'

Geoffrey Wellum didn't have time to visit us on set – but before the shoot, as I was scripting, we spent a huge amount of time together. And afterwards, during post-production, Geoff worked very closely with the CGI artists to make sure we got the tracer fire absolutely correct in the air battles. Geoff explained to the CGI folks that real tracer doesn't fly in straight lines – like *Star Wars*; it curves and snakes across the sky, governed by the motion of the aircraft and the air.

Working so closely with Geoffrey has made *First Light* a unique experience both for me as a director and I think, for the audience. The combination of Geoff's expert eye-witness guidance, and actually getting Sam up in the air – instead of in some faked-up studio cockpit – has made the film an incredibly rich experience for everybody. And, I guess, is just about as close as any of us would want to get to the nerve-jangling terrors of air combat, Battle of Britain style.

Creating the tension on the ground, however, was just as important as in the air. I love the waiting scene in dispersal before Geoff's first combat – the tinkling of teaspoons in cups, the rustle of a magazine and flight leader, Brian Kingcome, chewing on his match … And then the sudden shrill ringing of the phone – scramble! Geoff watched these scenes with great interest and said that he felt the film perfectly caught the mood and emotions he felt at the time, both on the ground and in the air. The war literally tore Geoff's emotions apart. If he had not been rested from flying before going back for a second tour of combat, I think he would be the first to say he would no longer be with us now. But at that time – as he reflects in the film – he was desperate to fight on until the bitter end. Geoff still carries a sense of guilt that he survived when so many he knew died. This was the truth for many soldiers – the feeling that they had been taken off the line before the 'job was done', and now were left to watch others die whom they could no longer help or protect.

Geoffrey hates to be called a hero, but his efforts, and that of all those around him seventy years ago, saved us from the terrors of Nazi occupation. I believe that his war – the Battle of Britain, was the key turning point of World War Two. If England had fallen to Germany, Britain could not have been used as the launching point for the D-Day landings and the liberation of Europe. I salute you, Geoff – however reluctant you are to be called a hero. I salute you and all those that fought alongside you. And I'm sure the audience will, too.

Sam Heughan, who more recently found fame in the excellent historical *Outlander* drama series, played Geoffrey Wellum in Whiteman's docudrama:

I have always been particularly interested in World War Two and the Battle of Britain. I guess my first contact was through my grandfather; he took me to the Imperial War Museum etc at an early age, and had himself been called up to fight. I think this influenced my career. I have always been cast in many period productions. My first job leaving drama school was *Island at War*, a big budget ITV drama focusing on the Channel Islands and the German occupation. I did a lot of research; there are a few documentaries and books on the subject.

We filmed on the Isle of Man, which in its own way lent itself to feeling like a small community removed from the mainland. I have also filmed several period documentaries and worked on many stage productions set in that period. I guess what fascinates me is the 'spirit' of the time. It seems to me that the British Isles were isolated and the war brought out the 'British' spirit, one where the people were industrious and collaborative, and learnt to survive. Also, the great tragedy, the bigger cause and the personal struggle.

I guess everything seems more poignant at wartime, time and life is precious, and should not be wasted. It lends itself to a great setting for drama – I guess that's why there are so many fantastic TV and film productions about the war. I also grew up watching the old 1940s movies, which all had a slight glamour, the uniforms and hairstyles. Only in more recent years, though, has the true grim reality of war been more accurately portrayed. To me, productions based on reality or history are a real gift to an actor, as you have so much research and source material.

When I was asked to audition for *First Light*, I read the script and instantly loved it. I did some research, saw that it was a book and read it. I think I finished it in one day; it was SO good, readable and touching. It became the whole casts' handbook. An insight into the world of 92 Squadron and the characters who fought, lived and died alongside each other. The pictures were evocative and the honesty in which Geoffrey revealed his inner most thoughts were a gift. I *had* to do it!

I met with Matthew Whiteman, the Director (also a pilot), and instantly felt that we got on. He has a great wealth of knowledge of the period, and, more than that, it's his passion. Matthew had also already done some great docudramas on the period (*Double X* is fascinating, I'd love to make it into a film), so had written and produced similar projects. In preparation, we talked, and had rehearsals. I re-read Geoffrey's book (the true inspiration and actually all we needed, it's all in there!), plus I wanted to understand more about Spitfires and what it meant to be a pilot. I found a reproduction of the Spitfire Pilot's Notes, an amazing pilot's aid. It was not a dissimilar way to how pilots learnt in those days. I studied the book and learnt all the controls for the cockpit and the start-up sequence. In the scene where I have my eyes closed and am being tested by the aircrew, I actually found I knew exactly where to find the 'Trim, brake, fuel select' etc. I also visited the Imperial War museum and RAF Museum site at Hendon.

However, again, on set it was Matthew who had the eye for everything. Much of the memorabilia in 'Boy Geoffrey's' home were Matthew's personal toys. I think in many ways, the film married Geoffrey's and Matthew's absolute love of flying. I felt that was the strong message in his book. Geoffrey's joy of flight, the freedom of the air. That's why the first flight in a Spitfire is such a large section of film. The ability to escape the dark goings-on of wartime and be free to glide anywhere, must have been amazing. These beautiful machines, being used for foul purposes. I was fortunate that we had a Spitfire to film in. I spent a large amount of time in the cockpit. It was a magical experience. I am six feet and three inches tall, not the perfect height for a pilot! However, once inside it felt very familiar. You can see what a great design it was, the mechanics beautifully engineered. The smell of grease, the ticking of the engine; I fell in love with the aircraft too. And when it fires up!

We also did some flying, an air sequence where I went up and did barrel-rolls, loop the loops etc. What a thrill! Terrifying also, to know these young men were put in charge of these powerful machines – fitted with guns – given comparatively little training, and then left to see if they'd survive ... I remember my first day, watching a Tiger Moth performing some aerial acrobatics and thinking how graceful and brave it was of the pilot. A young man's game, easier if one were less aware of the consequences. How those boys grew up quickly, we wanted the characters to age through the film. Experiencing the terrors and mundane side of the war, fraying our nerves and hopefully doing a little justice to what the real pilots went through. We can only imagine ...

The filming schedule was intense, maybe two-three weeks. I remember it was full on. We banded together as a team of young pilots. We drank beer in the evening, smoked cigarettes. The boredom of a filmset, waiting around, maybe not too dissimilar to the wait before being scrambled? (Without the threat!) The heavier themes of being at war were maybe found through our own personal experiences. We would discuss the book, the war, and I think everyone involved had some connection through relatives involved. As filming came to a close, we all felt deeply upset. We had all invested in it and knew how much we wanted to do Geoffrey a service.

Matthew had been working with Geoffrey for some time but thought it best I didn't meet him until after filming, so as not to try and mimic him, but find my own way into the part. Though Matthew knew him very well, and would answer questions or give me occasional insights into his character, I was desperate to meet Geoffrey and a few weeks after filming completed I did. We met at the RAF Club at Green Park. Geoffrey walked in, full of energy and humour. An amazing character, charming all around him, but yet clearly still living with the effects of living through World War Two. It's still with him and he'll never lose that, I also don't think he wants to. We must not forget.

The reason his book works, is his personal account of a tenacious young man surviving on his natural abilities during a time of great hardship. It doesn't feel dated, as it could apply to any period of history, however it was indeed a time of great change and high deeds. These days, challenges are different. I wouldn't say younger generations are forgetting, but I guess it's getting more distant, and more recent happenings (Afghanistan) are focused on.

I feel deeply honoured to have met Geoffrey Wellum. I'm lucky to have been able to work on this project and hopefully make sure people don't forget what these people did for us. Geoffrey wouldn't say he's a hero, he'd say that he and comrades did what they did just to survive. Yet we should be grateful – and celebrate their deeds.

The Lion Television docudrama *First Light* was broadcast on BBC 2 on 14 September 2010.

THE BATTLE OF BRITAIN ON THE BIG SCREEN

First Light: A Reading

0.00.09: The film begins with a black screen overlaid with white text, dating the film as being '70 years' after the Battle of Britain was fought (2010), in which 'Geoffrey Wellum fought', the film being 'based on his memoir'. So, from the outset we know exactly what this is all about.

Six seconds later the film's first scene shows a Spitfire pilot struggling to fly through heavy rain and thick cloud, in poor visibility. The pilot – 'Gannic Red 2' – is trying to communicate with the Sector Controller, 'Sapper' (echoes of *Angels One Five*) – and at 0.00.36 we get our first glimpse of 'Pilot Officer Geoffrey 'Boy' Wellum' (Sam Heughan). A few seconds later, a German aircraft's radio transmissions cut across the airwaves, and at 0.01.00 a He 111 suddenly appears passing very close overhead, narrowly missing and overtaking the Spitfire. 'Wellum' opens fire, hitting an engine, and the cries of wounded enemy airmen are heard over the radio.

In the book *First Light*, quite some pages are devoted to this sortie, flown in appalling weather in 'mid-January 1941', by Wellum and his friend, Pilot Officer Tommy Lund. Official records can be notoriously inaccurate and incomplete, however, and the 92 Squadron Operations Record Book makes no reference to any such sortie or combat. On 9 January 1941, 92 Squadron moved from Biggin Hill to Manston, a coastal airfield in Kent, which was, in fact, subjected that afternoon to a low-level strafing attack by Me 109s.

The following day, the weather closed in, largely preventing any flying of note throughout the remainder of the month. The daily record of flights, the 'Form 541', indicates, though, that at 12.45 hours on 18 January 1941, Pilot Officer Wellum took off in Spitfire X4779 'to intercept enemy aircraft'. There is no record of another pilot joining the sortie. The daily summary, 'Form 540', states that on that day, 'a section took off at 10.30 hours, but had to land on account of the weather which gradually became worse'. According to the

541, this was Pilot Officer Sherringham and Sergeant Havercroft, who abandoned an attempt to reach Duxford owing to deteriorating weather.

Between 12.15 hours and 14.00 hours, Pilot Officer Sanders and Sergeant Morris flew an uneventful 'standing patrol', but the 540 records that, 'By noon, snow was falling with a high wind. A blizzard was blowing for the rest of the day.' So, when Geoff took off for real that far-off day, the weather was terrible – and, according to the 541, he landed just ten minutes later, the enemy aircraft 'not seen'.

Geoff submitted no combat report that day, or one on any other date that could relate to this incident, although according to the book, a Ju 88 is claimed as damaged. This goes to show what a minefield official records can be for the historian, if relied upon as a sole source. In his book, Geoff describes the terrifying difficulties of trying to locate and return safely to base, which he eventually does, landing half an hour after Tommy Lund, his nerves stretched to breaking point.

Moving on, in a stroke of genius by director Matthew Whiteman, at 0.01.15 we join the real Geoff Wellum in the winter of 2010, then aged 88, at the small harbour at Mullion Cove, near his Cornish home. Using an interview with Geoff as a voiceover, we hear how deeply affected he remains by his wartime flying experiences, and the Battle of Britain especially. It is deeply moving.

Then, we go back in time to 1940, and the car transporting the newly trained fighter pilot, 'Pilot Officer Wellum', to report to his first squadron, 92 – who is using the journey to further study the *Pilot's Notes for Spitfire I & IA* – which he will soon fly in combat. Upon arrival at the airfield, Spitfires pass overhead – eagerly watched by the new replacement pilot – while passes are checked and admission gained.

At 0.03.04, 'Pilot Officer Wellum' reports to the 'Station Adjutant', 'Mac' (Gary Lewis, who also more recently starred in *Outlander*). We learn that the new pilot is 18 years and 9 months old, the following scene, in which the very young and naïve newcomer introduces himself, faithfully follows Geoff's description of this event in the book: 'I'm called Geoff.'

Pilot Officer Wellum joined 92 Squadron at Northolt on 21 May 1940, just before the squadron's operational pilots participated in the air operation covering the Dunkirk evacuation, and actually reported for duty in company with the 20-year-old Pilot Officer Trevor Sidney 'Wimpey' Wade. Both arrived fresh from completing service flying training at Little Rissington, and, as confirmed in the scene to 'Mac', Geoff (and Wade) had yet to fly a Spitfire. Geoff did, however, have an 'above average' rating from 'Rissy' and a willingness to learn – which 92 Squadron's CO, Squadron Leader Roger Bushell, found commendable, while pointing out that time to learn was something in short supply.

Before the Second World War, operational training was provided on squadrons, but in the event of hostilities there was neither time nor personnel available to deliver this. Consequently, in January 1940, three operational training units had been created to convert new pilots to the service aircraft they would fly operationally – but their combined output failed to either meet the demand for replacements during the Battle of France or create a trained reserve. Consequently, some pilots fresh out of service flying training schools did go direct to their fighter squadrons, as did Pilot Officers Wellum and Wade.

For many years it was believed, incidentally, that Geoff was the youngest of the Few, born on 4 August 1921, but more recent research has confirmed that mantle belongs to Pilot Officer Martyn Aurel King of 249 Squadron, who entered the world on 15 October 1921, and was also, sadly, the youngest of the Few to die during the Battle of Britain, on 16 August 1940.

Stepping outside and nervously taking in his new surroundings, at 0.04.35 'Geoff' is surprised by a flight lieutenant wearing the DFC ribbon: 'Who the bloody hell are you?' This is 'Flight Lieutenant Brian Kingcome' (Ben Aldridge), who decides that 'Geoff' must be known as 'Boy'. Having known Group Captain Kingcome personally, he was an extremely good natured and affable chap, the man I knew does not resonate, however, with this stuck up and arrogant portrayal by Aldridge, which is pretty much my only real criticism of the otherwise excellent film.

Nonetheless, Kingcome was a pre-war Cranwellian who had previously flown Spitfires with 65 Squadron before, in reality, becoming commander of 92's 'A' Flight on 27 May 1940 – six days after 'Boy' arrived at Northolt (Kingcome's first aerial victories were recorded on 2 June 1940, his DFC gazetted on 25 October 1940). The pair are joined at 0.04.44 by 'Pilot Officer Tommy Lund' (Alex Robertson). John Wilfred 'Tommy' Lund had read history at Oriel College, Oxford, before the war and was a member of the University Air Squadron, joining the RAFVR in June 1939. Called up in November that year, after training Lund's first operational squadron was 611, with whom he recorded a number of aerial victories during the Battle of Britain; he remained with the squadron until 2 October 1940, when he was posted to 92 Squadron. Although Geoff and Lund became friends on 92, like Kingcome the latter was not yet a member of the squadron when 'Boy' arrived. In the film, 'Tommy' is somewhat more welcoming than 'Brian', and invites the newcomer to join them at the local pub.

0.05.31 sees us join 'Brian' and the boys in a village local, more similar to that famous Biggin Hill fighter pilots' pub, The 'White Hart' at Brasted, with its famous blackboard signed by many wartime fighter pilots, than anything to be found in Northolt. As it happened, after the Dunkirk fighting and flying from Hornchurch, 92 Squadron was based at Pembrey in South Wales (with Kingcome's flight temporarily detached to Bibury in Gloucestershire), not arriving at Biggin Hill until 8 September 1940 – where the squadron remained until 9 January 1941, when it moved to Manston.

Nevertheless, this is a film spanning just an hour and fifteen minutes in which to tell a dramatic story taking place in real time over some months. Consequently, and not untypically, there is no option but to manipulate some of the facts and characters to fit the required timeframe – which is just the way it has to be. Back to the pub, the inexperienced 'Boy' looks in awe at the signatures on the blackboard – but is advised by 'Tommy Lund' not to sign it yet himself, the pleasure being reserved only for 'those who have seen the whites of the enemy's eyes' ... but when 'signed up', it's the one place 'nobody gets rubbed out'.

An interesting piece of dialogue, because living a comparatively normal life one minute, socialising and with decent accommodation and food, then fighting for your life the next is stressful in itself, something I spoke of at length to Polish Spitfire pilot, Flight Lieutenant Kazek Budzik. 'Tommy Lund' also introduces 'Boy' to 'The pilot's friend', a devilish cocktail ultimately leading to our teenage hero vomiting in front of his veteran Flight Commander, 'Brian'.

0.07.33 sees us out on the airfield the following morning, a fortunately much recovered 'Boy' excitedly approaching a waiting Spitfire and its engine fitter, 'Bevington' (Paul Kynman) and younger fitter, 'Davy' (Paul Tinto, also to later appear in *Outlander*). Now, this is quite a moment – to fly a Spitfire, the most superior RAF fighter of the day and every young fighter pilot's dream throughout training. This most significant of events for 'Boy' took place on 26 May 1940 – the day on which, on the wider stage, the decision was made to retire upon and evacuate from Dunkirk, and by which time 92 Squadron's commander, Squadron Leader Bushell, had already been shot down and captured (later to be executed by the Gestapo for his role in the 'Great Escape').

The Spitfire in which this maiden flight is to occur is in its correct camouflage for the period, while wearing the spurious (white, as opposed to the correct medium sea grey) fuselage codes 'AI-H', this being consistent with those used in *Battle of Britain* – giving us a clue that some flying scenes ahead are likely to be clips or out-takes from the 1969 classic. 'Boy's' flying kit and uniform is reasonably accurate, excepting the later pattern goggles and given that his 'Mae West' life jacket would most likely have been painted in the same yellow paint used on the aircraft's fuselage roundel, to assist identification in the water; the Spitfire also has the later, square-lensed, reflector gunsight. Does any of that really matter, though? In the bigger scheme of things, definitely not!

At 0.08.29, 'Boy' sits in the cockpit of a Spitfire for the first time – in itself quite a moment – and as he soaks it all up, is shown the controls and instruments, with a little banter thrown in. And so the moment arrives: 'Boy' is alone in his cockpit and starts the mighty Merlin, watched from a distance by 'old lags' 'Brian' and 'Mac': 'Fresh from the cradle and they're giving him a thousand horsepower and eight machine-guns to play with.' At 01.07.48, we see 'Boy' taxiing for take-off – in what is clearly a completely different Spitfire, a later example with colour scheme, cannon and codes to match.

In his excellent BBC blog on the making of the film (see bibliography), Matthew Whiteman explains that unfortunate and frustrating though this and other obvious continuity breaks are, there was no alternative, considering the limited budget available. Again, does it really matter in telling the overall story and raising awareness of it to an audience not exclusively comprising aviation experts? The main point is what follows: an 18-year-old pilot takes off in the RAF's most advanced fighter of the day – and an immediate love affair begins.

What follows is absolutely superb. The Spitfire in flight (from *Battle of Britain*) cut with footage of an airborne Sam Heughan filmed in the rear seat of a post-war Yak trainer, modified to look like a Spitfire, which adds a realism to the whole scene. As the Spitfire flies above cloud, looping and rolling to classical music, only the stonehearted could fail to be deeply moved. Then, at 0.12.23, Matthew really excels himself by cutting to in-car footage showing the real Geoff Wellum driving along a Cornish road, reflecting on that first Spitfire flight – in '*the* aeroplane'. Cutting back to the Spitfire flying over and around banks of cloud, with Geoff's voice-over, is absolute genius: 'It gets into your soul ... beautiful.' Truly, moving indeed.

On the ground in 'Mac's' office (0.14.33), 'Brian' awaits the new pilot's safe return, while 'Mac' writes a sympathetic letter to a casualty's relatives while hoping that, 'we are not heading for another "Bloody April"', referring to the so-called 'Fokker scourge' of 1917, in which British losses were high. Noteworthy is that 'Brian' has his top tunic button undone – the traditional eccentricity and mark of the fighter pilot. At 0.14.33, 'Boy's' Spitfire returns, 'Brian' and 'Mac' stepping outside to watch his landing – a bumpy one at that and a well-known scene from *Battle of Britain*. At 0.15.23, the Spitfire's propeller stops turning and we see a rather stunned 'Boy' – who has just achieved the ambition of a lifetime – to fly a *Spitfire*: 'Absolutely bloody marvellous!' – and walks off, almost disbelieving of what just happened.

Once more, we are back in the present, joining Squadron Leader Geoff Wellum, as he became, at the bar of his favourite watering hole (0.16.45) at Mullion Cove, explaining how committed he was to becoming a 'good fighter pilot', and the prevalent military situation of summer 1940, emphasising that Europe was dominated by Germany and the 'threat of invasion was very real indeed'.

Back on the airfield (0.17.22), we see an eager 'Boy' trying to persuade 'Mac' that he is ready to fly operationally, but the old sweat is unmoved. 'Tommy Lund' and 'Trevor Wade' (Jordan Bernarde) walking in from their Spitfires and discussing their latest combat, followed by a glum-looking 'Brian' – who enters the dispersal hut and scrubs the name of 'Pilot Officer Appleby' from the squadron's availability board – while 92 Squadron lost no 'Appleby' during the Battle of Britain (which for the film's purposes we must now assume has begun), the squadron did lose fourteen pilots killed in action between 10 July – 31 October 1940.

An interesting exchange regarding the casualty then takes place, 'Boy' asking who he was, 'Brian' answering 'Who was who?' As Flight

FIRST LIGHT

Lieutenant Harry Welford, a Hurricane pilot with 607 Squadron once said to me: 'It was a case of "You heard that so-and-so has bought it?", and that was that. Never mentioned again.' 'Boy' then joins 'Tommy' and friend for a game of chess, to while away the time, while 'Brian' has the sad duty of writing to the casualty's family. It is astonishing to think that this task fell upon the shoulders of flight and squadron commanders often no older than their early-to-mid-twenties.

For the record, after Squadron Leader Bushell's capture, the command of 92 Squadron had passed to a permanently commissioned pre-war officer, Squadron Leader P.J. 'Judy' Sanders, aged 25 – who led the squadron until 20 September 1940, when he landed a shot-up Spitfire doused in aviation fuel – and lit a cigarette with near fatal consequences. His place was taken by another squadron leader without combat experience in modern fighters, C.F. Lister DFC – until he was badly wounded four days later and at which point Brian Kingcome, as the senior flight commander, then led (but was not actually promoted to command) 92 Squadron; he was 23.

At 0.18.50 we join 'Boy' and 'Tommy' cycling to the pub down a quiet country lane, larking about like a couple of schoolboys – which both were, not so very long before. Then, war rears its ugly head abruptly when the pair encounter a parachute hanging from a tree – and a soldier guarding the dead body of an RAF fighter pilot. The casualty is not of 92 Squadron, but nonetheless a sobering experience somewhat lowering the mood and bringing the reality of war into sharp focus. No such event is recorded by Geoff in *First Light* – but nonetheless it is a very effective scene.

Back at the airfield we meet 'Drummond' (Alex Walmann), a newly arrived pilot moving in to share a room with 'Boy' – who arrives, surprised, not having been told (0.20.05). 'Drummond' is a portrayal of Flying Officer John Fraser Drummond DFC, a 22-year-old who had already seen action with 46 Squadron in the ill-fated Norwegian campaign, achieving several aerial victories, for which he had received a very early DFC; Drummond actually joined 92 Squadron at Pembrey, in South Wales, on 5 September 1940. Naturally, 'Boy' is very impressed with his august room-mate, who exhales cigarette smoke in preference to responding to 'Boy's' proffered hand (0.20.14) – clearly having already lost friends, 'Drummond' has no intention of getting close – but the veteran enquires as to whether 'Boy' has been trained on using the new reflector gunsight, and is nonplussed but unsurprised to discover not ...

At 0.20.57 we cut to the airfield and 'Boy' running through cockpit drills, with a bit of banter thrown in, with his Fitter, 'Bevington', and Rigger, 'Davey'. The groundcrews did a less glamorous but essential job, often working out in the open, without cover, for long periods. During the Battle of Britain, 312 RAF personnel were killed on the ground and a further 467 injured, so it is good to see the 'erks' included and not made to look stupid as per *Angels One Five*. 'Brian' is watching, and summons 'Boy' to give him the news the teenage fighter pilot has been eagerly awaiting (0.22.10): 'You are to report to ops at first light.' Quite a moment.

After all the months of training and wondering what combat would be like – 'Boy' will now find out for real, flying as his Flight Commander's wingman. This was common practice, new pilots flying as their section leader's No 2 at first, and – if they survived – increasing personal experience. We then see 'Boy' walking across the airfield, looking deeply thoughtful – and doubtless struggling with mixed emotions – while the real Geoff narrates and describes his feelings at the time, his duty being to stop the Germans bombing Britain's towns and cities. Moving indeed. Understandably it is an anxious night for 'Boy', the camera cutting to his interrupted night's sleep and bedside photo of girlfriend 'Grace' (Tuppence Middleton). Meanwhile, 'Drummond' is also having a restless night, clearly troubled by Norway.

0.24.24 sees us out on the airfield at dawn, the Squadron Transport conveying bleary-eyed pilots to dispersal and their waiting Spitfires. There is no conversation between 'Brian', 'Drummond', 'Tommy' and 'Boy'. Interestingly, all are officers, not a sergeant-pilot anywhere in sight, which is a pity: of the fifty pilots who flew with 92 Squadron during the Battle of Britain, seventeen were sergeants.

A few seconds later and we see 'Mac' chalking 'P/O Wellum' on the availability state board, replacing the casualty 'Appleby'. As the camera pans around the dispersal hut interior, we see pilots resting, trying to sleep, reading, talking, awaiting the call that will send them running to their fighters, and a corporal orderly clerk providing hot tea. It is a faithful recreation of both the interior and scene. The tension is under control but nonetheless palpable. The telephone rings at 0.26.24, answered urgently by 'Brian': 'Squadron scramble!' This is it. Chairs go flying and the pilots race to their Spitfires – 'Angels Twelve, Dover'.

We then cut to the *Battle of Britain* scramble scene, and a confused 'Boy' shoved out of the way and rebuked for getting in the way by 'Wade'. Great footage (0.26.47) of Spitfires' engines starting – with flame spitting from exhaust stubs – classic! Then we have 92 Squadron's pilots, including 'Boy', running to their Spitfires, cleverly mixed with the 1969 scramble footage and out-takes, and at 0.27.08 see a concerned and fatherly 'Bavington' preparing 'Boy' and his Spitfire for immediate take-off. 'Brian' leads them off, convincingly combined with more *Battle of Britain* out-takes, the Spitfires climbing to height in formation. With a colourful expletive, 'Boy' catches his first glimpse of the enemy – a mass formation of fighters and bombers (more *Battle of Britain* out-takes). 'Brian' leads the Spitfires into the attack, giving 'Boy' strict orders to 'Stick with me'.

The subsequent aerial combat scenes are more out-takes but machine-gun fire is exaggerated by laser-like illuminations, for effect. That said, every so many rounds were De Wilde tracer ammunition, which burned brightly upon striking the target and enabled pilots to immediately assess the accuracy of their fire. Inevitably, down come the 109s, which generally enjoyed the height and sun advantage.

THE BATTLE OF BRITAIN ON THE BIG SCREEN

The scenes of mass fighter combat above the clouds, from *Battle of Britain*, are, of course, superb, and we see 'Boy' successfully attack a He 111.

On 8 September 1940, 92 Squadron had arrived at Biggin Hill from Pembrey, finding the tempo of battle totally different to the comparative peace of southern Wales and Gloucestershire. The following day, Squadron Leader Sanders led 92 Squadron – including Pilot Officer Wellum – into battle, intercepting over 100 He 111s, Me 110s and Me 109s. The Spitfires, however, were 'bounced' by the Me 109s of III/JG26, two pilots being wounded while another was shot-up but unharmed. On the afternoon of 11 September 1940, Pilot Officer Wellum was in action again when 92 Squadron intercepted KG26's He 111s and their 100 strong Me 109 escort. Over the Kentish coast, Geoff claimed his first combat success – a He 111 destroyed, so in that respect the film is correct.

After attacking the He 111 (0.29.35), 'Boy' finds himself apparently alone in an empty sky – then spots another He 111 below and dives to engage. Attacking from astern 'Boy' expends his ammunition when suddenly strikes and bangs on his Spitfire indicate that while concentrating on shooting the He 111, an Me 109 has crept up unseen and opened fire on him (0.30.03).

What follows is absolutely superb. 'Boy' is pursued relentlessly by the German fighter, which he cannot shake off. In Geoff's book, this incident has to be the best piece of descriptive writing to ever emerge from the summer of 1940 – and Matthew Whiteman and Sam Heughan perfectly translate this into film. Half a minute later we see 'Boy's Spitfire, trailing a thin stream of white coolant, flying away, alone, and a second later a very shaken – but unscathed – 'Boy' is seen climbing out of his damaged Spitfire back at Biggin Hill. 'Bavington' and 'Davey' rush up – concerned. The damage to the replica Spitfire may be exaggerated in certain respects, but makes the point – the aircraft will have to be sent away for repair but clearly the pilot is lucky to be alive.

FIRST LIGHT

Undeterred, however, 'Boy' demands that another Spitfire is made ready as he needs to be 'ready for the next op', before shakily walking away. Geoff's voice then takes over, explaining that the 109 should, by rights, have killed him – and that having got away with it, he thought he could get away with anything. Without doubt, confidence had grown immeasurably from this traumatic incident. Why did the enemy pilot discontinue his attack, we must wonder? Well, the 109 only had fuel for twenty minutes over London, so that was very likely a factor, and maybe, like 'Boy', the German's ammunition was expended.

Geoff was flying Spitfire R6760 on that occasion; although as there is no record of the machine being damaged that day, we do know that Sergeant Bowen-Morris was shot-up in this aircraft and crash-landed back at base on 27 September 1940. Without a doubt, however, it was an incredibly lucky escape for Geoff and a story superbly told in print and on screen.

At 0.31.34 we join 'Trevor Wade', 'Tommy Lund' and 'Boy' arriving at the country local, where a pensive 'Brian' awaits: '"Boy" – you're a lucky sod … should be cinders now … ' Then, off to the party, the 'Boy' now an accepted, operational, member of 92 Squadron – and, rightly, looks about to burst with pride. Then, as if to completely make 'Boy's' day, 'Grace', who is working near Brasted, appears with friends – the only shadow over the happy reunion is that 'Grace's' brother was killed in France. The couple then join the party, where while the other pilots happily dance the night away, 'Brian' sits alone, still pensive, and chain-smokes. 'Boy' and 'Grace' kiss – as Battle of Britain Hurricane pilot Tony Pickering once told me, 'A big deal in those days, not like it is now!' – and the 'Boy' is clearly beginning to come of age. While the music from the party provides the backing – very effectively – at 0.35.07 the camera switches abruptly to the Air Ministry brass bell outside dispersal being rung, indicating another scramble, and we see more scenes of pilots running to their aircraft and Battle of Britain out-takes and in-cockpit footage of 'Boy', vividly making the point without narrative or further detail of ongoing aerial battles.

00.36.15 sees us watching the three friends 'Wade', 'Tommy' and 'Boy' pushing their bicycles down the country lane towards the pub, discussing loaning a 'fiver' to 'Boy', so he can purchase a 'Ford 10', a 'passion wagon' for his courting of 'Grace'. The car is duly purchased and in the next few minutes we join 'Boy' and 'Grace' on a date in the country.

00.39.35 sees an even more morose 'Brian', the responsibilities of command weighing heavily, wiping the name of another pilot from the availability board. Then 'Brian' and the rest of the pilots arrive in the Squadron Transport, back from another combat, which 'Boy' describes to 'Tommy'. Interestingly, 'Brian' moodily tells 'Boy' to ensure that he 'writes a report' about the 'Junkers' he has destroyed, from which there were no parachutes. Noteworthily, 'Boy', now a veteran himself, is wearing his top button undone.

Back in his room (0.40.12) we see 'Boy' telling 'Drummond' that this 'Junkers 88' was his 'first confirmed kill', which, as we have seen was actually a He 111. Aerial victories were categorised 'destroyed', when there was no doubt and witnessed; 'probably destroyed', when the final outcome was either not witnessed or uncertain but likely to have been destroyed, or 'damaged', suggesting that 'Boy's' previous claim was accredited as one or the other of the second and third categories.

In reality, during the Battle of Britain, Geoff destroyed the He 111 on 11 September 1940, then shared the destruction of a Ju 88 on 27 September. After the Battle's official conclusion, during November 1940 he damaged three Me 109s, and claimed more victories the following year, over France. The quiet 'Drummond' offers 'congratulations', the pair then finding common ground in the poetry of Kipling, specifically (and most appropriately) 'Tommy' (1890), in which the poet addresses the ordinary soldier sympathetically. After this, the clearly internally traumatised 'Drummond' opens up a bit, clearly a deep thinker otherwise destined for 'a quiet life', if not for a family tradition in the military – and, of course, the war. This is actually a moving scene. Countless young men found their lives not their own, their destiny dictated by greater events, and would certainly not have been in uniform – or even flying – if not for the war.

Back in the pub, 0.43.17, we at last see a sergeant-pilot, as 'Brian', in better spirits, holds court with his pilots of his 92 Squadron. It is unlikely that officers and NCOs would have used the same pub however, with ranks being segregated on the ground and having their respective messes and other places to socialise. As Wing Commander George Unwin, a flight sergeant in the Battle of Britain, said of his revered CO, Squadron Leader Brian Lane, 'We were as one in the air and frequently flew together, but were segregated by rank on the ground, so never socialised.' Moving on, while the pilots drinking, joking and signing ribald songs 'Drummond' sits alone, smoking, drinking – and brooding – before his leaving is only noticed by 'Boy'.

0.44.31 and we are back in the air, in action again, with Geoff narrating: 'We fought at first light, evening, dusk … it was a relentless ritual … all that mattered was fighting the war and surviving to fight the next day.' Moving indeed. At 0.45.17 we are back on the airfield ('Mae Wests' now painted yellow), joining the pilots of 92 Squadron, just landed after combat, outside dispersal.

Again, the dressing is excellent, the Lloyd Loom chairs and chess board with Spitfire parked beyond, reminiscent of a well-known photograph taken at Kirton-in-Lindsay during the Battle of Britain of 222 Squadron pilots. All are emotionally and physically exhausted – and feeling the loss of 'Drummond', who 'collided with another Spit'. This was the case. Sadly, on 10 October 1940, Flying Officer Drummond and Pilot Officer Dennis Williams collided while attacking a Do 17 over Tangmere. Both were killed, Drummond's parachute failing to open, the 21-year-old pilot dying in the arms of a priest who administered the last rites – nine days before his

22nd birthday. As 'Tommy Lund' rightly says, 'What a waste.' That night, the German bombing continues, the rumble and flash of anti-aircraft fire and exploding bombs lighting up 'Boy's' room – his room-mate now departed, his bed empty.

Next, we are outside dispersal again, pilots and groundcrew whiling away the quiet hours playing cricket – not uncommon in reality, and archery was also encouraged on some airfields. Unfortunately 'Brian' is plucked out of the game by 'Mac's' requirement for his presence, followed by the squadron taking off again (0.47.26), this being another Battle of Britain out-take, showing Spitfires scrambling from Hawkinge, near Folkestone, now home to the Kent Battle of Britain Museum and close-by the National Memorial to the Few.

A shot of the sky is overlaid by verbal radio transmissions of pilots in combat – very effective and atmospheric again – and more out-takes. 'Brian', however, is shot down (0.48.00), his Spitfire crashing and disintegrating on a Kentish beach. Poignantly, we then see his name being scrubbed from the blackboard. With their popular commander missing, a desolate mood settles over the airfield and 92 Squadron, 'Boy' particularly despairing at the apparent loss of his leader and hero. Geoff then resumes narration: 'Brian Kingcome *was* 92 Squadron … a *real* fighter pilot.' Concerned about 'Boy', 'Mac' checks on him (0.49.38), enquiring when he last had leave – having managed to get him a forty-eight-hour pass.

'Boy' then goes home, back to his parents, finding his room – that of a schoolboy's, cluttered with sporting kit and model aircraft – exactly as he left it. But now, of course, after his experiences in the service, killing and watching others die – violently – he is much-changed. His father (Richard Walsh), himself a First World War veteran, understands when, as Geoff explains, unable to adjust or comprehend, 'Boy' leaves early.

At 0.53.30, 'Boy' and 'Grace' are reunited, a date in the country, during which 'Boy' shares his despair and 'Brian's' apparent death in action and his difficulty being at home – breaking down. But then, a silver cloud, and Boy's love-life takes a very definite upturn – although that is not something we need to analyse!

0.55.28 and 'Boy' returns in his Ford 10 to the airfield – and is both astonished and delighted in equal measure to see 'Brian' hobble out of his office on crutches! 'Brian' explains that he 'baled out' near Dover. Frequently, pilots took to the silk, coming down in remote areas, miles from their base, it then taking hours for communications and administration to catch up, so it was not unusual for pilots to turn up safely in due course. In reality, on 15 October 1940, Flight Lieutenant Kingcome had led the squadron into action against fifty Me 109s. Afterwards, while returning to Biggin Hill, Kingcome, by his own admission, was 'breathtakingly stupid', having become over-confident, and prepared to practise a forced-landing on a dead engine. Throttled back, he had become a sitting duck for a marauding Me 109. Wounded in the leg, he baled out and was subsequently admitted to the Royal Hospital, Chatham. Although his fate was known at the time, Kingcome did not return to duty until his wounds had healed six weeks later. By that time, another squadron commander had rapidly come and gone, 92 Squadron then being led, from 26 October 1940 onwards, by Squadron Leader Johnny Kent, a tough Canadian.

'Mac' then appears at 0.56.06, handing 'Boy' an envelope with the other pilots looking on, clearly aware of the content – a somewhat embarrassed and surprised 'Boy' has been awarded the 'DF bloody C', or, according to 'Wade', 'Disastrous Fucking Clown'! 'Brian', however, concludes that it is a 'Good show'. In reality, Geoff's (well-earned) DFC was not awarded until August 1941.

At 0.56.52 we are back at the beginning, the bad weather patrol with 'Tommy Lund', 'Boy' seen back at base and in the Squadron Transport returning to dispersal after landing. Geoff then explains how by that time, which we know was January 1941, he and the other fellows all had 'combat fatigue' – without realising it. They were exhausted. Which was dangerous. In horrendously heavy rain the pilots then await events at readiness in their hut, nerves strained when the telephone rings – a routine administration matter, much relief – this scene flashing back to just before 'Boy' and 'Tommy' took off on that convoy patrol. 'Brian' breaks the news: 'Tommy' and 'Boy' are to fly the sortie. Neither are impressed; the others are relieved.

Kitted up, 'Tommy' is cheerful – 'Off we go'. Again, the paternal 'Bavington' is at hand to kit up his pilot, who takes off into horrendous weather and uncertainty. The pair of Spitfires are seen flying in a thunderous, rain-lashed, sky, visibility virtually zero and radio signal poor. Horrendous conditions. The Spitfire pair lose each other in cloud while the Controller reports a 'bandit' ahead.

At 1.03.52 we see the Ju 88, which, as we already know, 'Boy' nearly collides with and destroys. This is a duplication of what we have already seen, but now we follow 'Boy' trying to find home. Meanwhile, 'Tommy' has landed, explaining to 'Brian' that he has no idea what happened to 'Boy', because his radio had failed – receiving a rebuke because that being so, without communications the pilot should have turned back, which, in fact, 'Tommy' had.

The scene returns to 'Boy's' lonely and dangerous flight home in virtually zero visibility and rapidly expiring fuel reserves. He is overdue and 92 Squadron is concerned. Then, against the odds, 'Boy' returns to base – absolutely exhausted – explaining that he has shot down a Ju 88 and aggressively challenging 'Tommy's' whereabouts. This is the culmination, apparently, of months of danger and stress – but, as 'Brian' tells 'Boy' – 'You've got nothing to prove, Geoff.'

We then jump in time to August 1941 (0.01.18). More aerial combat scenes. Geoff explaining how busy the summer of 1941 was, and by which time he was an 'automoton'. 'Mac' counts the Spitfires back. 'Boy' returns, the paternal 'Bavington' gravely concerned about his pilot – and a great shot as 'Boy' slides back the hood and opens the cockpit door, very similar to a well-known press photograph of the great ace 'Sailor' Malan. In the pilots' hut, 'Boy' scrubs 'Tommy Lund's' name from the board, while Geoff explains that he was a 'Lovely chap and a very dear friend'.

Pilot Officer Lund was killed on 2 October 1941, when his section of three Spitfires were all shot down over the Channel while returning from an operation over France – he was 22, and remains missing.

By that time, in reality Pilot Officer Wellum had already left 92 Squadron, posted away on 'rest' in September 1941 as an instructor at a Spitfire Operational Training Unit. Only one thing for it in the film – as was so often the case – as 'Brian' says, get 'arseholed'. And so off to the pub to get drunk – and try to forget. 'Boy', however, sits in his car, in tears, deeply affected, while Geoff explains that upon reflection by that time he had reached the end of his tether.

01.11.25 sees a Spitfire pass overhead – 'Boy' returning from a sortie – and we then cut to 'Brian' and he walking together along the perimeter track. It is all over. 'Brian' breaks the news that 'Boy' is being posted away from 92 Squadron – devastating news, no matter how exhausted 'Boy' felt, because 92 Squadron had by then become both home and family. Geoff explains that at the time he felt that was it, he had reached the pinnacle of his achievement, the high-spot experience of his life – which it may very well have been for so many. Time to say goodbye, with a fond farewell from 'Mac' – whose respect the young pilot has earned. 'Boy' walks over to poignantly bid his Spitfire farewell, while Geoff asks whether it was 'worth it'. 'Mac' is then looking at the White Hart's signature-smothered blackboard with 'Wade', who remarks that 'Boy' never did get to sign it.

Finally, we see Geoff himself looking out over Mullion Cove in more peaceful times. The journey is over, with Sam Heughan reading a flying poem, *Under the Shadow of Wings*, while the Spitfire is looping and rolling over cloud, before the aircraft flies off into the distance. A wartime portrait of Geoff with a caption explains how he survived the war, married Grace, but suffered a breakdown in Malta during 1942. Similarly, we are told that Brian Kingcome survived the war to be invalided out of the RAF in 1954, retiring as a group captain, but died in 1994. We are not told what happened to Trevor

'Wimpey' Wade – who survived the war but was later killed as a test pilot in 1951. And so the film ends – more of which below.

Conclusion

Personally, I thought *First Light* excellent. The clever cutting between past and present, with Geoffrey Wellum appearing gazing out to sea and, in parts, providing a moving voiceover, produced, in my opinion, a very powerful programme indeed. Matthew Whiteman undoubtedly achieved as accurate and moving a tribute to 92 Squadron and Geoffrey Wellum as possible. Sam Heughan was perfectly cast in the part – and left a lasting impression.

Suffice it to say, *First Light* has raised the bar and set an entirely new standard. There is no doubt, then, that Matthew and his team achieved the tribute they had intended. If anyone wants to get a feel of what life must have been like as a young RAF fighter pilot during the Battle of Britain – watch and read *First Light*.

Sadly, Squadron Leader Geoffrey Wellum DFC left us in 2018, aged 96. In the winter of his life, Geoffrey had become an enthusiastic and perfect ambassador for the Few, and we often spoke of why he believed so passionately in ensuring that the Battle of Britain is remembered. We are fortunate indeed that Geoffrey left us his memoir – and that Matthew Whiteman made a docudrama of it.

Chapter 7

'Last Light?'

In this study, we have seen how the Battle of Britain has been represented over the years, through wartime newsreels, official 'shorts' and feature films, and beyond into post-war Britain. In this investigation we have considered the factors influencing production and representation, including propaganda, the state of society at a given time, financial constraints, and how the film industry became dominated not by Pinewood or Denham, but by Hollywood.

We have seen how long it took for anyone to attempt to tell the overall story, and that, to date, it has only been done once through Guy Hamilton's 1969 epic *Battle of Britain* – which has stood the test of time.

Although Matthew Whiteman's BBC2 docudrama *First Light*, based upon Geoff Wellum's best-selling memoir, was made for television and not cinema, which is really the focus of this book, it has been included here because whereas – so far as this historian is concerned – *Battle of Britain* remains the highpoint of the subject in cinema, *First Light* occupies that position on British television.

Whether we will ever see anything of the standard of *Battle of Britain* or *First Light* again remains to be seen – I am, it must be said, doubtful, mainly because CGI is simply not convincing enough and the vintage aircraft required are unavailable – and even if they were, the cost would doubtless be prohibitive, certainly for a British film-maker. As I write, Steven Spielberg and Tom Hanks are in the UK, filming their new mini-series *Masters of the Air*, concerning the American Eighth Air Force's daylight strategic bombing campaign, which I am sure will be a huge success. The problem is that the demise of the British film industry and domination by Hollywood means that the Battle of Britain simply does not resonate with, or inspire, Americans to see an investment in a movie featuring the great aerial battle.

There was talk several years ago of the Hollywood star Tom Cruise making a film based upon the life of Billy Fiske – the first American volunteer to die in the Battle of Britain – but so far this has not come to fruition; from what I read about the proposed plot, in which Fiske – who recorded one victory before his death in action – virtually wins the Battle of Britain single-handedly, it is probably a good job! So, it may well be that in terms of the Battle of Britain on screen, *First Light* actually represents a setting sun, and may actually in that respect be 'Last Light'.

Some may wonder why maintaining the currency of the Battle of Britain on film is important. Anyone wishing to know the answer needs only consider these lines written by Geoffrey Wellum:

> People say to me 'How do you remember these things?' How do you expect me to forget? You can't. I can remember it vividly, see things, see people, see aeroplanes. The experiences of being a Spitfire fighter pilot in the Battle of Britain stay with you forever. You can't do anything about it.
>
> Nobody wants a medal or a thank you – but it would be nice to be remembered, because then you must think of all of us, and not just those of us who survived.
>
> I asked myself 'Was it worth it?' All those young men I fought and flew with, all those chaps no longer with us. I asked myself that question and I can't answer it. I suppose it must have been. I am still struggling.

Acknowledgements

I would like to thank Matthew Whiteman and Sam Heughan for their contributions regarding *First Light*, provided initially for my book *The Final Few* of 2005.

As always, Martin Mace and the Pen & Sword team were a pleasure to work with.

Bibliography

Films mentioned in the text

Triumph Des Willens ('Triumph of the Will'), directed by Leni Riefenstahl (Universum Film AG, 1935).
Things to Come, directed by William Cameron Menzies (London Films, 1936).
The Gap, directed by Donald Carter (Gaumont-British Instructional, 1937).
The Warning, edited by R.Q. McNaughton (British National Films, 1939).
The Lion Has Wings, directed by Michael Powell, Adrian Brunel and Brian Desmond Hurst (London Films 1939).
Dangerous Moonlight, directed by Brian Desmond Hurst (RKO, 1941).
Target for Tonight, directed by Harry Watt (Crown Film Unit, 1941).
A Yank in the RAF, directed by Henry King (20th Century-Fox, 1941).
Mrs Miniver, directed by William Wyle (Metro-Goldwyn-Mayer, 1942).
The First of the Few, directed by Leslie Howard (British Aviation Pictures, 1942).
The Flemish Farm, directed by Jeffrey Dell (Two Cities Films, 1943).
Tawny Pipit, directed by Bernard Miles and Charles Saunders (General Film Distributors, 1944).
The Way to the Stars, directed by Anthony Asquith (Two Cities Films, 1945).
Twelve O'Clock High, directed by Henry King (20th Century-Fox, 1949).

BIBLIOGRAPHY

Angels One Five, directed by George More O'Farrall (Templar Film Studios, 1952).

Malta Story, directed by Brian Desmond Hurst (Theta Film Productions, 1953).

Albert RN, directed by Lewis Gilbert (Angel Productions, 1953).

The Sea Shall Not Have Them, directed by Lewis Gilbert, (Angel Productions, 1954).

The Purple Plain, directed by Robert Parrish (Two Cities Films, 1954).

The Dam Busters, directed by Michael Anderson (Associated British Picture Corporation, 1955).

Reach for the Sky, directed by Lewis Gilbert (The Rank Organisation, 1956).

The One That Got Away, directed by Roy Ward Baker (Julian Wintle Productions, 1957).

Battle of Britain, directed by Guy Hamilton (Spitfire Productions, 1969).

Dark Blue World, directed by Jan Sverák (Sony Pictures, 2001).

303 Squadron, directed by Denis Delic (Art Fiction, 2018).

Television

A Piece of Cake, directed by Ian Toynton (Holmes Associates, 1988).

A Perfect Hero, directed by James Cellan Jones (Havahall Pictures, 1991).

First Light, directed by Matthew Whiteman (Lion Television, 2010).

Websites

http://www.IMDb.com: The International Movie Database, an essential and comprehensive online database providing a host of information concerning films, television programme and other media.

http://www.screenonline.org.uk: 'The definitive guide to Britain's film and TV industry' by the British Film Institute.

http://www.impdb.org: The International Movie Plane Database, identifying aircraft used in films, television and video games.

https://www.bbc.co.uk/blogs/tv/2010/09/first-light-dramatising-there.shtml: Excellent blog by director Matthew Whiteman concerning *First Light*.

Books and Articles

Addison, P. and Crang, J. (eds), *The Burning Blue: A New History of the Battle of Britain*, Pimlico, London, 2000

Anon (Polish Air Force Association in Great Britain), *Destiny Can Wait: The Polish Air Force in the Second World War*, William Heinemann Ltd, London, 1949

Brickhill, P., *Reach for the Sky: The Story of Douglas Bader DSO DFC*, Collins, London, 1954

Burt, K. and Leasor, J., *The One That Got Away*, Collins/Michael Joseph, London, 1956

Calder, A., *The People's War: Britain 1939–45*, Jonathan Cape Ltd, London, 1969

_____, *The Myth of the Blitz*, Pimlico, London, 2008

Campion, G., *The Good Fight: Battle of Britain Propaganda and the Few*, Palgrave Macmillan, Basingstoke, 2010

_____, *The Battle of Britain 1945-1965: The Air Ministry and the Few*, Palgrave Macmillan, Basingstoke, 2015

Clapson, M., *The Routledge Companion to Britain in the Twentieth Century*, Routledge, London, 2009

Clarke, J., *War Films*, Virgin Film, London, 2006

Dando-Collins, S., *The Hero Maker: A Biography of Paul Brickhill*, Penguin Random House Australia Pty Ltd, North Sydney NSW, 2016

Donnelly, M., *Britain in the Second World War*, Routledge, London, 1999

BIBLIOGRAPHY

Foreman, J., *RAF Fighter Command Victory Claims of World War Two, Part One 1939–1940*, Red Kite, Walton-on-Thames, 2003

Franks, N.L.R., *RAF Fighter Command Losses of the Second World War, Volume 1, Operational Losses: Aircraft and Crews, 1939–41*, Midland, Hersham, 2008

Fyne, R., *The Hollywood Propaganda of World War II*, Scarecrow Press Inc., Maryland, 1997

Galland, General A., *The First and the Last*, Cerberus Publishing, Bristol, 2001

Hurd, G. (ed), *National Fictions: World War Two in British Films and Television*, BFI Publishing, London, 1984

Kallis, A.A., *Nazi Propaganda and the Second World War*, Palgrave Macmillan, London, 2008

Kellett, Wg Cdr R.G., Memoirs, unpublished, 1978

Kingcome, Grp Capt B.F.A., *A Willingness to Die*, Tempus, Stroud, 1999

MacKenzie, A.J., *Propaganda Boom*, The Right Book Club, London, 1938

MacKenzie, S.P., *The Battle of Britain on Screen: 'The Few' in British Film and Television Drama*, Edinburgh University Press, Edinburgh, 2007

Mitchell, G., et al, *R.J. Mitchell, World-Famous Aircraft Designer: Schooldays to Spitfire*, Nelson and Saunders Publishers, Olney, 1986

More, K., *More or Less*, Hodder and Stoughton, London, 1974

Mosley, L., *Battle of Britain*, Pan Books, London, 1969

O'Shaughnessy, N.J., *Politics and Propaganda: Weapons of Mass Seduction*, Manchester University Press, Manchester, 2004

Overy, R., *The Battle*, Penguin, London, 2000

Ponting, C., *1940: Myth & Reality*, Hamish Hamilton Ltd, London, 1990

Popple, T., 'Angels-One-Five', *After the Battle* 30 (1980), pp. 11-18

_____, 'Reach for the Sky', *After the Battle* 35 (1982), pp. 38-53

Ramsey, W. (Ed), *The Blitz Then & Now: Volume 1*, Battle of Britain Prints International Ltd, London, 1987

Rudhall, R., *Battle of Britain: The Movie*, Ramrod Publications, Worcester, 1999

Sarkar, D., *The Few: The Battle of Britain in the Words of the Pilots*, Amberley Publishing, Stroud, 2009

_____, *Douglas Bader*, Amberley Publishing, Stroud, 2013

_____, *The Final Few: The Last Surviving Pilots of the Battle of Britain Tell Their Stories*, Amberley Publishing, Stroud, 2015

_____, *The Bader Wings: The Duxford Wings Controversy*, Pen & Sword Ltd, Barnsley, 2021

_____, *Sailor' Malan: Freedom Fighter, the Inspirational Story of a Fighter Ace*, Pen & Sword Ltd, Barnsley, 2021

Smith, M., *Britain and 1940: History, Myth and Popular Memory*, Routledge, London, 2000

Truesdale, D., and Esler Smith, A., *Theirs is the Glory: Arnhem, Hurst and Conflict on Film*, Helion and Company, Solihull, 2016

Turner, J.F., *The Bader Tapes*, The Kensal Press, Bourne End, 1986

Welch, D., *Nazi Propaganda*, first edition, Barnes and Noble, New Jersey, 1983

_____, *Propaganda and the German Cinema 1933–45*, second edition, IB Taurus and Co. Ltd., London, 2001

Wellum, G.H.A., *First Light*, Viking Books, London, 2002

Other Books by Dilip Sarkar

Spitfire Squadron: No 19 Squadron at War, 1939–41
The Invisible Thread: A Spitfire's Tale
Through Peril to the Stars: RAF Fighter Pilots Who Failed to Return, 1939–45
Angriff Westland: Three Battle of Britain Air Raids Through the Looking Glass
A Few of the Many: Air War 1939–45, A Kaleidoscope of Memories
Bader's Tangmere Spitfires: The Untold Story, 1941
Bader's Duxford Fighters: The Big Wing Controversy
Missing in Action: Resting in Peace?
Guards VC: Blitzkrieg 1940
Battle of Britain: The Photographic Kaleidoscope, Volumes I-IV
Fighter Pilot: The Photographic Kaleidoscope
Group Captain Sir Douglas Bader: An Inspiration in Photographs
Johnnie Johnson: Spitfire Top Gun, Part I
Johnnie Johnson: Spitfire Top Gun, Part II
Battle of Britain: Last Look Back
Spitfire! Courage & Sacrifice
Spitfire Voices: Heroes Remember
The Battle of Powick Bridge: Ambush a Fore-thought
Duxford 1940: A Battle of Britain Base at War
The Few: The Battle of Britain in the Words of the Pilots
Spitfire Manual 1940
The Sinking of HMS Royal Oak In the Words of the Survivors (re-print of Hearts of Oak)

THE BATTLE OF BRITAIN ON THE BIG SCREEN

The Last of the Few: Eighteen Battle of Britain Pilots Tell Their Extraordinary Stories
Hearts of Oak: The Human Tragedy of HMS Royal Oak
Spitfire Voices: Life as a Spitfire Pilot in the Words of the Veterans
How the Spitfire Won the Battle of Britain
Spitfire Ace of Aces: The True Wartime Story of Johnnie Johnson
Douglas Bader
Fighter Ace: The Extraordinary Life of Douglas Bader, Battle of Britain Hero (re-print of above)
Spitfire: The Photographic Biography
Hurricane Manual 1940
River Pike
The Final Few: The Last Surviving Pilots of the Battle of Britain Tell Their Stories
Arnhem 1944: The Human Tragedy of the Bridge Too Far
Spitfire! The Full Story of a Unique Battle of Britain Fighter Squadron
Battle of Britain 1940: The Finest Hour's Human Cost
Letters from The Few: Unique Memories of the Battle of Britain
Johnnie Johnson's 1942 Diary: The War Diary of the Spitfire Ace of Aces
Johnnie Johnson's Great Adventure: The Spitfire Ace of Ace's Last Look Back
Sailor Malan – Freedom Fighter: The Inspirational Story of a Spitfire Ace
Spitfire Ace of Aces – The Album: The Photographs of Johnnie Johnson
The Real Spitfire Pilot
The Real Hurricane Pilot
Bader's Big Wing Controversy: Duxford 1940.
Bader's Spitfire Wing: Tangmere 1941

Index

10 Group, 8, 152, 178
11 Group, 8, 72, 77, 79, 93, 95, 101, 110–13, 124–5, 131, 152, 157–8, 161, 163–5, 168, 170, 174, 177–8
12 Group, 8, 72, 108, 110–12, 118, 124, 128, 131–3, 152, 161, 163–5, 174, 178
19 Squadron, 21, 32, 92, 94, 108–109, 123–6, 163, 165
56 Squadron, 19, 37, 77, 93, 171
74 Squadron, 19, 25, 160
92 Squadron, 115, 125, 185, 191, 194, 196–8, 200–201, 203–205, 207–12
149 Squadron, 18, 24
242 Squadron, 86, 109–11, 118, 126, 129–31, 134–5, 164–5, 170
302 Squadron, 161
616 Squadron, 72, 133, 135, 138

Air Ministry, 2, 9–10, 15–16, 27, 35–6, 39, 44, 52, 59–62, 66, 69, 77, 99, 108–109, 112, 123, 146, 166, 205
America, 14, 18, 38–9, 41–2, 44, 54, 70, 72, 74, 114, 143, 148, 161, 180
Angels One Five, 67, 75, 77–8, 80, 99, 105–107, 142, 182, 194, 202
Archie, Pilot Officer, 176, 180
Attlee, Clement, 114
Avro,
    Anson, 19
    Lancaster, 23, 66

Bader, Squadron Leader Douglas, 86, 105, 107–11, 113–41, 145, 161, 164–6, 170, 174

Baker, Roy Ward, 142
Baldwin, Stanley, 3–4
Bartley, Flight Lieutenant Tony, 47–8
Beachy Head, 67, 96, 137, 156
Belgium, 34, 71, 146
Bentley Priory, 8, 151, 160, 164, 173, 181
Berlin, 26, 147, 167
Biggin Hill, 44, 76, 94, 125, 136, 158, 185, 194, 197, 204, 209
Bletchley Park, 33
Boothman, Flight Lieutenant J.N., 9, 56
Boret, Group Captain Jack, 134
Brickhill, Paul, 115–17, 123, 133, 137
Bristol,
    Bulldog, 9, 22, 118, 121
Brook, Lyndon, 118, 120
Brunel, Adrian, 17
Burt, Kendal, 142
Burton, Squadron Leader H.F. 'Billy', 135
Burton, Richard, 117
Bushell, Squadron Leader Roger, 125, 196, 198, 201

Calder, Angus, 1, 143
Camm, Sydney, 9, 69
Capra, Frank, 41, 72–3
Chamberlain, Neville, 23–4, 35
Churchill, Winston, 4, 16, 18, 34, 35, 42, 44–6, 59, 68, 78, 104, 114, 147, 149, 152, 165, 167, 178, 181
Cinema, 12–16, 27, 31, 36, 43, 69–70, 74, 105, 143, 158–9, 183–4, 213

Cranwell, RAF, 82, 86, 91, 108–109, 118, 120, 123, 127–8, 135, 197
Crowley-Milling, Air Marshal Sir Denis, 109, 117–18, 126, 128, 133, 135, 139
Currant, Squadron Leader Christopher 'Bunny', 44, 46, 67

Dalrymple, Ian, 17
Dangerous Moonlight, 17, 37–8, 71
Day, Group Captain Harry, 114, 117–18, 120–1, 123
Dornier,
  Do 17, 10, 68, 97, 109, 147, 171, 176, 207
Douglas, Air Chief Marshal Sholto, 44, 112, 165–6
Dover, 1, 5, 19, 79–80, 102, 151, 156, 209
Dowding, Air Chief Marshal Sir Hugh, 6–7, 9–10, 27, 60–1, 111–12, 118, 129, 146, 150–2, 155, 159–66, 168, 172–4, 179–81
Drummond, Dlying Officer John Fraser, 201–202, 206–207
Dundas, Group Captain Sir Hugh 'Cocky', 133, 135, 137, 139
Duxford, 32, 44, 69, 86, 92, 108–111, 118, 123–4, 130–3, 161–2, 165, 195
Dynamo, Operation, 92, 124

Emmett, E.V.H., 15, 17, 19–27, 29–31

First Light, vi, 185, 188, 190, 193–4, 201, 212–14
First World War, 1, 5, 13–14, 17, 26, 49–50, 60, 208
Fisz, Ben, 143, 181–2
Focke-Wulf,
  Condor, 29–30
France, 11, 166, 32, 34–5, 71, 78, 109, 113, 124, 127–8, 136–7, 139, 144–8, 150–1, 162, 174, 196, 205–206, 211

Germany, 4–5, 11, 13–14, 16, 18, 20–3, 25, 31–2, 34–5, 40, 42–3, 45, 57–9, 73, 124, 142, 147, 149, 181, 189, 200
Gillen, Fight Lieutenant, 46–8
Goebbels, Dr Josef, 14, 42, 46
Göring, Herman, 46, 167–8, 175, 179–80, 182
Gossage, John, 75–6
Gracie, Flight Lieutenant 'Jumbo', 37
Guernica, 6–7, 11–12, 15–16, 34, 64

Hamilton, Guy, 143–4, 181–3, 213
Harris, Squadron Leader Paul, 18
Harvey, Section Officer Maggie, 153, 157–60, 166, 176–7
Hawker,
  Fury, 11, 22, 29
  Hurricane, 6, 9–12, 16, 19, 23, 28, 37–8, 69, 71, 74, 76–7, 79–84, 89–97, 101–103, 105, 108–109, 111, 119, 124, 126–8, 131–2, 137, 144–6, 149, 152, 154, 159, 162, 169, 171, 174–8, 183, 201, 205
Heinkel,
  He 51, 7, 26, 30
  He 111, 10, 30, 37–8, 44, 67–8, 102, 109–11, 126, 147, 156, 159–60, 174, 176, 179, 194, 204, 206
Holden, Squadron Leader Ken, 137
Hollywood, 14, 40, 43, 72, 74, 143, 213–14
Hornchurch, RAF, 17, 19, 25, 76, 124, 157, 178, 197
House of Commons, 4, 54
Howard, Leslie, 43–5, 47–8, 64, 70
Howell, Squadron Leader Frank, 44, 47
Hungary, 15
Hurst, Brian Desmond, 17–18, 37, 91

Ibsley, RAF, 44, 46
Isle of Man, 190

INDEX

Jericho, Operation, 40
Johnson, Air Vice-Marshal Johnnie, 72, 135–7, 139
Junkers,
    Ju 52, 28–30
    Ju 88, 46, 93, 97–8, 102, 195, 206, 210
    Ju 88C6, 70

Kellett, Wing Commander, 170–2
Kenley, RAF, 76–7, 80, 83, 97, 106, 108, 118, 120–1, 123, 126
Kent, Wing Commander Johnny, 172, 209
Kiel, 18, 23, 25
King, George, 43–5
King, Pilot Officer Martyn Aurel, 176, 196
Kingcome, Flight Lieutenant Brian, 47, 189, 196–7, 201, 208–209, 211
Kinkead, Flight Lieutenant S.M., 53
Korda, Alexander, 15–18, 31, 33, 43

Lane, Flight Lieutenant Brian, 32, 92–3, 125, 207
Leasor, James, 142
Leigh-Mallory, Air Vice-Marshal, 108–109, 111–12, 118, 126, 131–4, 163–6, 174
Lloyd George, David, 2
Lund, Pilot Officer Tommy, 194–5, 197–8, 200, 205, 208–211
Luxembourg, 34

MacDonald, Flight Lieutenant Peter, 126, 135, 137
MacDonald, Ramsay, 55
Malan, Wing Commander 'Sailor', 68, 129, 136, 145, 150, 154, 210
Malta, 185, 211
Manton, Squadron Leader G.A.L. 'Minnie', 37, 93
Marshall, George C., 72
McRae, Flying Officer Bill, 18

Mermagen, Squadron Leader 'Tubby', 109, 124, 126
Metro-Goldwyn-Mayer (MGM), 41, 43
Mildenhall, 18, 24–5
Ministry of Information, 16, 37
Mitchell, Reginald Joseph, 9–11, 43, 45, 48–70
Mrs Miniver, 40–3, 70, 73
More, Kenneth, 117, 120, 128, 157

Netherlands, 34, 40
Nicolson, Flight Lieutenant James Brindley, 176
North Weald, RAF, 37, 118, 131, 133
Northolt, RAF, 48, 161, 170, 196–7

O'Ferrall, George More, 76
Observer Corps, 8, 26–7, 29, 32, 111, 156, 182
One of Our Aircraft is Missing, 27, 40
Orlebar, Squadron Leader A.H., 54–5

Park, Air Vice-Marshal, 72, 77, 95, 101, 110–12, 124, 154, 158–9, 163–6, 169–70, 172–3, 178
Paskiewicz, Flying Officer Ludwik, 170–3
Pearl Harbor, 41, 72
Peck, Gregory, 74, 118
Pelham-Groom, Wing Commander A.J.C., 76–7
Pembrey, 197, 202, 204
Pickard, Percy Chalres 'Pick', 40
Pickering, George, 65
Pinewood Studios, 118, 166, 213
Pinkham, Squadron Leader Philip, 93
Poland, 11–12, 16, 23, 32
Ponting, Clive, 143
Powell, Michael, 17–19, 40
Prelude to War, 41
Pressburger, Emerich, 40

Quill, Supermarine Test Pilot Jeffrey, 48, 51, 66

Rafter, Pilot Officer Robin, 178
Reach for the Sky, 107, 116, 140–2, 166, 182
Richardson, Wing Commander Ralph, 17–18, 22, 24, 29–31, 148
Richthofen, Manfred *Freiherr* von, 17
Rolls-Royce,
   Goshawk, 60
   Kestrel, 60
   Merlin, 10, 28, 42, 59–60, 64–5, 147, 149, 155, 199
Russia, 12, 38, 57

Sanders, Squadron Leader P.K. 'Judy', 195, 201, 204
Seelöwe, Operation, 133, 154
Seven Sisters cliffs, 79, 137, 156
Southampton, 9, 49, 51–2, 176
Spain, 5–7, 26
Spitfire,
   Mk I, 28, 64, 70, 77, 119
   Mk II, 64, 70–1, 74, 81, 119, 136
   Mk IIA, 46, 64, 68, 149
   Mk IIC, 77
   Mk V, 64, 119
   Mk VB, 64
   Mk XVI, 119
Stafford, John, 43–5
Stainforth, Flight Lieutenant G.H., 9, 56
Stephenson, Squadron Leader
   Geoffrey, 108–109, 114, 118, 124–5
   'Sanderson', Johnny, 118, 120–1, 123–4, 126, 130, 132–3, 137, 139–40

Tangmere, 113, 118, 128, 134–7, 207
   Tangmere Wing, 113, 134–5, 137–9
The Dam Busters, 115–16
The First of the Few, 27, 40, 43, 68–71, 107

The Flemish Farm, 71
The Great Escape, 115
The Lion Has Wings, 12, 17–18, 31–4, 37, 40, 72–3, 75
Tenant, Cecil Gordon, 75
Tracey, Flight Lieutenant 'Treacle', 18–19, 26–7
Trenchard, Air Chief Marshal Sir Hugh, 2–3, 5–6
Tuck, Flight Lieutenant Robert Stanford, 125
Tunisia, 115
Twist, Derek, 75–7

Uxbridge, RAF, 77, 79, 122, 158, 168–9, 178

Versailles Treaty, 4, 57–8
Vickers, 21, 53
   Wellington, 18, 23–5, 40, 167
von Werra, Oberleutnant Franz, 142

Waghorn, Fligh Lieutenant H.R.D., 54
Walton, Sir William, 178, 182
Warmwell, RAF, 44
Warsaw, 11–12, 34, 38
Weaver, Flight Lieutenant Percy 'Squeak', 37
Welford, Flight Lieutenant Harry, 201
Wellum, Geoffrey Harry Augustus, 185–9, 193–6, 199–200, 204, 211–14
Whiteman, Matthew, 185, 189, 191, 195, 199, 204, 212–13
Wicks, Pilot Officer J.B., 171
Woodhall, Wing Commander A.B. 'Woody', 86, 108–11, 118, 130–4, 136, 161, 165

Zanuck, Darryl F., 39